The Butterfly Effect in China's Economic Growth

Wei-Bin Zhang

The Butterfly Effect in China's Economic Growth

From Socialist Penury Towards Marx's Progressive Capitalism

palgrave
macmillan

Wei-Bin Zhang
Ritsumeikan Asia Pacific University
Beppu-Shi, Japan

ISBN 978-981-15-9888-3 ISBN 978-981-15-9889-0 (eBook)
https://doi.org/10.1007/978-981-15-9889-0

This Palgrave Macmillan imprint is published by the registered company Springer Nature Singapore Pte Ltd.
The registered company address is: 152 Beach Road, #21-01/04 Gateway East, Singapore 189721, Singapore

Our greatest glory is not in never falling, but in rising every time we fall.

Confucius (551–479 BC)

When things thus find the proper point to which to come, they are sure to become great.

The Yi Jing

It seems to never occur to fools that merit and good fortune are closely united.

J. W. von Goethe (1749–1832)

In a game of mutual deception an Englishman or an American can beat a Chinese nine times out of ten.

Bertrand Russell (1922: 210)

Fool me once, shame on you; fool me twice, shame on me.

Chinese Proverb

It is easy to hate and it is difficult to love. This is how the whole scheme of things works. All good things are difficult to achieve; and bad things are very easy to get.

Confucius (551 BC–479 BC)

When cleverness and knowledge arise, great lies will flourish. When relatives fall out with one another there will be filial duty and love. When states are in confusion there will be faithful servants.

Laozi (6th–4th BC?)

Preface And Acknowledgments

My aim in writing this book is to reflect on China's economic growth from 1978 till 2018. I have never stopped thinking about the issues about China's modern history even a few days once I began to be concerned with it from 1983. After I graduated from Department of Geography, Beijing University in 1982, through passing the examination in engineering I was sent by China's government as a graduate student to study at School of Civil Engineering, Kyoto University (the name of which I had not known before I was told to go). Soon after I landed in Japan in 1983, my shocks by the differences in the two countries were unspeakable. I had been brought up in the isolated China and had heard almost nothing about capitalist societies before coming to Japan. Since I came to Japan, I have spent much time on understanding a few questions. One is why China has been behind Japan's economic development so long, even though Japan learned so much from China over the many centuries. How was it possible that in the early 1980s my diligent father who graduated, as law major student, from a Japanese University in Northeastern China in the 1940s, was earning the monthly salary that a young worker was receiving by washing dishes only two hours in a fast-food restaurant in Japan (in nominal exchange rate)? In the early 1980s, an unskilled Japanese worker was paid for one hour's work as much as a young Chinese worker's monthly salary in Shanghai or Beijing. I was further shocked at China's poverty, after I had observed that Japanese students in Kyoto

University were neither more diligent, nor smarter, nor more academically advanced, nor more respectable as student (with regard to respect and passion for learning), than Chinese students in Beijing University. Ever since I started asking these questions, I have endeavored to understand dynamic changes in income and wealth, ethics, institutions, firms, and behavior in China and Japan for the sake of understanding in my leisure times over years.

Unpredictability is only certainty in important events in human history. Nowadays I often hear Chinese tourists' joyful exclamations "太便宜啦" ("too cheap") in Japan. The reduced gaps in the living conditions between China and Japan within such a short time period were beyond anyone's expectations in the 1980s. By 2018, China was the world's second-largest economy with its 9 percent average annual growth rate of GDP in the previous four decades. Its share of the world economy rose from merely 2.7 percent to currently 16 percent. The per capita GDP jumped from $100 to over $1,0000 in 2019. Eight hundred million people have made a great escape from poverty. Since the late 1990s, each year many articles and books have predicted immediate collapses of China's economy. These predications were often based on well-established theories and observed facts. No news is good news. No single year has shown any success of those predications.

The study of history is, mathematically speaking, to solve higher dimensional partial differential equations with initial conditions. The fundamental job of studying history of human societies is to find the equations, i.e., mechanisms, of historical evolution. Historical variables are nonlinearly interdependent. This implies that equations are nonlinear, multidimensional, and dynamic. Any historian, even if he is smart, diligent, and well-informed, may solve wrong equations—"wrong" in the light of new knowledge. Equations are possibly so complicated that no generation so far could establish and solve true equations for important historical events. Hence, no generation could solve historical issues with certainty as there is no true equation available. Wrong equations with correct historical factors lead to, almost certainly, wrong conclusions. This asserts why new knowledge, new assumptions, and new perspectives, not to say new facts and new biases, will change the history. Each generation has its ancestor history. Occurrence is invariant but the written history of the occurrence changes with time. History is constantly re-written as man, except his new biases due to brainwashing of his contemporary culture, knows more about himself and dynamic mechanisms of human societies.

This book reflects on China's 40 years economic reform with modern chaos theory on social and economic dynamics and new interpretations of Confucianism. Chaos theory reveals complexity and unpredictability of evolution (Zhang, 1991), while Confucianism is the basic cultural stock of Chinese civilization. This book is also based on my books in 1998: *Japan versus China in the Industrial Race*; in 1999: *Confucianism and Modernization*; and in 2007: *New China's Long March from Servility to Freedom*. It is a continued part of my research on applying modern knowledge and economic theory to interpret Chinese thought and Chinese history. I have been interested in ancient Confucianism and its implications for modernization of East Asia since the late 1990s. This book quotes extensively from the Confucian classics to illustrate what I mean by that Confucius, as the cultural stock of China, is important for understanding China's recent development.

Most of Chinese names are expressed in pinyin, except a few names, such as Confucius, Mencius, Lao Tzu, and in the citations, in Romanized Chinese. By ancient Confucianism, I mainly refer to the Confucian doctrines developed by Confucius (Kongzi in pinyin, 551–479, BC), Mencius (Mengzi in pinyin, 382 BC–279 BC), and Xun Zi in pinyin (Hsun Tzu in Romanized Chinese, 298–238 BC). The quotes of Deng Xiaoping are from: https://quotes.thefamouspeople.com/deng-xiaoping-4263.php. There are some quotes which I don't provide sources as almost all of them are from https://www.brainyquote.com, with a few expectations which can be identified by googling. I am deeply gratitude to the websites. I am thankful to the valuable comments and suggestions of the anonymous referee. I am very grateful to Editor Jacob Dreyer and Manager Ashwini Elango for effective co-operation. I completed this book at the Ritsumeikan Asia Pacific University. I learn much from the campus life sustained collectively by the colleagues, students, and staffs from over 100 countries. I am grateful for the university's supportive environment in research.

Beppu-Shi, Japan Wei-Bin Zhang

Contents

List of Figures

List of Tables

CHAPTER 1

Mao Zedong and the Preconditions for the Butterfly Effect

Nothing affects the life of a child so much as the unlived life of its parent.
Carl Jung (1875–1961)

If one examines rapid progress period of developed economies, one finds that these economies started them mostly from poverty and low education with social and political order. Before WWII, German and Japanese economies were growing from poverty and low education. After the war, the two economies grew swiftly from poverty, even though human capital was not totally lost in the war. They had social and political stability under American protection. The USA, great as it is today, was built by poor and uneducated immigrants of low social status from their original countries. This is true for Australia, Canada, and New Zealand. Before WWII, the modern industrial economies became developed in association with colonization. The colonization played an important role for social and political stabilities as "trouble-makers" in their own countries could make fortunes in other lands. Wars might also help political and social stabilities. Singapore, Hong Kong, and Taiwan were developed by immigrants of low social status in their original provinces back in mainland China. They enjoyed relatively orderly social and political reliable environment under Western powers. South Korea had swift growth after being liberated from a colonized state and subject to American protection. China's initial state was poverty and low education with social and political stability and order under a single party's control.

W.-B. Zhang, *The Butterfly Effect in China's Economic Growth*,
https://doi.org/10.1007/978-981-15-9889-0_1

When Chairman Mao was passing, Chinese people were not only poor, but also had no dream to become rich; they were not only lowly educated, but also had no hope to receive any formal higher education. Mao created a worst type of poverty: no hope for a better life. China has experienced meteoric improvement in national economic conditions since it launched the economic reform and opened to global markets in 1978. The per capita GDP jumped from $100 in 1978 to over $10,000 in 2019. Eight hundred million people made a great escape from poverty. By 2018, China was the world's second-largest economy from its 10th position in 1978 with its 9% average annual growth rate of GDP in the previous four decades. Its share of the world economy rose from merely 2.7% to 16%.

A great challenging question in the history of civilizations in general, and economic development in particular, is why China could have achieved such rapid economic progress with the one-fifth global population and little resource (in terms per capita) from the bottom of the world (in terms of per capita income and per capita higher education received). The Nobel Laureate in Economics, Coase, jointly with Wang claim: "It will take us decades, if not centuries, to fully explain why China became capitalist the way it did, resolving all intriguing puzzles." (Coase and Wang 2012: 202). There is perhaps no precise solution of the black swan event. But it is worthy to study China's economic reform as Fernand Braudel (1902–1985) points out: "Everything must be recaptured and relocated in the general framework of history, so that despite the difficulties, the fundamental paradoxes and contradictions, we may respect the unity of history which is also the unity of life." China's economic proliferation is a short period of China's history, but an exciting one. It is the bifurcating point into modern social and economic structure from the traditional one.

The Chinese economic structure has experienced catastrophic changes due to a well-known idea in the ocean of economic knowledge—market mechanism. Traditional economic theory cannot explain how a "trite" political economic idea can lead to an unprecedented change in human history. This kind of change needs modern chaos theory or theory of complexity to rigorously explain. Chaos theory mathematically exhibits how a small change can lead to dramatically structural change. "Mathematically" implies that the theory demonstrates rigorously not only beautiful phenomenon, but also, perhaps more importantly, the mechanisms controlling the system, the structure, and the status under which the phenomenon is observed. Traditional Newtonian natural science and neoclassical economics predict that a small change can only result in small changes. Traditional sciences cannot explain structural changes with small exogenous changes. Chaos theory demonstrates how a butterfly flaps its wings in Okinawa may subsequently cause a storm which ravages Japan. A touch of a friend's dog in a small town may cost many human lives and originate a global economic crisis due to virus diffusion. Sources of structural changes in human societies are not necessarily big shocks such as revolutions, storms, nuclear bombs, earthquakes, great liars, and great politicians. Revolution, even if it succeeds in the destructive purpose in the short term, often does not lead to permanent structural changes in the long term. There are plenty of examples that a society, or an industry, or an organization experiences structural changes due to seemingly unimportant events. The chaos theory also tells why so many economists in the world who have been trained and done research so many years and are equipped with most advanced mathematics, valid data, and computers can predict only these phenomena which people without professional training roughly know. This is similarly for weather forecasting. An old man should know what it means the best doctor is oneself. Young people do not need sophisticated doctors if they catch a cold; old people with complicated health problems can hardly find a useful one among many well-trained doctors. Politicians should do little in improving economic performances if an economy is in healthily growing stages; politicians often worsen economic performances if the economy is in deep troubles. Chaos theory help us to understand the complexity of nonlinear dynamic phenomena.

The most intellectually challenging question about the butterfly effect is not the unpredictable and amusing phenomenon, but the complexity of structure and preconditions under which a nuance brings about large-scale changes. A butterfly must flap at the right time within the right structure, and at the right state of the system to generate the big effect. Political economic ideas for improving human societies are abundant and applied in varied parts of the world. None has brought about the butterfly effect in scale, scope, and speed as Deng's idea about economic reform in entire human history. In fact, Deng had once advocated the idea in the 1960s, together with his superior Liu Shaoqi (1898–1968). They were together labelled in the late 1960s as China's foremost "capitalist-roaders". Their idea was proposed at the wrong time, even though China's socioeconomic structure in the 1960s was the same as in the late 1970s. Deng's early application of market mechanism to China's reality had no great impact on China's economic advancement. He had to wait for fortunes before switching China's modern path of development to the track of rapid economic progress.

Liu Shaoqi—the Chairman of the People's Republic from 1959 to 1968—deemed that a limited market economy and the retention of private ownership (which is the idea that Deng practiced after 1978) is not against socialism and should promote socialist development. The basic idea was what the CCP (Chinese Communist Party) now calls market economy with Chinese characteristics. Liu, rather than Deng, is still considered by some Chinese as the pioneer of market economy in the New China. Liu and Deng failed to introduce market mechanism to Chinese economy due to the wrong time within the same economic structure as in 1978. Mao Zedong was China's most powerful man and he had no concern about market economy. Under Mao's leadership, China remained poor in terms of per capita income and lowly educated. Mao had begotten the structure and state for Deng's butterfly effect.

A great success of man occurs as a combination of his character, efforts, and fortune. Talent, diligence, and virtue do not lead to great fruits if no fortune falls. After the death of Mao (who never lived in an industrializing economy except the short visit to Russia), Deng (who experienced 5-years "hard-work and frugal study" in many parts of France) was the right person with the belief in market economy and in the nation's top position to bring about the socioeconomic structural changes in the New China left behind Mao.

Mao as the Leader of China from 1949 to 1976

> Many are stubborn in pursuit of the path they have chosen, few in pursuit of the goal.
>
> Friedrich Nietzsche (1844–1900)

Mao Zedong (1893–1976) was the founding father of the New China. He became the national leader after his forces defeated the Nationalist government and forced Chiang Kai-shek's government to withdraw to Taiwan. He ruled the country as chairman of the CCP from its establishment in 1949 until his death in 1976.

Mao was born in the village of Shaoshan in the Hunan Province of China. He was brought up by his peasant father and Buddhist mother. His family was fairly well-to-do. He received Chinese classics education.

He attended his village's primary school at the age of eight, focusing on Confucian classics. He then worked in his family farm at the age of thirteen. He soon went to study in a neighboring county and then moved to a secondary school in Changsha at the age of 17. In the capital city of the province, he got some Western ideas. He joined a unit of the revolutionary army for 6 months as a soldier. Then he began to study at a Hunan Provincial library on his own. He read the Western works by, for instance, Darwin, Mill, and Rousseau. He then joined a teaching course, completing his course in 1918. In the same year he went to Beijing where he got a poorly paid job as assistant in the library of Beijing University. He knew the library chief Li Dazhao, and a professor of literature, Chen Duxiu, in the university. The two men were radical Chinese Marxists and the founders of the CCP. Mao soon became a Chinese Marxist, as he portrayed himself: "I had become in theory, and, to some extent, in action, a Marxist." Influenced by the May Fourth Movement, he believed that all Chinese traditional cultures should be abolished. China should be moved to an egalitarian and communist stage.

Mao liked to read Chinese literature of tales about bandits and heroes. His vision of social order and national management was perhaps much framed by the socioeconomic structure in the Qing dynasty. Gray (1990: 19) describes the Qing dynasty as follows: "It was China's political culture rather than her political institutions, which kept life going. The object of that culture was the maintenance of peace and stability in an agrarian society, in which change was neither sought nor anticipated. The highest value recognized in China was social harmony. The method by which the Chinese sought to realize this value was the control of conflict by the imposition of hierarchically organized authority." Mao's belief and vision constructed as a failed student and a farmer in the countryside, a soldier in local regions, a lowly paid worker in youth in the capital city, and killing fields in chaotic China would later frame China once he grasped the absolute power over the country.

In 1920, Mao took a job as principal of a primary school in Changsha. He joined a group in setting up the Changsha branch of the CCP. In 1921, he was one of 12 delegates at the First Congress of the CCP. In the 1920s, Mao concentrated on political work in his native Province and Jiangxi Province. He was elected chairman of the newly established Soviet Republic of China, based in Jiangxi province in 1931. During the Second Sino-Japanese War (1937–1945), the CCP battled the Japanese invaders. Mao and Jiang (Chiang Kai-shek in Romanized Chinese and

Jiang Jieshi in pinyin) decided to start a full-scale civil in 1946. Jiang won initial victories. But corruption and inflation sabotaged his effort. In 1949, Beijing fell, and Jiang was forced to withdraw to Taiwan. On the 1st of October in 1949, the People's Republic of China was established.

Plato describes a way to become a tyrant: "This and no other is the root from which a tyrant springs; when he first appears he is a protector." Plato's logic illustrates how Mao could die as the "triumphant" tyrant. Before he got absolute power, he was quite democratic and co-operative with his superiors and equals. His democratic attitudes earned trust and followers. Once he got absolute power, he would reasonably comeback to his nature as a powerful politician born into poverty and survived in brutal chaos. Mao would not change the traditional way about how to rule China as Kant describes (Schwarcz 1986: 283): "Revolutions may be able to abolish despotism, profit seeking. But they are unable, by themselves, to reform ways of thinking. New prejudices, like the old ones they replaced, will emerge to enchain, to control the great unthinking mass." Brutality is the only human capital he truly mastered after he got the absolute power.

The Kangxi emperor describes the Chinese emperor's absolute power as (Spence 1992: 29): "Giving life to people and killing people – those are the powers that the emperor has." Mao inherited this mentality. The Chinese emperor had monopolistic power over the country, including human life. Beginning in 1949, the CCP claimed that political power depends on control of political and legal institutions. The party is the law. A leader in the legal field, Peng Zhen (1902–1997) illustrated the party's view: "Is law subordinate to actuality, or actuality to law? Who is the mother? Who are the children? Actuality is the mother. It produces law. Law and theories of law are the children" (Yu 1989: 74). As the party has the power to determine actuality through information control, it could have defined the law according to its concrete needs among the Chinese cultural soil formed under the Manchus. The Manchu ruler did not treat Han Chinese as humans. the political tradition during the Qing dynasty left almost no positive influence on introduction of human rights. Han Chinese were used to cruel treatment of the government. Unlike the Japanese people who had never been under control of a monopolistic power (perhaps except a short period during WWII), Chinese people have been under a monopolistic power (except domestic or international war times) over thousand years.

During his political and military career, Mao's victories relied on mobilizing peasants and young people in large scales. By adopting situation-dependent strategies, he overcame the better-armed and better educated Chinese Nationalist Party armies. He considered people as easily available substitutes for weapons and military training— late Mao extended this substitution to substitution between the number and productivity, between the number and natural resources, and between the number and knowledge. He conceived that by making people to use their lives for his goals, he could win any war. In economic development, he forced people to grow grains in futile lands without basic cost and benefit calculations. After he controlled China, the number of people was his key resource and class struggle was his strategy of maintaining his political monopoly.

When he was confronted with America's nuclear weapons, Mao claimed that the US was unable to wipe out China as he had 600 million people and 9,600,000 square kilometers of land. In his visit to Moscow, he shocked Soviet Premier Nikita Khrushchev (1974: 255) by saying: "We shouldn't be afraid of atomic missiles. No matter what kind of war breaks out – conventional or thermonuclear – we'll win. As for China, if the imperialists unleash war on us, we may lose more than three hundred million people. So what? War is war. The years will pass and we'll get to work producing more babies than ever before." Li Zhisui (1996: 125), Mao's physician, reflected on Mao's attitude to human life: "I did not immediately understand, because it was so hard to accept, how willing Mao was to sacrifice his own citizens in order to achieve his goals… It was not until the Great Leap Forward, when millions of Chinese began dying during the famine, that I became fully aware of how much Mao resembled the ruthless emperors he so admired. Mao knew that people were dying by the millions. He did not care." There is a relationship between the people and the leader. The people support the leader. Today China still nationally admires Mao. Today his body lies at China's most symbolic place and his photo appears in China's bill with the highest value. Mao is a shallow individual with unstopped revolutionary passions. This type of individuals destroys himself simultaneously as he hurts the people associated with him. It is the race's fate to have such personality to control China. His revolutionary passion not only left almost nothing for his family, but also the entire country with huge poor and uneducated population. This tends to be the final result of a shallow-minded leader who has great passion in youth and great power in old age. His granddaughter, Kong Dongmei, illustrates the lasting impact of his revolutionary passion:

"it shows his influence, that he exists in people's consciousness and has influenced several generations of Chinese people's way of life. Just like Che Chevara's image, his has become a symbol of revolutionary culture." (Duncan 2009). Some people are "drug-addicted" to some passionate persons. In Chinese case, nothing could change their unlimited love for Chairman Mao.

Marx's Theory and Chinese Marxism

> If anything is certain, it is that I myself am not a Marxist.
>
> Karl Marx (1818–1883)

> The least initial deviation from the truth is multiplied later a thousandfold.
>
> Aristotle

Great thought tends to come back to influence man in intervals of a few hundred years as human collective stupidity is repeatedly corrected and reversed in changing forms in the name of actuality. Human nature is almost invariant at least seen from ancient Greek and Chinese civilizations. Great thinkers who have lasting reputations are not wrong in the sense that their conclusions are correct if the situations satisfy their (explicit or implicit) assumed conditions. When Marx's doctrine was applied China, the assumed conditions of replacing a mature capitalism with communism had nothing to do with China's reality. To a great degree, communism was applied to the New China during the Mao time as a religion which "is the masterpiece of the art of animal training, for it trains people as to how they shall think" as described by Schopenhauer. Mankind is still too young to evaluate Marx with human histories. Russia' and China' communist realities have nothing to do with Marx's communist theory as these societies have no history of mature capitalism upon which Marx's dream about communism is made of. China's economic reform is to follow Marx's ideas about capitalism—capitalism may be economically effective, even if it creates negative consequences. China's economic reform is nothing but by admitting the wrongdoing of following the faked Marxism and making returns from socialism towards Marx's early stage of capitalism in the name of Chinese socialism with possible negative consequences of capitalism.

A rigorous economic theory, which is repeatedly analyzed by many scholars, is not wrong as far as reality is concerned. A scientific theory consists of the assumptions, the relations built on the assumptions, and the analytical results derived from the relations. If the theory failed to explain or play the supposed role in improving society, it might not be the invalidity of the theory but the wrong application of the theory. History recodes that man collectively learns from neither theory nor history. Man in power often seeks after power, sex, wealth, reputation, or personalized dream, rather than improving social welfare as he claims. Rational theory for society is constructed on the assumed purpose of improving welfare, neglecting the stupidity or the evil human nature of applicants. In natural sciences theory is effective in explaining and predicting natural phenomena as the assumptions are "satisfied" by nature and natural motion. Human motion itself is disorderly because of man's enhanced abilities to lie as well as unsteady human emotion. If human nature is structurally unstable (man is naturally adaptive to environment in unlimited possible combinations of known or unknown basic instincts), there would be no deterministic mathematical equations to accurately describe human behavior. Theory in social sciences often seems irrelevant when it is applied to explain, predict, or plan real world due to the complexity of nonlinear interdependence between multiple forces. Some contemporary economists had confidence to advise poor non-Western societies by applying very refined economic theories created in the West. It is easy to find examples of destructive consequences that academic economists brought about by applying political economic theories suitable for advanced economies to developing economies. China's application of Marxist socialism is an obvious example.

The key reason for Confucian regions to economically succeed is to learn from the West carefully, passionately but not purposelessly, and scrupulously plant the Western seeds in their own soils. China once failed as China learned haphazardly either from Russia or the West. Except the complexity of human behavior and social dynamics which implies irrelevance of social theory built on too simplified assumptions with too simplified structures, another important reason for often disastrous consequences in applying theory in social sciences is that people who apply the theory have no capacity to know the assumptions and to follow the logic in the theory. They apply conclusions from the theory to the reality which does not even approximately satisfy the basic assumptions in the theory.

Some powerful politicians who claim to believe in a theory are not interested in the theory at all but use some conclusions seemingly derived from the theory to justify their own behavior to appeal the public to satisfy their own needs. In this sense, social sciences and economics are not useful as they should be.

Marx appreciates capitalism as it speeds up accumulation of wealth and makes technological change due to profit optimization and private ownership of capital. He argues that capitalism is a progressive historical stage of human society. Nevertheless, like people will eventually die, capitalism will be eventually replaced by socialism which is characterized by public ownership of property. For Marx, capital is not simply machine, but a social and economic relation between people. Marx considers social structure in terms of its major classes. Rather than income or status, the ownership of property is the main indicator for class. Marx argues for intrinsic existence of class struggle between proletariat and bourgeoisie in capitalist industrial society. In association with capitalism development class struggle between capitalists and workers for political and economic power is intensified. Class consciousness is strengthened. Within each class there are common interests. Interest conflicts between heterogeneous classes affect political relations. For Marx, the distribution of political power is closely related to the ownership of capital. In a well-developed capitalist society, the ruling bourgeoisie class uses the state power and dominates the power distribution. As the disparity between the classes' conditions is widened, the worker class will carry out a proletarian revolution. Private property will be eliminated and replaced by public ownership. Society will not be based on classes due to the ownership of property.

When the New China was established in 1949, China had never experienced a stage of mature capitalism. Marx's theory on establishment of socialism had nothing to do with China's reality in the 1940s, the New China under Mao's ruling jumped from an agricultural society to a socialist economy. China followed Marx's idea on communism: "The theory of Communism may be summed up in one sentence: Abolish all private property". China applied Marx's idea without satisfying Marx's conditions for socialism. There was little capital and technologies in the New China. The application of Marx's theory resulted in a collective tragedy during Mao's time.

Mao's Economic Thought Bred the Orderly Equality in Poverty

> Suffering by nature or chance never seems so painful as suffering inflicted on us by the arbitrary will of another.
>
> Arthur Schopenhauer (1788–1860)

Mao holds that thumans could force nature into obedience. In May 1958, he wrote: "'Make the high mountain bow its head; make the river yield the way.' It is an excellent sentence. When we ask the high mountain to bow its head, it has to do so! When we ask the river to yield the way, it must yield!" (Shapiro 2001: 68). Becker (1996: 308) observes the central fallacy in farmer-poet Mao's thought: "Mao wanted to modernize China but could not grasp the basis of modern thought, the scientific method: that the way in which the natural universe behaves can be proved or disproved by objective tests, independent of ideology or individual will."

Mao had little knowledge about modernization of industrial economies. He did not seem to have carefully read any book of economics, even though he read many things. He did not experience living abroad, except a short visit to Russia. His whole adult life was about political struggle in a chaotic and brutal environment. Sympathy is perhaps what he never experienced himself or observed. He strongly believed that men could obtain victory if they had the right ideology. Technology and other discrete economic problems would be simply solved with proper ideologies. His economic principles can be summarized as follows. (1) Local, regional, and national economies should be self-sufficient. There was little dependence on foreign trade or assistance. This implies that possible economic gains from division of labor and scale and scope economies due to international interactions were neglected. In his ideal society there is no effective division of labor and specialization. Mao held that there should be no class differences. The government forced equalities between industry and agriculture, and city and countryside. (2) There were enforced egalitarianism and normative incentives, including mass campaigns, and a reduction in the direct relation of individual, small group, and unit income to the quality and quantity of work they accomplished. Aspirations for improving one's conditions better than the rest were under check. Motivations for improving productivity were limited. (3) The government eliminated the 'vestiges' of capitalism or reduced activities generating private income outside the socialist sector. Yielding possible fruits from market economy were impossible. (4) The government conducted mass participation in decision–making and elimination of an explicit hierarchy of authority and responsibility based on expertise and job assignment. Professional knowledge and potentials of experts were not to be full use. The impact is described by Alexis de Tocqueville: "It is the dissimilarities and inequalities among men which give rise to the notion of honor; as such differences become less, it grows feeble; and when they disappear, it will vanish too." (5) The politicization of economic decision making, behavioral rules, and policy determination, and reduced emphasis on economic rationality in the sense of economic cost and benefit calculations. In 1959, Mao admitted his ignorance: 'I understand nothing about industrial planning'. But he would neither learn economic nor change his vision in managing national economy. The farmer-poet's ignorance on modern economics would be continued to his death.

Mao launched the Great Leap Forward in 1958. He urged to construct backyard steel furnaces to exceed Western steel production with miserable failures. There was a campaign to re-establish Mao's ideological line culminated in the Cultural Revolution (1966–76). He hoped to eliminate the three great gaps between workers and peasants, between rural and urban areas, and between manual and mental labor. These gaps are, fortunately or unfortunately, further enlarged by Deng's economic reforms. Mao dispatched millions of educated youth to the countryside to solve urban problems and reduce the gaps. He easily equalized income and wealth among the urban people across country. At the end of his life, Chinese had no aspirations to become rich. Millions of Chinese who have now succeeded in multifarious fields have a common upbringing during Mao's period: brought up in extreme poverty and their parents had low education or no education at all. Mo Yan (1955-), the Nobel Prize laureate in literature in 2012, was born to a family of poor farmers. He described the living conditions of his youth: "Loneliness and hunger were my fortunes of creation." Many of the generation born in the 1950s and 1960s consider themselves "born to" be reformers. They lacked everything when Mao died, except hopes, dreams, and passions, for living an enriched—perhaps decent—human life.

Mao's Cultural Revolution Terminated Higher Education

> To put the people to death without having instructed them – this is called cruelty.
>
> Confucius

Mao's lifetime activities in China give a showcase about what Hegel says: "people and governments never have learned anything from history, or acted on principles deduced from it." Hegel was partly true as uneducated people tend to memorize their stupidities and thus often collectively repeat them. A society that attempts to deny and forget its ancestors is lost. China's loss under Mao has made Chinese race too painful and too shameful to officially recode it in official documents. Mao tried to create a society with the type of equality which Aristotle called the worst: "The worst form of inequality is to try to make unequal things equal." Mencius expresses similarly: "It is the nature of things to be of unequal quality.... If you reduce them all to the same standard, that must throw empire into confusion."

As his vision about economy was based on his family farm, social organization on Chinese communism, and maintaining government by guns, Mao logically nationalized the rich's wealth to follow the condition of Chinese communism. His cultural revolution was to vanish Chinese higher education. A Chinese proverb says: "To study is to become an official; to be an official is to become wealthy." This proverb describes Chinese cultural character. China's education is traditionally freely competitive. There were high risks but high economic returns in investing in education. Performances in different levels of education were clearly measured by official examinations, at local levels, provincial levels, and national levels, and finally in the front of the emperor. Mao reasonably sent intellectuals to the countryside to make a revolution against the traditional Chinese culture; and made the country as ignorant as possible to continue highest political power over his beloved people.

At the onset of the New China, Mao did not abolish higher education. Its first higher education entrance examination was conducted in 1952. But the government began to apply stricter political censor in entrance after 1958. The entrance examination system was then abolished in 1966. The government recruited students to higher education institutions not based on academic performance. From 1967 to his death, Mao sent both senior and junior secondary school graduates to countryside, working together with and receiving re-education by peasants. There was only a small number who were selected to enter universities based on political and family backgrounds. Millions of young people from urban areas were forced to work and live in the countryside as peasants almost without any hope of either returning to cities or receiving proper higher education. Peasants' land was shared by urban young people and urban burdens with over population were lightened. Mao's political strategy through making the population as ignorant as possible was carried out "effectively" due to the party's centralized organizational system.

Most of the first two leadership generations did not receive higher education. Mao did not receive any formal higher education. The leaders under Mao were almost all soldiers, peasants, and urban lower-middle classes. Zhou Enlai and Deng Xiaoping did not receive formally higher education even though they lived abroad some years before returning. Liu Shaoqu, Ye Jianying, and Yang Shankun attended college in the Soviet Union but received only military training and Marxist doctrines. The party's members and government officials were recruited by: (1) seniority in joining the party and the revolution; (2) ideological commitment to Chinese Marxism and Mao Zedong thought; (3) political loyalty and activism in the class struggle; and (4) poor and uneducated family background. Formal education was often a negative factor in the selection process. The educational level of party cadres and members was low during Mao's period. In 1955, only 5% of the top leaders had a junior high school education or above (Schurmann 1968: 283).

Since the early 1910s till 1970s, China widely criticized Confucianism, blaming Confucianism for China's underdevelopment. Hu Shi (1891–1962) played a significant role in criticizing Confucianism. Like many of his generation's Southern intellectuals, he rejected Confucianism but failed to find any meaningful suggestion for China's modernization. His followers also severely attacked Confucianism. Lu Xun (1881–1936, 1980: 43), an influential Chinese writer, related in the words of the madman in *Diary of a Madman:* "Everything requires careful consideration if one is to understand it. In ancient times, as I recollect, people often ate human beings, but I am rather hazy about it. I tried to look thus up, but my history has no chronology and scrawled all over each page are the words: 'Confucian Virtue and Morality.' Since I could not sleep anyway, I read intently half the night until I began to see words between the lines.

The whole book was filled with the two words – 'Eat People'." Mao stated (Rummel 1991): "What's so unusual about Emperor Qin Shihuang? He had buried alive 460 scholars only, but we have buried alive 46,000 scholars.... I had an argument with the democratic personages. They say we are behaving worse than Emperor Shihuang of the Qin Dynasty [221B.C.-206 B.C.]. That's definitely not correct. We are 100 times ahead of Emperor Qin Shihuang in repression of counter-revolutionary scholars."

Emperor Shihuang united many states to form China. Although the first emperor did not promote Confucianism, he provided "proper conditions" for development of Confucianism after he passed. Under Mao, little modern knowledge accumulated during Mao's time. Mao's death brought about the beginning of an epoch of agile progress of science and technology in China. The first emperor and Mao represented the turning points of two main socio-economic structural changes in China's civilization. Jones (2001: 76) observes that "the transformation of China from a model of moral rule to the 'sick man of the east' offered the enticing prospect for additional reflection on the impact of evolution, environment, nutrition and race upon civilizational progress and decay."

Mao's National Isolation

The real tragedy of life is when men are afraid of the light.

Plato (423-347 BC)

Since China had been under monopolistic power of the emperor, individualistic and liberal aspects of ancient Confucianism were abolished. Rather than open societies where the ancient Confucianists lived, the emperor ruled an almost isolated country. The emperor kept power through selecting talented officials via the controlled examination system and killed anyone, including his brothers and relatives, who would even potentially threaten his power.

In his essay *Of the Rise and Progress of the Arts and Sciences* published more than 200 years ago, the British philosopher and historian, David Hume (1711–1776, 1994) observes: "In CHINA, there seems to be a pretty considerable stock of politeness and science, which, in the course of so many centuries, might naturally be expected to ripen into something more perfect and finished, than what has yet arisen from them. But CHINA is one vast empire, speaking one language, governed by one law, and sympathizing in the same manners. The authority of any teacher ... was propagated easily from one corner of the empire to the other. None had courage to resist the torrent of popular opinion. And posterity was not bold enough to dispute what had been universally received by their ancestors. This seems to be one natural reason, why the sciences have made so slow a progress in that mighty empire." The vast land within the Great Wall and diligent and obedient people were enough for the emperor to enjoy power, wealth, and sex, until his empire was broken by fierce nomadic invaders. Mao isolated China again, following the past emperors' dreams to have a self-sufficient economy for him to enjoy power.

China was basically isolated from the West during the Mao time. Chinese people had almost no opportunity to travel abroad except official relations. To travel to USA or Europe as a tourist was beyond Chinese people's dream. Even books about the West were not available at least in 1976 when Mao died. From 1949 till President Nixon's visit to China, direct conflicts regularly occurred between America and China, the Korea War of 1950-1953, the Taiwan Straits Crises of 1954-55 and 1958, and the war in Vietnam from 1965 to 1974. Mao (1977, V: 152) related on January 25, 1955: "The United States cannot annihilate the Chinese nation with its small stack of atom bombs. Even if the U.S. atom bombs were so powerful that, when dropped on China, they would make a hole right through the earth, or even blow it up, that would hardly mean anything to the universe as a whole, though it might be a major event for the solar system." After Nixon's visit to China in February 1972, China's relations with America were much improved. There was increasingly more collaboration, especially, in economic fields. America wished to ally with China to be against the Soviet Union. The Shanghai Communiqué between Nixon and Zhou Enlai of February 1972 states the U.S. and China would both work towards normalization. The U.S. recognized Taiwan as a part of China. Jiang Jieshi (1887–1975) regarded this new development as a "shattering blow to 'Free China' and as an incomprehensible act of betrayal by the Nixon administration." (Garver 1997).

The Pro-Conditions Left by Mao for Deng's Butterfly Effect

Stay hungry, stay foolish.

Steve Jobs (1955–2011)

Failure is the mother of success; necessity is the mother of invention; cruel fathers bring up fortunate children; kind parents have spoiled children; civilized state with seemingly secured prosperity creates mediocre citizens and breeds decline. As far as life is concerned, bad performances may provide conditions for good results, and vice versa. Process of civilization flows on its accumulated cultural stocks. Civilization repeats itself and at the same time takes new elements, either through creativity or imitation by forces within or outside, into its organs. It often takes years or generations for foreign elements to become a part of the cultural capital stock. Some cultures make quick advances by quickly adapting to new environment, while some others can hardly make any essential "progress" with cultural isolation. Japan and the four Asian tigers learned quickly from the West partly due to the political geography and "shallow" but rationality-dominated historical and cultural stocks.

Mao wanted to destroy Chinese culture perhaps because his teacher generation had said nothing positive about Chinese civilization and China had been under the Manchu control until 1911 and had been humiliated by Western and Japanese powers till the mid-1940s. Mao blamed all these disadvantages as consequences of Chinese culture, especially Confucianism. Majority of the Chinese people who had neither education nor travelled far beyond their birth places trusted him. Mao dreamed a "prosperous" economy with equality perhaps this was only what a Chinese farmer-poet could really understand as an effective, desirable, easily operable system. A man easily makes errors if he has a sense of virtue, but no knowledge. If a man has neither virtue nor knowledge but unlimited power, he will perform any kind of evils imageable for his own gains.

The cultural, social, and economic destruction that China had experienced from the Opium Wars to the end of the Cultural Revolution created a great opportunity to do something positive and to end the trend of further destruction. Mencius (382 BC-279 BC) gives a condition for wealth accumulation and economic prosperity which China has followed after the economic reform: "Without effective protection of the citizens' to property, it will be difficult to attract and accumulate valuable capital." Mao established the New China, eradiated intellectuals, and equalized income. His socioeconomic vision and way of governing were like those emperors in the Qing dynasty—there was no social fairness and only one available way, killing, in controlling the vast country. Mencius (14: 12) describes Mao's lifetime achievements: "If men of virtue and ability be not confided in, a state will become empty and void. Without the rules of propriety and distinctions of right, the high and the low will be thrown into confusion. Without the great principles of government and their various business, there will not be wealth sufficient for the expenditure." Over the cycles of Chinese dynasties over more than two thousand years, bad time was the mother of peace and prosperity, while golden age was the mother of disasters. Malthusian economic theory gives some reasons for the Chinese cycles. The Mao period led China to the bottom of the world in terms of per capita income and national higher education per 1000 persons. Jobs' condition of progress: "Stay hungry, stay foolish" was replaced by Mao's condition for stability under his will: made hungry, made foolish. Mao laid a solid precondition of "being hungry, being foolish" for Deng's miracle.

Social Stability Under Centralized Government

> Knowledge which is acquired under compulsion obtains no hold on the mind.
>
> Plato (423–347 BC)

Teamwork is a common feature for winning sport games, military battles, organizational efficiency, and economic prosperity. National development relies on teamwork. Adam Smith holds that in enriching the nation national teamwork can be effectively conducted through free market with invisible hand. Karl Marx's socialism implies that a centralized rational government can effectively organize the co-operation of the people as a single team with national planning. Keynes synthesizes the two systems in his approach to national development. In the last hundred years economists see one failure after another in these three approaches. Due to Mao's style of control, China had a social stability under the single organization, the CCP. The social stability and forced social harmony are essential determinants that China could have achieved rapid economic progress. A simplified and centralized government implies that reasonable ideas and policies can be implemented nationwide with little frictions caused by multifarious interest groups and intellectuals brainwashed with invalid thought and ideas for economic development.

Conditions for Perfect Competition

> A nation that is afraid to let its people judge the truth and falsehood in an open market is a nation that is afraid of its people.
>
> John F. Kennedy (1917–1963)

Perfect competition is generally considered an ideal situation for improving economic efficiency with profit-motivations. American industries are dominantly imperfectly competitive, and wealth is concentrated in a few families. China's conditions in 1978 were quite different. Monopolistic power due to wealth, skill, and knowledge did not exist, at least not strong enough to greatly distort conditions for perfectly competitive conditions. Hence, if the government relaxed its control over the national economy, the power of invisible hand would enable China to improve productivities through, for instance, Marx's spirit of animals, learning by doing, or learning by co-operating with proper partners through free formation of team. By 1978 there were almost no rich men and rare professionals with modern knowledge (perhaps except in a few military industries) due to Mao's way of controlling the country. Among most important factors that might distort perfect competition were the CCP itself and economic institutions (which were to be reformed slowly but steadily). This condition plus social stability implies that Chinese potentials of desire for material and diligence could be easily explored once they got opportunities to enrich themselves. Since China suffered from international humiliations and domestic wars from 1911 to 1949, and experienced poverty and Mao's "governing by gun" from 1949 to 1976, the obedient Chinese people could be easily satisfied if they could make some, even slight, improvements in life. During the Mao era, crime rate was low. There was almost nothing to be snitched in society, and punishment for any crime was severe. "When a society opens up and reforms," said a fifty-year-old nurse (Levy 2002: 47), "there will definitely be some people who seek personal gain. ... Before 1978, we never heard that Guangzhou had prostitutes, drugs, or those kinds of things. At that time, we were very pure. … No one stole things; no one sold guns; there was no smuggling. Really, the whole society was very peaceful, but … we were very poor. … After the reforms, these types of things entered society." Official barriers to markets mechanisms and corruption network were not very sophisticated in the earlier years of the reform.

Relative Equality in Income, Medical Care, and Education

The real tragedy of the poor is the poverty of their aspirations.
Adam Smith (1723–1790)

When Mao died, China had almost nothing left for class struggles, except people's lives. There were not very large gaps between rural and urban areas, among families. As higher education was almost abolished in the Mao time, there were not great gaps in human capital. Although they had high social status, officials were mostly just re-recruited and not yet smartly corrupt. In 1976, people lived at mere survival level, most of the population was poorly educated, cultural heritages were ruined, and environment deteriorated. China's social safety net was extended only to about 20% of the population. Most rural areas were seriously underdeveloped in 1978. People's communes which were the main political and economic institutions in rural areas offered few social benefits to their members. Peasants had no access to state pensions or subsidized housing. Equalized poverty of the country implied great opportunities for common people to improve their living conditions. Poor infrastructures plus all the land practically owned by the state enabled the country to quickly build infrastructures with best ideas and technologies on the earth with little local conflicts. Low level of capital stock implied high returns from saving and more effective use of machines. "Empty" positions in the academic world and government encouraged millions of young people to sustain their passions for receiving higher education and making investment in human capital under relatively fair competitive conditions. Young generations had the hope, the belief, and the conviction that they would have a better life, and they could improve China, even though many middle-aged people, who was labeled as the lost generation, in the earlier years of the reform had mixed feelings when watching national bright futures and thinking of losing best times for dream building, for learning, for love, for working, and for family building.

The Homogeneous Poor Population for Scale Effects of Animal Spirits in Deng's Era

> Those who undertake learning become men; those who neglect become as wild beasts.
>
> Xun Zi (298-238 BC, 1: 8)

During the Mao period, China's population nearly doubled from 540 million to 969 million. Mao had the idea about controlling population change by the early 1970s. The government recommended two children per family in cities and three or four in the rural area. In the late 1970s and earlier 1980s, when economic reform started the population had strong desires to become rich. One was called a rich man in the earlier 1980s if he had 1000 US dollars when a profession's monthly salary was about 15 US dollars. The passion for receiving a higher education was also high. All these demands for working hard and higher education and suddenly allowed "capitalist" lifestyles would have positive interdependent relations to encourage China's growth. Chinese youth in 1978 had cost almost nothing to their family and society, in comparison to contemporary Chinese youth, before they made great contributions to socioeconomic development. Moreover, there were many opportunities and the government was not yet equipped with highly educated officials in the earlier years of the reform so that talented people from any part of China and from any family background could almost certainly make improvement in life via diligence, and even often with honesty (China was socially "clean" and environmentally not so polluted in the earlier years of the reform). Mao thought enabled Deng to easily achieve what Abdul Kalam (1931–2015) describes: "One lesson that every nation can learn from China is to focus more on creating village-level enterprises, quality health services and educational facilities."

Mao Established Relations with the Capitalist Economies

Mao re-opened relations with the United States. U.S. President Richard Nixon visited China in 1972 after the diplomatic isolation since 1949. It was also the first time that a U.S. president visited the New China. The visit ended the history of no communication and diplomatic ties between the two countries over 25 years. It is all the first time for the American public to view China during the visit from February 21 to 28. Although he was in poor health, Mao met with the president once in Beijing. This visit made it much easier for China to establish relations with capitalist economies. Mao opened China under his leadership partly to the West. When watching China, the developed world felt a great sympathy over the poor China. Many overseas Chinese felt happy to have immigrated abroad. Many oversea Chinese made investment in their past homeland soon after Deng opened the door. Some Chinese whose life was only closed tied with China also tried to make positive contributions to China's development in the early years of the reform.

A Few Men's Decision on the One-Child Policy Greatly Reduced the World Population

> The power of population is indefinitely greater than the power in the earth to produce subsistence for man.
>
> Thomas Malthus (1766–1834)

In the last few years of his life, Mao introduced population control policy, which was later strengthened to the one-child policy under Deng. The one-child policy had a complicated impact on economic development during the period under consideration. For instance, it reduced the number of labor but might have increased human capital as the parent could have concentrated the family's resources on bringing up the child and spent more time on working and improving themselves. Mao also promoted the status of Chinese women, improving health care in egalitarian sense (like in education). Under his leadership life expectancy of the Chinese people increased. But all these improvements seem to be slow in comparison with Japan and the overseas Chinese regions during the same period. More people were born but many lost lives due to mass repression, starvation, mass execution, prison labor and persecution. China's population has now reached over 1.4 billion. The number was 1 billion in 1982. The population change from 1960 to 2015 is plotted in Fig. 1.1. Now the population has a relatively small youth component partly due to the one-child policy. Over 91% of the population was Han Chinese. After 1979 the government advocated a one-child limit for all Chinese, except special circumstances for two children per couple. Minority nationalities were generally allowed two children per couple. It was recognized by the government that general swift improvement in material living conditions and education were impossible without population control. In association with sustained and steady economic advancement, Chinese people live longer. The population policy implies that there will be a decline in the labor force in near future. To alleviate problems associated with declining birth rates, on January 1, 2016, the government changed its fertility policy from a selective two-child policy to a universal two-child policy. The new policy has an uncertain impact on encouraging people to have more children. Many urban young couples choose not to have child. Quite a high percent of married couples craves only one child partly due to high costs of fostering and education.

A successful event involving intrigue interdependence of multiple forces rarely occurs without fortune. Mao left a "harmonious" country with social and military stability, almost without any significant group of

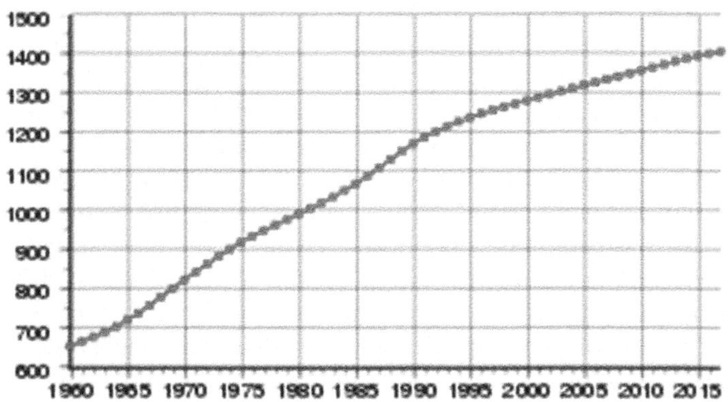

Fig. 1.1 China's Population since 1960 in millions (*Source* https://en.wikipedia.org/wiki/Demographics_of_China)

the rich and the elite. This might turn to a proper initial condition for the economy to make a agile take-off both through Adam Smith's invisible hand and Karl Marx's effective state planning. Rapid economic progress from a poor state is well observed in modern economies. Taiwan and Hong Kong developed from culturally uncultivated regions with immigrants from the Confucian regions. West Germany, Japan, and South Korea experienced swift growth from devastated conditions. There were few strong cultural and institutional barriers in these regions for "immigrants" to build new economies with their own home-land cultural values and tradition. China has been experiencing an economic miracle after the deep devastation by the Cultural Revolution. The devastated destruction provided the "refreshed" soil suitable for seeds of modernization. A baby grows fast because each part has potentials to grow. An uncultivated land or devastated region with proper cultural seeds is capable of being quickly developed because each part of the society has great potentials for improvement.

The short-term and long-term merits and demerits of an important person in history are always difficult to evaluate with accuracy and certainty. This is an interesting feature of human life, a life with demand for high reasoning as well as for natural emotional playfulness—life is worthy to live and to examine because of its unfathomability, uncertainty, seriousness, and playfulness. Deng was fully aware of what Mao left to him. He evaluated Mao: "We should not lay all past mistakes on Chairman Mao. So we must be very objective in assessing him. His contributions were primary, his mistakes secondary." No single man makes history as man is a social animal. Man's wrongdoing could not be carried out without million people' supports. Deng knew that Mao's mistakes enabled him to easily improve the country. Mao's vision about life and society was built in farm and chaotic China with brutal and cruel reality even without a short-term experience of orderly and prosperous socioeconomic environment, while Deng's primary vision was formed in France (and perhaps Russia). As a politician, Deng might have suffered much from Mao's Chinese peasant vision of life and society. It is very difficult for young enriched and educated generation to imagine how Chinese people in Deng's generation could tolerate each other with their own views to live, work, and get together for a lifetime. Deng was a great survivor from Mao's passionate personality with cruelness.

History changes forward or backward, rapidly or slowly, and orderly or chaotically, with the same forces. Like life cannot be still, history moves all the time if the society does not vanish. If Mao had lived another 10 years, probability for China to initiate economic reform in the later 1970s would be almost zero. The Cultural Revolution under Mao gave a deep destruction of China's economic and social systems. China had become potentially a highly mobile society due to equalized conditions. There was no strong interest group due to repeated class struggles during Mao's period. Sophisticated networks with mutual trust in keeping power or stealing government money were not yet formed. There was deep distrust in Chinese society. People were not yet united together by profits and long-term benefits. A simplified society implies great potentials for improvements. Chinese people could become entrepreneurs and accumulate wealth through diligence with little sophisticated constrains. They could become politically powerful, especially via education first, in a short period from obscurity as parentage was not very significant barrier. Chinese people were geographically mobile in search of fortunes as they had no special, cultural, political, social as well as economic, attachment, except the officially fixed *hukou*, to a place.

The death of Mao put China at turning points as different ideas had chances to be effectively implemented. China was going to either continue the Mao's line or do something else. Even when we look back to the turning point, the human capital of China's top politicians at Mao's death does not provide any hint on a great economic prosperity in near future. There is no certainty for China to select a special one among paths at the bifurcating point. With the collective mindset of Chinese people, possible new leaders were given a chance to structurally change China. Luck visited China with the rise of Deng to the national power. Poverty implies great potential for rapid economic advancement. Low education implies possible agile progress of knowledge without biased interests due to professional barriers (as almost no professors in any field left after Mao's death). Rapid economic advancement in wealth and knowledge tend to lead to social consensus, happiness and harmony among people who had lived in poverty and had never received proper education. Centralized social order without conflicts of interest groups implies that a proper decision - luckily Deng provided as the history proves—can greatly advance the nation in modern economies filled with opportunities of scale and scope economies. Long-term isolation implies that society can focus its thought and energy to do a single task with a single-minded determination. Mao's control over China left a historical memory, if China could have a proper collective memory of history at all, of great values for the future in Carl Jung's sense: "The most intense conflicts, if overcome, leave behind a sense of security and calm that is not easily disturbed. It is just these intense conflicts and their conflagration which are needed to produce valuable and lasting results." China, if opened once, could never be back to its traditional society because of the last destructiveness and collective memory of brutal and shameless past during Mao's China. As far as the meaning of life and sense of shame are concerned, no foreign invasion can teach Chinese people more effectively than the national self-humiliation in a scale and scope during Mao's period. Chinese people now know what Galbraith means: "Under capitalism, man exploits man. Under communism, it's just the opposite." It is human nature that man exploits man. Human nature may manifest in any type of society. Capitalism kept smiling and playful faces with unequal wealth, while socialism produced bored and stupidly serious faces with equal poverty.

References

Becker, J. (1996). *Hungry Ghosts: Mao's Secret Famine*. New York: Free Press.

Coase, R., & Wang, N. (2012). *How China Became Capitalist*. Hampshire: Palgrave Macmillan.

Duncan, M. (2009, September 28). *Granddaughter Keeps Mao's Memory Alive in Bookshop*. Reuters.

Garver, J. W. (1997). *The Sino-American Alliance - Nationalist China and American Cold War Strategy in Asia*. Armonk: M.E. Sharpe.

Gray, J. (1990). *Rebellions and Revolutions—China from the 1800 s to the 1980s*. Oxford: Oxford University Press.

Hume, D. (1994). *Political Essays* (edited by K. Haakonssen). Cambridge: Cambridge University Press.

Jones, D. M. (2001). *The Image of China in Western Social and Political Thought*. New York: Palgrave.

Khrushchev, N. (1974). *Khrushchev Remembers—The Last Testament* (translated and edited by S. Talbott). Boston: Little, Brown.

Levy, R. (2002). Corruption in Popular China. In P. Link, R. P. Madsen, & P. G. Pickowicz (Eds.), *Popular China—Unofficial Culture in a Globalizing Society*. New York: Rowman & Littlefield Publishers.

Li, Z. S. (1996). *The Private Life of Chairman Mao—The Memoirs of Mao's Personal Physician* (translated from the Chinese origin by H. C. Tai). New York: Random House.

Lu, X. (1980). *Selected Works* (in four volumes, translated from the Chinese origin by X. Y. Yang and G. Yang). Beijing: Foreign Languages Press.

Mao, Z. D. (1977). *Selected Works of Mao Tse-Tung* (in five volumes, published in varied years). Beijing: Foreign Language Press.
Rummel, R. J. (1991). *China's Bloody Century - Genocide and Mass Murder since 1900*. London: Transaction Publishers.
Schurmann, F. (1968). *Ideology and Organization in Communist China*. Berkeley: University of California Press.
Schwarcz, V. (1986). *The Chinese Enlightenment: Intellectuals and the Legacy of the May Fourth Movement of 1919*. Berkeley: University of California Press.
Shapiro, J. (2001). *Mao's War Against Nature—Politics and the Environment in Revolutionary China*. Cambridge: Cambridge University Press.
Spence, J. D. (1992). *Emperor of China—Self-Portrait of K'ang-his*. London: Pimlico.
Yu, X. Z. (1989). Legal Pragmatism in the People's Republic of China. *Journal of Chinese Law, 3*, 29–51.

CHAPTER 2

Deng Xiaoping Triggered off the Butterfly Effect

> *Da Guo* suggests to us a beam that is weak. There will be advantage in moving under its conditions in any direction whatever; there will be success. … Great indeed is the work to be done in this very extraordinary time.
>
> *I Ching: Da Guo*

Mahatma Gandhi's following saying is well mentioned, "A small body of determined spirits fired by an unquenchable faith in their mission can alter the course of history." The Chinese bible, *I Ching* (the *Book of Change*), says that this kind of change is possible but rare as a miracle depends on fortune. A man can change the course of history positively even without a faith. A faithful man craves improving the world, but with miserable consequences, if not helped by fortune. In Chinese way of thinking, everything is closely connected with everything else, logically as well as randomly.

A national leader, like a medical doctor, proves his value only when the nation is faced with serious problems and structural changes. Both in ancient Confucianism and Taoism, if the nation is in healthy order, the people are not aware of the existence of government. In prosperous America, any kind of professionally untrained person could become a reputed president as the nation was healthy and jokes of a shallow mind made common happy. As far as fairness of power distribution is concerned, during some periods of its history Chinese society was not

W.-B. Zhang, *The Butterfly Effect in China's Economic Growth*,
https://doi.org/10.1007/978-981-15-9889-0_2

superior to monkey society in the sense that the new master in monkey society gets its social power through its ability, spirit, and energy for leading the society. The Chinese emperor transferred his political and economic power through heritage. In this video-connected world, a national leader, who cannot easily make up biased stories to play with the public and other countries, can shame his country immediately and globally due to his ignorance, rudeness, and immaturity in handling with important domestic and international problems. A national leader can also lead a country to great advantage in a short period. No other man in human history, as Deng Xiaoping, had changed living conditions of so many people in the last two decades of his life with a well-known ("trivial") idea in economics. If Mao lived a few years more, or if Mao had a talented son alive, or if Deng passed away before Mao, millions of Chinese scholars, teachers, engineers, and rich people in many parts of global metropolitan areas might be, perhaps even happily, digging land in countryside in China earning money merely for survival. Real history is never associated with "ifs"; history in textbooks of a half-civilized and half-barbarian country is made of collectively agreed upon lies.

Neoclassical economic growth theory predicts if a market economy is initially located at poverty with low productivity (or education) with market mechanism, it is possible for the economy to experience rapid economic advancement period by saving more, having more labor force, and learning effectively. The theory implicitly assumes social and economic stability guaranteed, even though it explicitly requires the condition of market economy. If an economy is in civil wars, society is in chaos, and people cannot secure fruits of their efforts and investment, there is no secured prosperity. Social order and free market are the preconditions of modern industrial growth. Deng, who held the military and political power, proved to be right person at the right time to lead the country to agile progressive track by unconditionally and alacritously switching the command economy to a market-oriented economy without any blueprint.

Deng Launched Economic Reform and the Open-Door Policy

> The best government is a benevolent tyranny tempered by an occasional assassination
>
> Voltaire (1694–1778)

In 1976, the three most powerful leaders, Zhou Enlai, Zhu De (Hakka), and Mao Zedong passed one after another. China was basically an underdeveloped agrarian economy, plagued by the devastating consequences of the Great Leap Forward (1958–60) and the Cultural Revolution (1966–76). Chairman Mao lost his son, Mao Anying, on November 25, 1950, in the Korean War. He was killed by the 3rd Bomb Group of the United States Air Force. It was said that has was cooking when he was killed in a makeshift building near caves. By October 1976, the Cultural Revolution had ended. With the strong backing of Ye Jianying (Hakka) and other veterans, Deng was appointed as Vice-Chairman of the Central Committee, Vice-Premier of the State Council, Vice-Chairman of the Military Commission and Chief of the General Staff of the People's Liberation Army at the Third Plenary Session of the Tenth Central Committee in July 1977. In March 1978, he was elected Chairman of the Fifth National Committee of the Chinese People's Political Consultative Conference. Deng soon encouraged the country to adopt an enlightened environment for discussing miscellaneous social and political issues after Mao's dark era. In December 1978, the party discarded the notion of class struggle and announced the party's main goal would become economic development.

Although he had worked many years under Mao in the New China, Deng did not hold Mao's vision about how to lead and manage a country. Ideas change paths of history. Formation of ideas comes from creativity, education, and learning from environment. Both Deng and Mao did not receive formal higher education. Deng did not seem to be interested in reading. Mao had a life-time interest in reading. Deng spent his youth in France, while Mao spent some of his youth in cleaning floors in the library of Beijing University. The differences in ethnicities (Deng was Hakka and Mao was Han) and human capital information experiences between the two most influential figures in the last seventy years might explain much about the differences of how the two old men led and managed China in their final years.

By 1978 Deng Xiaoping had become the paramount leader of China till his death in 1997, replacing Mao's chosen successor, Hua Guofeng. From 1977 to early 1979, he resumed the college entrance examination in China and launched the reform and re-opening of China. The former has increased the education and human capital and the latter has enhanced China's productivity both in scale, scope, and speed unpreceded in human history. He reversed China's direction of development, backwards this time, in Marx's historical progress, by introducing capitalism into China. After almost half a century of Mao's communism, China finally turned to Marx's historically determined progressive stage, capitalism, under Deng's leadership. Today Deng is reputed to be the architect of modern China.

Chance favors the prepared. Deng had ideas for economic reform long before he became the top man. Liu Shaoqi and Deng aspired to introduce individual responsibility for increasing the incentives for agricultural production in the 1950s. They were defeated by Mao. But Deng did not change the point of view about organizing a state: let people pursue economic activities freely and maintain social order by the means of guns. Einstein says: "A person who never made a mistake never tried anything new." Having seen the failures in Mao's attempts and knowing possible progresses both from Marx's doctrine and life in France, he began to put this vision into practice as soon as he seized power. Deng seldom said anything about himself and even disliked debating with others as he described himself: "Do not debate! is one of my inventions." There are little known certainly about the inner life of the man. In contrast to Mao whose youth was spent on a Manchu-reformed or a Manchu-controlled Chinese way of thinking in which ethics and obedience are the most important determinants of social order and power and lived in the environment that foreigners from many countries humiliated the weakened country, Deng spent much of his youth in a main center of Western civilization and had opportunities to observe behavior of people and socioeconomic structures in France. He also spent some time in Russia which might have provided him environment to properly study Marx's ideas on revolution and capitalism. The foreign experiences might explain why this farmer boy who had never formally received higher education could have changed China's history, and historical path of mankind as well.

Deng's Early Life in France and Late in China

> The least of things with a meaning is worth more in life than the greatest of things without it.
>
> Carl Jung (1875–1961)

> The power of intuitive understanding will protect you from harm until the end of your days.
>
> Lao Tzu

Deng had a clear vision for China when he opened China's door: market economy with public dominant ownership, open nation, spread of education, and development of science and technology. This vision was perhaps formed in youth in one of the main Western civilization centers, France.

Deng Xiaoping (Deng Xiansheng) was born in Paifang Village in Xiexing Town, Guang'an County, Province Sichuan, on Aug. 22, 1904 (died on Feb. 19, 1997). His father, Deng Wenming, was a small landowner. He wished his eldest son to receive education. At five, he entered a private pre-school, at seven a modern primary school, and then a middle school in his native county. In 1915, he studied mathematics, science, and geography at a higher-level primary school. In 1918, his father sent him to Chongqing for a programme of work and study in France. He left the primary school and went to Chongqing to prepare his journey to France. In the summer of 1920, he graduated from the Chongqing Preparatory School. On September 1920, he sailed on a ship for France from Shanghai. He arrived at Marseilles on 19 October. He got his first job as the rolling-mill of the Schneider works. He worked fifty or more hours a week with daily wage 6.6 francs, the wage being lower than for apprentices. He quit the job after three weeks. He went to Paris at the age of sixteen. He worked most of time with numerous unskilled jobs. Since January 1921, he worked as temporary and unskilled worker in the rest of his five years in France. He worked hard to survive with little income, without any other financial support. His dream to study in France was not realized. He had no opportunity to receive higher education there. The lack of French influences via high academic education might be a main determinant for him to know not much about academic interpretations of Marxism in Europe. It was a fortune for China as a wrong understanding might be worse than not study at all.

When he was in France, Marxism and other schools of socialist thought were widely spread. Under the influence of Zhou Enlai and others, Deng began to be interested in Marxism. In 1922, he joined the Chinese Socialist Youth League in Europe. In June 1923, he was elected to the executive committee of the association. In the second half of 1924, he joined the CCP. In 1925, he was appointed as special representative to the Lyon Area Party Branch when he was working in Lyon. He lived five years in France from age 16 to 21. He had become a revolutionary Marxist. His early concept and understanding of Marxism is more European in nature than mainland Chinese.

During the long stay in France, he should have observed and had a basic understanding of modern industrial economy. His confidence in China's course with Marxism and belief in science and technology might have been formed under French environment. He thought that China would not have a bright future without learning from the world. Once he was in power, he soon opened the closed country to global economies with advanced science and technology. This vision was unlike Mao's, even though he had been Mao's follower for many years. What affect one's vision about life and society are intangible. These effects are often invisible, deep, multiply dimensional, and long lasting. As Deng did not say much about his personal life, it is difficult for contemporary people to know accurately the impact of French experiences on the youth.

France showed him what life meant for being Chinese in an enriched capitalist society with liberty and freedom. The experience might explain why he reformed China in his France-experienced way with the unshaking faith in science and technology, but little interest in Western democracy. This is similarly true for many Chinese who returned from America after having lived there many years. As a poor young man in France without receiving higher education and finding a fair-pay secured job, he might not have faith in what liberal ideas could bring about for life. Man trusts and learn from in what he sees and experiences, not in what he reads about. In his time, democracy had little to do with Chinese people in France.

On 7 January 1926, Deng traveled to Moscow to study in the Communist University of the Toilers of the East. He late studied at the Sun Yat-sen University. He came back to China in 1927. Deng joined Chinese comrades in the spring of 1927 in Xi'an at the Sun Yat-sen Military and Political Academy. He soon went to Hankou in Hubei Province, working as a secretary for the Central Committee of the CCP. From

1932 to 1948, Deng was appointed many positions. After the PRC was founded on October 1, 1949, he spent a few years in the Great Southwest. In July 1952, Deng was appointed as both executive Vice-Premier of the Government Administration Council (which was to become the State Council in 1954) and Vice-Chairman of the Financial and Economic Commission. He was then appointed as the Director of the Office of Communications and Minister of Finance. In 1955, he was elected to the Committee's Political Bureau. In his report to the Party's Eighth National Congress in 1956, Deng pointed to the necessity for the Party to face reality. He suggested democratic centralism. He also asked that the Party improve collective leadership at all levels of Organizations. In the Cultural Revolution, he was twice removed from office. Deng was labeled the "No.2 Capitalist Roader in China". In October 1969, he was dismissed from all his posts and sent a County in Jiangxi Province. He did manual labor, living with his wife and his aged stepmother. In September 1971, when Lin Biao was disgraced from power, Deng came to be in office again. In 1973, Mao restored him to his post as Vice-Premier of the State Council. In January 1975, he was reappointed Vice-Premier and appointed Vice-Chairman of the Central Committee, Vice-Chairman of the Central Military Commission and Chief of the General Staff of the PLA. By 1975, he called for developing the national economy. But Mao Zedong disliked Deng's deviation from his course. In 1976, Deng was dismissed from all his posts inside and outside the Party.

Hakkas as the Seeds in Modernizing Chinese Societies

He who is not a good servant will not be a good master.

Plato (423-347 BC)

Historical bifurcations are often caused by short men, sick men, discriminated men, famous losers, neglected minorities, small groups of people, children of brute fathers and drunken mothers, or small countries. History is full of empires built by an ethnic group of people with small population. The Mongolian empire and British empire are examples with mighty. The last dynasty of China, for instance, was controlled from 1664 to 1911 by the Manchus whose population was less than one percent of China's population. In academic fields Jewish people have made great contributions in the last 150 years. By 2017 902 individuals were awarded Nobel Prizes, of whom 203 were Jewish people. The percentage of Jewish Nobel laureates is 11,25% above average of the global populations. By 2018, 37% of Nobel laureates in economics were Jewish descent (List of Jewish Nobel Laureates 2018). Karl Marx, Einstein, Freud, Samuelson, and many other Jewish people influenced much of the contents of modern textbooks in higher education. Intellectual contribution and wealth accumulation by Jewish once discriminated in the white-people-dominated world and wealth accumulation by Hakka once discriminated in Asia gave suitable examples of bitter discrimination in one generation leading to the fruitful life in another generation.

Jewish Karl Marx argues: "Men's ideas are the most direct emanations of their material state." The Hakka sub-ethnicity within China are often called the "Jewish of Asia". Hakka people have commonly been labeled as "the guest people" in China for several hundred years. Their economic conditions and social status in traditional China were somehow like the European Jewish before WWII. European Jewish Karl Marx advocated communism and many American Jewish Nobel laureates in economics advocated free market. Hakka Hong Xiuquan (1814–1864) self-proclaimed brother of Jesus Christ and leader of the Taiping Movement that conquered Southern areas of China. Hakka Sun Yat-sen in the 1910s advocated socialism to destroy the Qing dynasty. Hakka Deng introduced market-mechanism with socialist character to enrich China and his family. Hakka Taiwanese wanted to be independent of mainland China. These Hakka people were the leaders in China in exercising all the Western dominant ideologies one by one, according to their social status and material conditions, in the Chinese soil. Hakka highly valuated diligence, co-operation, wealth, and education. Hakka did not achieve academic achievements and recognitions like the Jews. Hakka people have accumulated huge wealth.

Another great Hakka Lee Kuan Yew (1923–2015) informed Deng about how to have a prosperous market economy under centralized government. Deng visited Singapore in November 1978. The economic development of Singapore at that time was perhaps not very impressive for Deng because he was in France before and visited Japan in October 1978. But Singapore's influence on his ideas about economic reform was perhaps much more inspiring and deeper than France's romantics and liberty, America's prosperity and democracy, and Japan's skyscrapers. He met with Lee Kuan Yew, Singapore's founding father, the first Prime

Minister of Singapore from 1959 to 1990. Lee told Deng that Singapore was mainly built by descendants of lowly-educated poor Chinese coolies. Lee studied at the London School of Economics. He graduated from Fitzwilliam College, Cambridge, with double starred-first-class honors in law. Under his leadership Lee led his country from a developing economy into a developed economy within a single generation. Lee was also the only overseas Hakka leader who explicitly advocated Confucianism in Singapore. Unlike Hakka in Singapore, Hakkas in Taiwan now seldom mention Confucianism but explicitly advocate American values. Smart "guests" know how to use, benefit from, and play with the environment. Like Jewish in white societies, Hakkas in Chinese societies have made positive contributions to the societies and had gains from their contributions.

In his first and only official visit to Singapore, Deng met with Lee for three hours. He was interested in how the backwater fishing village could have been transformed into a leading global city. In 1978 alone some 400 delegations from China visited Singapore. Deng asked Chinese officials to learn from Singapore on his well-known *nanxun* in 1992. During the rest of his life, China learned much from Singapore's developmental experience with Lee's gleaned lessons in dealing with the West and South Asia in the Hakka manner. The influences of Hakka Singaporeans were perhaps far more important than America and Japan. Vogel (2011: 290) describes the relation between Deng and Lee as follows: "Deng admired what Lee had accomplished in Singapore, and Lee admired how Deng was dealing problems in China. Before Deng's visit to Singapore, the Chinese press had referred to Singapore as the 'running dogs of American imperialism.' A few weeks after Deng's visit, ... Singapore was described as a place worth studying. ... Deng found orderly Singapore an appealing model for reform, and he was ready to send people there to learn about city planning, public management, and controlling corruption." Lee visited China 33 times over 37 years. In December 2018 Beijing conferred the "China Reform Friendship Medal" on the late Prime Minister Lee for his deep involvement in China's reform and opening-up journey at the Great Hall of the People to celebrate China's 40-years reform. Lee's comments and suggestions were politically and culturally more suitable for China's development than any Japanese or Western people.

The significance of Hakka in Chinese societies is illustrated by a list of some well-known names: Sun Yat-sen, Deng Xiaoping, Zhu De, Ye Ting, Zhang Guotao, Chen Shui Bian, Lee Teng-hui, and Annette Lu in

Taiwan, Lee Kuan-yew family in Singapore, and many prosperous businessmen in Asia. Many of Taiping Tian Guo's leaders were Hakka: Hong Xiu Quan, Yang Xiu Qing, Shi Da Kai, Wei Chang Hui. Zeng Guo Fan (the Qing official) often referred to Hakka women as "Big foot hillbilly witch" since the Hakka females never bound their feet like other Han Chinese girls. In war they often fought side by side with men. We have also other famous Hakkas as Han Suyin and the Song family. Han Suyin (1965: 24) described how Hakka fled southward to escape the invasion of Chinggis Khan during the 13th century: "The Hakkas were driven further south, or to mountainous poor areas. … Because of their mobility, hardihood and fierceness, the dynasties began to regard the Hakkas as potential pioneers, good or resettling the sub-populated areas. … Circumstance thus defined their group character: clannish, thrifty, loyalty to each other, bad neighbors and ready fighters, the name Hakka stuck to them and they became proud of it."

In 1929, Hakka historian Hsieh T'ing-yu (Constable 1996: 10; Hsieh 1929) portrays the stereotypical Hakka as such: "The character of the Hakkas is shown quite clearly in their name and history. They are a strong, hardy, energetic, fearless race with simple habits but a very contentious and litigious disposition. Self-reliant and active, their rapid expansion and fondness of property have often brought them into conflict with their neighbors. … The Hakkas are proud of the literary accomplishments of their ancestors; they claim many well-known literati. … The Hakkas are a 'people of the future,' unhampered by the prejudices or the easy-going slackness of the old land owners. … Fundamentally the Hakka is a farmer, forced by poverty to struggle with the unproductive soil. …The women folk are strong and energetic and have never adopted foot-binding as a custom."

Sometimes events appear accidental, but there are invisible reasons behind their occurrence. Karl Marx points out: "Men make their own history, but they do not make it just as they please; they do not make it under circumstances chosen by themselves, but under circumstances directly found, given and transmitted from the past. The tradition of all the dead generations weighs like a nightmare on the brain of the living." Differing from Han Chinese Mao's emphasis on morality, Hakka Deng knew the importance of wealth for development. The Hakkas were accustomed to never being fully free as they always lived as guests with low social status until modern times. They know the importance of wealth and are masters of accumulating wealth in difficult social and economic conditions.

Hakkas played a significant role in Mao's revolutionary course. Many Hakka heroes, Deng Xiaoping, Zhu De, Chen Yi, Li Lisan, Guo Moruo, Fu Lianchang, Hu Yaobang, Ye Jianying, Tan Zhenlin, all assumed important roles in the New China. Some of them suffered greatly during the Cultural Revolution. Deng's return in 1977 resulted in many influential Hakka leaders being rehabilitated. Deng secured military power with his re-appointed General Ye Jianying, also a Hakka. Hakka Hu Yaobang became the new chairman of the party, replacing Mao's chosen successor. In 1984, "Hakka individuals made up half the Standing Committee of the Politburo, eleven of the 105 top leaders, and many of the lower rank." (Erbaugh 1996: 225). Many Hakka leaders in Chinese societies are well known for emphasizing Confucian value on education and for being skillful at accumulating wealth. The great Hakka leaders made miscellaneous strategies in modernizing Chinese societies, perhaps with the exception of fostering genuine democratization.

Deng's Pragmatic Approach to China's Reality

> The man who reads nothing at all is better educated than the man who reads nothing but newspaper.
>
> Thomas Jefferson (1743–1826)

> Every form of addiction is bad, no matter whether the narcotic is alcohol, morphine or idealism.
>
> Carl Jung (1875–1961)

Deng is known for his joy in playing cards, not like Mao for reading books for teenage. He is known for having no fixed ideology, not like Mao who spread his own Mao's thought. Deng had the three pre-eminent qualities which Max Weber considered a decisive important for the politician: "passion, a feeling of responsibility, and a sense of proportion." Deng's reasoning for his economic policy is: "It matters not whether a cat is white or black; as long as it catches mice, it is a good cat." This may be interpreted his own understanding Marx's well-known saying: "The philosophers have only interpreted the world, in various ways. The point, however, is to change it." Deng did not receive formal higher education.

His style of reasoning was apprehensible to hundred million of common Chinese people who had no idea yet about higher education, not to say a dream to receive one. Unlike highly educated, rich or born into loyal, leaders among the poor in poor countries, Deng was a common among the Chinese people, at least in terms of birth, education, and wealth.

From the setout of his reforms Deng progressed with a clear vision but without a blueprint in mind; instead, he followed his instinct formed via rich experiences in life struggles and calamities to search for power and wealth for his country and his people. He is exemplified as a bee who can build a perfect beehive without a premeditated map. Lao Tzu says about how to wisely manage: "anticipate the difficult by managing the easy." As a man who was educated with Marxism which informs positive consequences of enhancing productivity and enlarged inequality in capitalist system, Deng knew that capitalism leads to inequality and results in injustice in many aspects. He put possible consequences of his market economy in his non-academic manner which every Chinese understood: "Let some people get rich first. Poverty is not socialism. To be rich is glorious". He had confidence in that what he was doing was to enrich China and was not against Karl Marx's idea as far as China's reality was concerned. One of his most notable sayings remembered by the Chinese people in a manner like American's adhere to the concept of freedom was, "A fundamental contradiction does not exist between socialism and a market economy."

Deng played the decisive role in leading China from its slumber and poverty to dramatic changes and rapid economic progress. He argued for the necessity of modernization through economic reform. Unlike Mao, he emphasized the significance of intellectuals for modernization. Deng rehabilitated the intellectuals purged by Mao and released those living in prisons, labor reform camps, and 'stinking ninth hell' into which Mao had sent them. From 1978 on, he had selected young officials with proper education to replace ageing cadres. The system of life tenure for leading cadres was gradually abolished.

In 1979, China began to have the formal exchange of diplomatic recognition between the People's Republic and the United States. On December 15, 1978, the US and China announced to exchange diplomatic recognition on January 1, 1979. Diplomatic relations between the US and the Taiwan were to be terminated. The new foreign policy was implemented to help China to obtain economic gains from international trade. Trying to minimize possible conflicts due to ideological differences, Deng opened China to foreign economic investment, technology transfer, trade, books, and education. As China had become ever further behind advanced economies during the Mao regime, Deng could speed up economic reform with peaceful relations with advanced economies partly because nobody could have perceive China to become a strong competitor with Western advanced economies in such a short time-period. China could explore its relative advantage—cheap labor and humble servility under the party's surveillance (which guaranteed social stability and reduced labor costs due to, for instance, strikes organized by labor union)—in global division of labor(Fig. 2.1).

Although he advocated some reforms in politics, Deng did not have faith in Western democracy and individual freedom, like most Hakkas, perhaps, with the exception of Hakkas in Taiwan. His political reforms were basically for speeding up and nursing economic development. He reconstructed the political system which had functioned properly for his target. In 1986, Deng claimed: "We cannot do without dictatorship. We must not only affirm the need for it but exercise it when necessary. … if some people attempt to provoke bloodshed, what are we going to do about it? We shall first expose their plot and then do our best to avoid shedding blood, even if that means some of our own people get hurt."

Fig. 2.1 Deng visited America in 1979 (*Source* http://www.sohu.com/a/133768166_513610)

(He 2001: 45). He compared China's centralized power with America's division of power as follows:

> I have often criticized people in power in the United States, saying that actually they have three governments. Of course, the American bourgeoisie uses this system in dealing with other countries, but when it comes to internal affairs, the three branches often pull in different directions and that makes trouble. We cannot adopt such a system.
>
> The greatest advantage of the socialist system is that when the central leadership makes a decision it is promptly implemented without interference from any other quarters. When we decided to reform the economic structure, the whole country responded; when we decided to reform the economic structure, the whole country responded; when we decided to establish the special economic zones, they were soon set up. We don't have to go through a lot of repetitive discussion and consultation, with one branch of government holding up another and decisions being made but not carried out. From this point of view, our system is very efficient.

After the 1989 Tiananmen massacre, China's foreign relations were severely affected. Many countries with revulsion and disgust at the killing of people by the government and the PLA. There were many economic sanctions on China. China's door to the outside world was mostly closed after 5th June till the early 1990. By 1991, China had made efforts to restore diplomatic engagement, support international organizations, and encourage foreign investment and trade.

Soon after 1990 China's economic development had not slowed down partly because Deng understood the masses and the Chinese culture. The protest movement from Beijing was partly due to rising prices in Beijing and Shanghai and fixed wages of intellectuals and urban workers who had enjoyed the pride over the farmers and other regions and received extra gains from the centralized planning economy. Deng solved the main social conflict by freeing markets in Beijing and Shanghai as well as other Chinese cities. Even until today one seldom hears strong demand for implementing democracy in highly educated and smart Beijing and Shanghai. Beijing's and Shanghai's "citizens" enjoyed benefits from high prices of houses and other special welfare from the government. In recent years, many residents from the two cities sold apartments (or rent them) and immigrated to America, Canada, and Australia. A retired couple can spend comfortably the rest of their lives in America with the money from selling an apartment of a few hundred square meters in either of the two cities.

Deng carried out economic reform steadily and gradually. He also changed policies slowly and partially. The Chinese revolutionary leader was aware of the complexity of social and economic changes. Instead of carrying out reform in a ubiquitous manner, he scrupulously selected certain regional areas for initiating reform. The initial areas were chosen in a way that they could remain socially orderly and controllable under the party. A city like Shanghai or Beijing was not the logical choice (as risks were too high). After knowing the consequences of the reform, he would spread the successful policies to the country. Political stability and national harmony enforced by guns if needed were his unshakable principles. The Chinese people had been collectively obedient. The obedience to authority was formed due to the history of Manchus ruling, the (quasi) colonization experience by multiple countries, and Mao's further unification with modern guns. Deng launched economic reform only in provinces of Sichuan and Anhui. He started to establish four special economic zones. Fourteen coastal cities were allowed open to the outside world. He insisted on economic co-operation with foreign countries, absorbing foreign capital, and learning science and technologies and managerial skills. His style of reform rapidly enlarged gaps in income and wealth between households, urban and rural areas, and Southern and Western regions. Deng had perhaps little idea that those initial differences would become permanently enlarged due to scale and scope economies in modern economies which he perhaps knew little about. His initial promise to the Chinese people of "someone becoming rich first and others following" would "naturally" become a broken promise in the market economy.

Deng held that a single party should lead the country. But the contents of the party should be modernized. He initiated political reform. In August 1980, he argued for socialist democracy and reformation of legal system. By 1986, he revitalized the whole state apparatus, increased efficiency by stimulating the initiative of the people and of the grass-roots units. In the Central Committee Leading Group for Financial and Economic Affairs in September 1986, Deng (1994) said: "We have to discuss what the content of political reform should be and work out the details. In my opinion, its purposes are to bring the initiative of the masses into play, to increase efficiency and to overcome bureaucratism. Its content should be as follows: First, we should separate the

Party and the government and decide how the Party can exercise leadership most effectively. This is the key and should be given top priority. Second, we should transfer some of the powers of the central authorities to local authorities to strengthen our relations between the two. At the same time, local authorities should likewise transfer some of their powers to lower levels. Third, we should streamline the administrative structure, and this is related to the devotion of powers." The Thirteenth National Congress in October 1987 declared reform of the political structure. The party decided on separating the functions of the party and the government, delegating powers to lower levels, reforming government organs and the personnel system relating to cadres, establishing a system of consultation and dialogue, and improving a number of systems relating to socialist democracy and strengthening the socialist legal system. Deng asked for abolishing permanent tenure in leading posts. At the Party's Thirteenth National Congress and the First Plenary Session of the Thirteenth Central Committee, he withdrew his candidacy for membership in the Central Committee and its Political Bureau and kept the reappointment as Chairman of the Central Military Commission.

Deng deemed that officials should be educated for effective management. He abolished Mao's vision of class struggle by the barrel of a gun and highly valued education in recruiting cadres. He considered intellectuals as the core of a modernization program. In the early 1980s, the top leaders, Deng, Chen Yun, Hu Yaobang, and Zhao Ziyang did not have technical background. Technocrats began to form a new leadership in the Twelfth Party Congress in 1982. There was a massive turnover of Chinese leaders at all levels in the 1980s. From 1980 to 1986, more than 1,370,000 senior cadres recruited before 1949 retired. The state replaced them with more than 469,000 college-educated young people above the county level. This also encouraged young people to receive higher education. China had been largely led by technocrats and engineers turned politicians. The three top leaders in the third generation, Jiang Zemin, Li Peng, and Zhu Rongji, and in the fourth generation, Hu Jintao, Wen Jiabao, and Zheng Qinghong, were all trained engineers.

At the National Science Conference in March 1978, Deng told the nation that science and technology are productive forces of national modernization. His subsequent statement was received as a great surprise to the country brainwashed by Mao's thought: "we cannot demand scientists and technicians to study a lot of political and theoretical books, participate in numerous social activities and political meetings not related to their work." The message to separate science and technology from the area of political struggle was revolutionary for people who had just experienced the Cultural Revolution. Younger generations of Chinese today cannot appreciate how and why so many people with higher education were full of tears when reading Deng's statement. Hundreds of thousands of Chinese intellectuals were enlightened and soon would make great contributions to the achievements of the reform even they lacked sufficient human capital and physical capital. The government switched its policy from the anti-professional ideology to the values of efficiency, educational achievement, and technical competence. From 1977, young people began to enter colleges and universities through competitive entrance examinations based on academic performance. From May 1980, postgraduate study was also introduced to campus. Under Deng's leadership China had made great achievements in economic and educational reforms. By the time that Deng died, China had established the foundation for long-term development and spread of education, advances in science and technology.

In the late 1980s, Deng began to transfer powers to younger generations, even though he retained the final say on policy decisions until his death. Brook describes him in this manner: "Deng Xiaoping was a pragmatic administrator rather than an inspired thinker, a deft politician rather than a Greater Helmsman. But he was also a confirmed Leninist, committed to the concept of a vanguard Communist Party leading the nation toward socialism rather than mediating among competing interest groups. If he and Chairman Mao share anything, it is the presumption that policies can be assured only by monopolizing power at the top" (Brook 1998: 20–21).

The One-Party System of the Elite, for the Elite, and by the Elite

> Freedom of opinion can only exist when the government thinks itself secure.
>
> Bertrand Russell (1872–1970)

China was conquered, expanded, controlled, and managed by the Manchus from 1664 to 1911. The Manchus co-operated with the

Mongols and Han Chinese in the national management. The close relations with the Mongols were maintained through marriage and other methods and with the Han Chinese through education and respect and utilization of Han Chinese culture. Even when a Han Chinese was successful in the examination system, the system did not "automatically" guarantee a secured official position. If a talented Han Chinese was critically creative and spoke out openly and honestly, not only he but also his enlarged family (including his and his wife's relatives) might be exterminated. If he was critically creative and *mo yan* (keep one's mouth closed), he might have his and his family lives spared. Only extremely talented Han Chinese who could give proper suggestions and write ethnically and politically correct articles could work together with the Manchu masters. While the Manchu emperors were well-educated, talented, diligent, and (most of them) not even corrupt, few creatively and honestly talented Han Chinese could have survived in such a leadership model over centuries. This style of national management has kept China, for better or worse, politically integrated, and socially orderly even in the New China after the Cultural Revolution. This was also a key factor for China to be able to have experienced economic growth with social stability without invading other lands. A nomadic group of people could conquer great territories because of inner unification with mutual trust and cruelness towards outsider. The modern prosperous democratic economies were domestically co-operative and invaded other countries in their initial stages of modern development. Colonization was not only economically beneficial but also played important role in maintaining social order and increasing domestic securities. Over many hundred years, farmer Han Chinese, when not under invaders' control, used all methods, often very cruel, to maintain social order (harmony). The Chinese government had little sense about human rights within China, but appeared to behave nicely, and sometimes even humanely (at least, without calculating monetary gains) in international affairs. This farmer mentality or way of political gaming was formed over centuries.

The CCP does not spouse any comprehensive theory for national management; it has developed a strategy of 'deception', prefixing 'Chinese' to any Western theory, which was to be diffused among the unquestioning Chinese people. One reads: 'Chinese Marxist legal theory', 'Chinese market economy', 'Chinese socialism', and so on. The common character of these "Chinese" theories is not rationally based. One might be surprised at how this practice could have been pervaded on Chinese cultural soil over so many years. An obvious reason is that the party has had monopolistic power over almost all aspects of Chinese life. Historically speaking, a consequence of the Manchu ruling over China was that Chinese people tolerate almost anything that the central authority stipulates in the name of national harmony or social stability. The achievements of the one-child policy and economic reform can hardly be understood without noticing the formation of Chinese collective mindset formed during the Qing dynasty. Mao ruled China in many ways similar with how the Manchus ruled China during 1644 to 1911.

Gray (1990: 19) describes China's political culture as follows: "The object of that culture was the maintenance of peace and stability in an agrarian society, in which change was neither sought nor anticipated. The highest value recognized in China was social harmony. The method by which the Chinese sought to realize this value was the control of conflict by the imposition of hierarchically organized authority." This tradition is continued. However, how to play political games with the same goal (that is, to stabilize social order under one party) varied between Mao's China and Deng's China. The key difference between Mao and Deng was that Mao employed people with little formal education, while Deng employed people with higher formal education (especially in natural science and engineering). The CPC has changed from a poor and non-educated-based party to a party of the educated. This profound transformation has been described as "mass to elite" (Brodsgaard 2018). In Mao's time, one could join the party only because he was born into a poor family and had none or very basic education. Mao's people are ignorantly and destructively passionate; and Deng's people are constructively and cunningly rational. Like endings of some love stories, the former leaves a passionate, fruitless, and sad story, while the latter builds a prosperous family with properly educated children.

Han Chinese Mao utilized morality as tool to control power, while Hakka Deng applied market economy to enrich the nation and his family. Mao did not leave wealth to his children and relatives. His wife was put in prison soon after he died. Deng, like many of Hakkas in the world, enriched his country as well as family. China's politic system has changed greatly after the death of Deng. However, there was no structural change, especially as far as economic policies are concerned. In his report to the 19th Party Congress in October 2017, Xi said: 'the Party exercises overall leadership over all areas of endeavor in every part of the country' (Xinhua

News Agency 2017/10/18). The new leader is said to be "back" towards Mao's line from Deng's line. As China is today not at a structurally turning point, one individual can make some influences in socioeconomic evolution, but not structurally.

A basic condition for a long-term prosperity in any economy is securing social conditions that allow one's short-run and long-term gains from efforts in work, education, learning, investment in property markets, and saving to be fruitful. China has had a relatively orderly social environment in recent decades. This stability has been important for bolstering the economic advancement that China has achieved.

Social Order Maintained by the Legal System and the *Guanxi*

The single party controls the country. The party is the law in China. This is a partial improvement in Chinese life as there was not even any law nationally valid over some centuries before the party unified the country. Mao, who survived from partially colonized China and domestic wars, had trust in governing by gun, and did not respect law. Deng insisted on the significance of law for modernization. He considered law essential to socialist modernization. After assuming supreme power in late 1978, he abolished Maoist legal nihilism. The government reformed and restructured the legal system. The State Constitutions were revised, law was re-designed, and judicial organs were reorganized. By 2000, China made substantial progresses in civil and economic law. China adopted constitutional and administrative law or criminal law and procedure (Keller 2001; Chen 2002). Many new rules, such as rules on the regulation of securities and futures markets, consumer protection, intellectual property, banking, and insurance, were introduced.

Since 1949, the party has continued its political power by controlling political and legal institutions. Deng and the leaders after him have maintained the party's monopolistic political power. Since the onset of economic reform, legal systems have been improved, especially with regards to economic fields. From 1979 to 1997, China enacted 311 laws, issued 700 sets of regulations and 4000 sets of administrative rules covering a wide range of political, economic, and social areas (Burns 1999: 27). China first introduced new rules, such as rules on the regulation of securities and futures markets, consumer protection, intellectual property, banking, and insurance. Many new institutions were also established to enforce regulations.

The Chinese character of the law under the party has remained the same. As demonstrated by Yu (1989: 71–72), the CCP's legal system was characterized by: "(1) it overemphasizes instrumental facets of law, (2) it regards law as an outcome of actuality, (3) it treats law as a servant of policy, and (4) it does not treat individual legal rights seriously." The contemporary situation is not much changed as described by Clarke (2003: 93) below: "Contract laws are full of mandatory provisions, while tax laws seem to be largely negotiable; judges until recently wore military-style uniforms in court; and the constitution does not in fact constitute." "Chinese law", Jones (2003: 7–8) who has worked in the area of Chinese and comparative law for more than thirty years, observes: "is very easy to misunderstand. It is not at all certain that anyone – Chinese or foreign – understands it. The reason for this is that when we think about law, we think about a formal legal system of the western type. We look at China and expect to find such things as a law of contracts, a bench and bar, and all the other paraphernalia that we associate with law. At present, one can find such institutions in China, but they are modern imports. … Although on paper modern China has all of the apparatus of a western system, it is a country that is still heavily influenced by tradition, and any study of Chinese law that concentrates solely on the statutes and institutions copied from the West is bound to come to wrong conclusions." "The pragmatic approach towards developing a legal system in China has never been systematically explained by Chinese leaders or legal scholars. … [T]he approach towards legalization is actually purely pragmatic, and despite much rhetoric, Marxist theory is largely ignored. It is ironic, therefore, that PRC legal scholars began in the early years by criticizing legal pragmatism and ended up adopting many of its basic tenets." (Yu 1989: 71). As legal scholars make designs of law under the condition that law is to continue monopolistic power of the party over the country and the party is mainly controlled by a few (if not a single), often uneducated, top leaders, scholars make the design under changeable, and often arbitrary, will of the few. The typical Chinese farmer had never known anything called reliable law over thousand years until recent years, as the Chinese law was traditionally designed for the emperor to manipulate and control rather than to fairly govern. It takes generations for a Chinese society to develop a modern culture of respecting law rather than a personal authority or party. Chinese political culture is deeply rooted in servility. For traditional Chinese farmer, there was no gaming or playfulness, but a set of unlimited duties subject to superior's will.

Although law does not protect human relations as in the West, this does not mean that Chinese society is without order. Chinese society is closely connected by *guanxi*, the Chinese social networking. The *guanxi* is built with emotion, tradition, and usual cost-benefit calculations over one's lifetime. The complexity is not only one's own network as it also related to, for instance, one's parent networks. Chinese people spend huge time, money, and other resources on creating, maintaining, expanding, and destroying *guanxi* in lifetime. One's *guanxi* network links relatives, friends, former classmates, teachers, co-workers, bosses, and all other social relations. The relationships are long-term calculations. The networking has recently rapidly changed due to changed economic relations, social mobility, and improved living conditions. In a recent study on Chinese *guanxi*, Weng and Xu (2018) focus its implications on labor market (see also Xiong, et al. 2017). The importance of the "iron rice bowl" or life-long employment has increasingly declined. China abolished the job assignment policy for university graduates and allowed state-owned enterprises to lay-off workers in the late 1990s. University graduates now search for jobs in the labor market. Fired workers can self-employ or search for other jobs. Job market mechanisms have become more transparent. Nevertheless, the *guanxi* still strongly affects China's labor market. An unqualified person may be unfairly selected for the job due to his *guanxi*. In many situations, *guanxi* reduces the efficiencies of government and companies. As an informal institution maintained and operated over centuries, *guanxi* bring about multifarious social and economic consequences. The complexity of this Chinese social networking may partly explain inefficiency of the Chinese legal system. "What ethnic Chinese", Lee Kuan Yew, stated in his opening statement at the Second World Chinese Entrepreneurs Convention in 1993, "from Hong Kong, Macao and Taiwan did was to demonstrate to a skeptical world that *guanxi* connections through the same language and culture can make up for a lack in the rule of law and transparency in rules and regulations. This *guanxi* capability will be of value for the next 20 years at least, until China develops a system based on the rule of law, with sufficient transparency and certainty to satisfy foreign investors." (*International Herald Tribute*, 23 November 1993).

The *Hukou* System for Social Order and Stability

> It is virtuous manners which constitute the excellence of neighborhood. If a man in selecting a residence does not fix on one where such prevail, how can he be wise?
>
> Mencius (13: 13)

People cannot choose where to live permanently in China since the party took over the country. The Chinese people don't consider this as a discrimination policy due to birthplace. Rapid growing inequalities between households, rural and urban areas, cities, and regions are closely related to this Chinese socialist market economy institution. The institution, like most of other economic, political, and social institutions, has been slowly but steadily reformed over decades to free Chinese people and to associate the overall development of China. The institution has gargantuan economic implications for housing markets, especially in large cities, as Chinese people's wealth is largely stored in housing markets. In recent years many people, who held Beijing or Shanghai *hukou*, sold their apartments and immigrated the USA, Canada, Australia, or New Zealand to enjoy (the rest of their) life with the gains from housing markets. The *hukou* system has also greatly "distorted" Chinese marriage markets as the urban *hukou* has great additional values in people's entire life.

Contemporary economics has little to say about how to balance economic prosperity and political/social stability. Stability, somehow interpreted as sustainability, is one of the most important concepts in understanding social and economic evolution. Social sciences still lack sufficient knowledge about relations between efficiency, fairness, economic stability, and political stability as no theory can systematically examine these issues within a single comprehensive framework. If a system is steady, its behavior is predictable. But if the system is unstable, its behavior is unpredictable. Unstable systems are characterized by catastrophes, chaos, bifurcations, lock-ins, and multiple equilibria. We daily observe both political and economic catastrophes in many poor economies and economic chaos in stock markets in developed economies. A rapid (potentially structurally chaotic) economic progress needs relatively orderly social and political environment. It is a great challenge for any society to have a (predictable) orderly social and political system for economic advancement in association with instabilities. China with the largest population on the earth could have continued rapid economic progress over the last four decades mainly because of its political stability and social order which had been established during Mao's time.

A significant institution for maintaining China's social stability is the *hukou* system. The government uses the system to locate, control, and move people. The system requires every Chinese to be registered at the place of permanent residence. Transfer of this registration requires official approval. It is quite difficult for common people to get approval for moving from the countryside to urban areas, or from smaller urban places to larger cities. Through the system the government could control population distribution over the country. The state could effectively force rural migration of 20 million workers in the years 1961–62 back to rural areas. There were some 17 million urban youths who were forced to spend many years in the countryside without opportunity to receive higher education during 1964-77. The *hukou* system enabled the state to effectively reduce urban burden. It was closely associated with strict control over employment and housing. Rationing of necessities such as food was nationally planned under the *hukou* system. The *hukou* system denies one of most important freedom in life in one's own country—freedom of where one wants to live and to work. The system divided Chinese society into spatial hierarchies with the division of agricultural and non-agricultural *hukou* status. People had social status of either "eating state grain" or "growing their own grain". By 1970, the non-agricultural population was 16%, while the agricultural population was the rest. The agricultural population basically obtained their livelihood on their own labor, while the state cared for almost every aspect of the welfare of urban *hukou* residents. The urban citizen had accesses to lifetime employment, subsidized housing, inexpensive food, education, medical care, and pensions, which were denied to peasants. As there was much urban welfare associated with the system, the state made efforts in denying most of Chinese people to access to urban *hukou*. *Hukou* is an inherited status. One might also obtain status with government jobs at commune or higher levels or other conditions. This system has helped China to make the greatest economic structural transformation in mankind, safely so far, in a very short period.

By the second half of the 1980s, many millions of migrants were then working in cities and rural industrial areas. By the later 1980s, the national floating population is estimated about 50 to 70 million (Ke 1988; Chan and Zhang 1999). As some of the controls over population mobility were relaxed, peasants searched new opportunities in cities. Many of these people are de facto urban residents for years but do not have urban or non-agricultural *hukou* status. This implies that the government could move these people out of cities if it wanted at any time. Flood of people into cities challenged the traditional system and forced the government to adjust its policies. The *hukou* system gave workers few rights or protection when they left their designated place of residence. Citizens did not feel at home when they migrated other places in their own country. The practice of the *hukou* system has also made *guanxi* more complicated in recent years.

The people in a city without its *hukou* are called floating population. They are mostly peasants. They no longer work and dwell in places where they were initially registered to live. Without the *hukou*, farmers stay in the 'temporary' category and thus cannot enjoy normal urban life. As their legal position is at best ambiguous, they are easily exploited. Many of these migrants live two worlds—they work and live in city, but socially and economically they preserve ties with their home community. The *hukou* system has been an important rule for the government to institutionalize exclusion of the rural poor out of China's cities. The government has made reforms of the *hukou* system; but its function to control migration to cities is not changed. People with non-agricultural *hukou* are generally better off than those with agricultural *hukou*. Non-agricultural *hukou* holders are also differentiated basically according to urban sizes. It is difficult to move from smaller to larger cities, but not vice versa. Due to the rigid system, the *hukou* system force millions of married couples to live permanently apart far away from each other. Urban couples might meet once or twice and each time often a few days in one year. The government has constructed complex new barriers to migrants' entry into large cities and a web of discriminatory rules that effectively put them in a similar situation to guest workers or illegal immigrants.

The family is the social unit and the responsible element in one's life in traditional China. The primary economic and social group is the household (*hu*). It consists of the element family (*jia*), plus domestic servants, laborers, or apprentices who live with the family. The family might include a married couple, their sons or adopted sons, unmarried (or adopted) daughters, the wives of married sons, children of married sons, the parents of the male member of the married couple. The Chinese family is a co-residential kinship group with common ritual practices. The members have division of labor, pooled income, and shared its expenditures. Other members of the household have their tasks and are paid on agreed conditions. An important feature of Chinse household is that the family property is equally divided among the sons. The eldest son retains the family headship and certain ceremonial duties.

Families are tied together with family lineage. This is another major social institution in traditional China. It is an exogamous patrilineal clan or lineage (*zu*). The lineage varies from a few to hundreds of constituent families. It is a group of males from a founding ancestor, plus their wives and unmarried daughters. It holds ancestral estates and performs periodic rituals. Every child from birth joins a strictly ordered system of relations with elder brothers, sisters, maternal elder brothers' wives, and other kinds of aunts, uncles, cousins, grandparents, and in-laws. These relationships are well defined and associated with rights and duties. As people in villages often have little mobility during lifetime, they tend to follow the rules of the system. Domination and submission are well defined and follow within the system. Families and kinship have played important role in creating, operating, and maintaining social networking. These grassroots social and economic relations have provided security for profits and trust for co-operation in a society which has no proper legal systems and trustful financial institutions. Weber (1951) holds that the extensive lineage organization creates obstacles to rational entrepreneurial development. It discourages individualism and independence.

For some people loyalty to the family and continuation of family name imply the meaning of life. To study hard when young, to work hard and earn living for family, to have children and to properly bring them up, and to take care of parents occupy most of active parts of one's life in traditional China. For the family, luxury is discouraged, and saving is considered virtue. The family also tends to optimize cultivation and use of more talented members. In a social environment with low trustfulness to the outsiders, few institutional protections, and few financial securities, the family provides home place, securities for future, meaning of study and work, and many other social, economic, and cultural activities.

References

Brodsgaard, K. J. (2018). China's Communist Party: From Mass to Elite Party. *China Report, 54*(4), 385–402.

Brook, T. (1998). *Quelling the People—The Military Suppression of the Beijing Democracy Movement*. Stanford: Stanford University Press.

Burns, J. P. (1999). The People's Republic of China at 55: National Political Reform. In R. L. Edmonds (Ed.), *The People's Republic of China After 50 Years*. Oxford: Oxford University Press.

Chan, K. W., & Zhang, L. (1999). The Hukou System and Rural-Urban Migration in China: Processes and Changes. *The China Quarterly, 160,* 818–855.

Chen, A. H. Y. (2002). *An Introduction to the Legal System of the People's Republic of China*. Hong Kong: Butterworths.

Clarke, D. C. (2003). Puzzling Observations in Chinese Law—When Is a Riddle Just a Mistake? In C. S. Hsu (Ed.), *Understanding China's Legal System*. New York: New York University Press.

Constable, N. (1996). Introduction—What Does It Mean to Be Hakka? In N. Constable (Ed.), *Guest People—Hakka Identity in China and Abroad*. Seattle: University of Washington Press.

Deng, X. P. (1994). On Reform of the Political Structure. In *Selected Works of Deng Xiaoping*. Vol. III. Beijing: Foreign Language Press.

Erbaugh, M. S. (1996). The Hakka Paradox in the People's Republic of China—Exile, Eminence, and Public Silence. In N. Constable (Ed.), *Guest People—Hakka Identity in China and Abroad*. Seattle: University of Washington Press.

Gray, J. (1990). *Rebellions and Revolutions—China from the 1800 s to the 1980s*. Oxford: Oxford University Press.

Han, S. Y. (1965). *The Crippled Tree*. New York: G.P. Putnam's Sons.

He, B. G. (2001). *The Democratization of China*. London: Routledge.

Hsieh, T. Y. (1929). Origins and Migrations of the Hakkas. *Chinese Social and Political Science Review, 13,* 208–228.

Jones, W. C. (2003). Trying to Understand the Current Chinese Legal System. In C. S. Hsu (Ed.), *Understanding China's Legal System*. New York: New York University Press.

Ke, C. (1988). The Problem of the Floating Population in Large Cities and Countermeasures. *Cengxiang Jianshe* 5.

Keller, P. (2001, edited). *Chinese Law and Legal Theory*. Dartmouth: Ashgate.

List of Jewish Nobel Laureates. (2018). Retrieved from https://en.wikipedia.org/wiki/List_of_Jewish_Nobel_laureates.

Vogel, E.F. (2011) *Deng Xiaoping and the Transformation of China*. Cambridge, MA: Harvard University Press.

Weber, M. (1951). *The Religion of China—Confucianism and Taoism* (translated from the German original by H. H. Gerth with an introduction by C. K. Yang). New York: The Free Press.

Weng, Y. L., & Xu, H. (2018, October). How Guanxi Affects Job Search Outcomes in China? Job March and Job Turnover. *China Economic Review, 51*, 70–82.

Xiong, A. L., Li, H. Y., Westlund, H., & Pu, Y. J. (2017, April). Social Networks, Job Satisfaction and Job Searching Behavior in the Chinese Labor Market. *China Economic Review, 43*, 1–15.

Yu, X. Z. (1989). Legal Pragmatism in the People's Republic of China. *Journal of Chinese Law, 3*, 29–51.

CHAPTER 3

Confucius as Cultural Capital in Sustaining the Butterfly Effect

The way to gain a good reputation is to endeavor to be what you desire to appear.

Socrates (470–399 BC)

Who has fully realized that history is not contained in thick books but lives in our very blood?

Carl Jung (1875–1961)

Three men's photos are seen in world more frequently than any superstar in sports and arts. Benjamin Franklin, Fukuzawa Yukichi, Mao Zedong, who are honored in their countries by having their photos on the bills with the highest values of their currencies, 100 USD, 10,000 JPY, and 100 CNY, respectively.

Benjamin Franklin (1706–1790) was one of the founding fathers of the United States. He was an American polymath, a politician, diplomat, writer, printer, political philosopher, scientist, inventor, humorist, statesman, and civil activist. He was an important figure in the history of physics for his discoveries and theories regarding electricity. He was against religious and political authoritarianism. He advocated for the scientific and tolerant values of the Enlightenment. He is repeatedly selected as the symbol of America.

W.-B. Zhang, *The Butterfly Effect in China's Economic Growth*, https://doi.org/10.1007/978-981-15-9889-0_3

Fukuzawa Yukichi (1835–1901) was the most influential expert on the West in Japan in his lifetime. He was a comprehensive exponent of the doctrines of Enlightenment. He has been widely considered the key thinker of Japan's modernization even since he became famous in Japan. He was prominent educator, writer, and propagator of Western knowledge during the Meiji period (1868–1912), founder of Keio Gijuku (now Keio University), a modern public speaker, and founder of the newspaper *Jiji Shimpo*. Even when his countrymen had little idea about the West, he began to explain almost every important thing in Western civilization. He persistently demonstrated that if Japan were not to become westernized and become strong enough to be a match for the Western nations, Japan would suffer humiliations under the Western powers like India and China had. My 2010 book, *Fukuzawa Yukichi: The Pioneer of East Asia's Westernization with Ancient Confucianism,* analyzes why he has been selected over years as the symbol of modern Japan. His family bible is the *Yi Jing*. His visions and ideas are essentially ancient-Confucian. He is the first man who extensively studied and understood the essentials of Western doctrines and still positively appreciated Eastern thought.

The man on his country's bill represents the national value and contemporary respectability of the country. No nation is perfect; they are happy and proud in similar contents but ugly in their own manner. These men's visions and values explain largely the per capita income differences between the three countries from the end of WWII till now.

Life is a game. The model or value system for a society is important in a similar way like the rules of a game. It determines, at least strongly influences, social status, respectability, worthiness, contents of leaning and behaving, reward and punishment, exchange markets in emotion and wealth in the society's interconnected value systems. The national value system involves relations of all individuals' lives from birth to death in a society. Alexis de Tocqueville describes role of religions: "The main business of religions is to purify, control, and restrain that excessive and exclusive taste for well-being which men acquire in times of equality." In sport games, some follow the rule while some play with dishonesty. National ideology is a lie that collectively agrees upon. Like the foundation of a building, the value system is a key determinant for national sustainable development. The deep parts of a value system are periodically visible or invisible. Its effects are tangible or intangible. It is difficult to explicitly judge and statistically measure the impact of a value system on socioeconomic evolution. But its long-term effects on societies are definite.

Irrespective of all possible negative consequences in association with each value system, democracy is accepted by many to be the most suitable value system for an open mobile rational society, while Confucianism was accepted by the rice-based land-locked rational societies, such as China, Korea and Vietnam. The two Confucian masters, Confucius and Mencius, were widely read and differently interpreted under a variety of social and economic conditions in China, Japan, Vietnam, and Korea. They were the "textbooks" in China, Vietnam, and Korea over many hundred years for selecting officials. Japan had no national examination to select officials and Confucianism had never deeply diffused into Japanese political culture before modern times. That is perhaps a main reason that Japan could properly see the positive aspects of ancient Confucianism, while the other Confucian cultures which had used Confucianism as the standard of selecting officials were interested in abolishing Confucianism. Any value system tends to be wrongly interpreted and biasedly applied by the powerful and interest group over time.

The dominant value system of Chinese civilization is Confucianism, while Taoism and Chinese Buddhism co-existed with Confucianism to satisfy other demands of people before the West began to influence China. The Chinese societies over history in the last two thousand years have been constructed and destroyed in association with Confucianism. To understand the butterfly effect in such a scale and scope in such a sustained manner one need to study the Chinese cultural capital, which is stored in philosophies, great scholars, artists, literature men, value systems, thought, national projects, dresses, buildings, and so on. As far as possible effects of socioeconomic structures, values and ethics on Deng's reform are concerned, Confucianism is perhaps the most important Chinese cultural capital for explaining why Deng's simple idea could lead to structural changes in China.

There are three main rational economic theories, capitalism, socialism, and Keynesianism (with blurred boundaries between capitalism and socialism) and many religions in the Western civilization. After WWII, one economic miracle after another has occurred in East Asia. National progress with millions of participants cannot happen without reasons. Ideas about social changes might come about from any place. But for seeds to grow up into trees, soil, climate, nutrition, water, and other conditions should be properly compounded over the entire development process. Initiation of socioeconomic changes may be from multiple sources. Sustainability of the changes does come from cultural values and peoples' states of mind. Economic ideas are globally public goods in the sense any culture freely applies economic knowledge. But a question is why economic development occurs culturally convergently either in the culturally similar parts of the West or East Asia. In many developing economies with large populations and even rich resources, important social and positions are held by those people who have received high education and lived in developed economies and can speak English frequently. But these economies have not continued their economic development. There is no unique way to prosperity. But a long-term prosperity over years need certain conditions. A simple faith, or pure fortune, or unlimited diligence, or animal spirits for plundering, an orderly social environment, a functional law, or durable family, or a "decent" political ideology, or good education, or rich resources does not solely lead to a long-term economic development in industrial, information-based, or knowledge-based economies. It is synergetic effects of multiple forces that sustain a complicated social system over years. Deng's idea about market economy for increasing national wealth is following Adam Smith's invisible hand and Karl Marx's economic theory for unfledged capitalist economy. What is miracle is that the application of the simple idea causes a butterfly effect in China's economic development. Mao provided the initial state for China to experience agile development. Deng flapped at the right time. Confucianism is the cultural stock for encouraging and diffusing the effect. The butterfly flapped at the right time within the right structure, and at the right state of the system.

Confucius

> I admire Confucius. He was the first man who did not receive a divine inspiration.
>
> Voltaire (1694–1778, Seldes, 1985)

Confucius (Kong Qiu, 551–479 B.C.) was born in humble circumstances in the state of Lu in modern Shandong Province. Kong He, his father, was an elderly commandant of the Lu garrison. His father died when he was at the age of three. He was brought up by his mother in poverty. He was educated at schools for commoners. At age 19 he married and had three children. He was poor and fond of learning in his youth. He is said to have various government jobs during his early 20s. His mother died when he was aged 23. He is a philosopher and politician of the Spring and Autumn period (771–476 B.C.). He left his homeland in 497 B.C and travelled around the principality states of north-east and central China. He tried to expound his political beliefs at the courts of these states without success. He returned to homeland at the age of 68. He spent his last years on teaching via the Five Classics, *Classical Poetry*, *Book of Documents*, *Book of Rites*, *I Ching* (also called *Yi Jing, Book of Changes*), and *Spring and Autumn Annals*. He sometime also gave advices to several government officials in Lu about governance and crime. He died at the age of 71 or 72, after he lost his only son and favorite disciples.

Confucius considered himself as a transmitter rather than creator or inventor. He emphasized study. His teachings on morality and ethics are focused on self-cultivation, emulation of moral exemplars and situation-dependent judgements. He did not have faith in governance through strict law. In the Chinese way of reasoning, his taught through *yin-yang* manner. A typical case is that he extensively examined the little man and gentle man and left other great, if not unlimited, varieties between the two extremes loosely alluded or remarked with innuendo. A typical example is given as follows: "When the stables were burnt down, on returning from court Confucius said, 'Was anyone hurt?' He did not ask about the horses." The paragraph is to demonstrate that the gentleman values human beings over animals. It leaves the reader to decide what one should do when faced with similar situations. People behave through self-reflection and moral cultivation, rather than following unlimited regulations in life. In the *yin-yang* system, there is not such a thing called a well-defined all-powerful deity or a universally true set of fixed principles for personal life as well as society.

Confucius was living in an age with the beginning of a process of moral reflection which had been provoked by the crisis of aristocratic society and the decline of ritual. New combinations of wealth, power, rules, and virtue were demanded in association with technological changes and server competition between states. He tried to construct a system which identified personal culture with the public good based on classical works left by the past sages. He refused to insist on certainties and refused to be inflexible. Confucius did not claim to be either superior in intelligence or in moral qualities. He was an "international" scholar. He traveled to and worked in different states with heterogeneous cultures. He has been widely considered as an influential thinker in human history. His teaching and philosophy still have a strong impact on some parts of the world.

Confucius has no foregone conclusions, no arbitrary predeterminations, and no obstinacy. He is much concerned with the administration of the state. The virtues he sought to inculcate are not those of personal holiness, nor are they designed to secure salvation in a future life but are rather those which can lead to a peaceful and prosperous community. He rarely speaks about extraordinary things, feats of strength, disorder, and spiritual beings. For him, if one does not even know life, why is one concerned with death. There are four things which he teaches: letters, ethics, devotion to the soul, and truthfulness. He is fond of learning and music. Confucius's thought emphasizes co-operation, dynamic unity, and harmony. He follows the *Yi Jing* vision and way of thinking. Things which oppose each other are complementary in the basic vision in almost all ideas called Chinese. His ideas and thought re compiled by his disciples and followers into the *Analects*. Confucius leaves no book written by himself. The *Analects* is the basic source for what is called Confucianism. His two followers deviated from their master in assuming that human nature is certain. Mencius in the fourth century B.C. assumes that human nature is good. Xun Zi in the third century B.C. assumes that human nature is evil. Whether or not man is self-interested in modern economics, there is no definitive answer about human nature to be found in Chinese philosophy from the fourth century B.C.

The Principles of Ancient Confucianism

> Success depends on previous preparation, and without such preparation there is sure to be failure.
>
> Confucius (551–479 BC)

The history of Confucianism has been politically like that of an indestructible bone toy for dogs since the appearance of the first emperor in China. The bone has been thrown around by numerous types of dogs. Each dog satisfies its idiosyncratic pleasures by playing and biting different parts of the bone. The dogs were gone but the bone reminds. The emperors who control how ancient Confucianism are interpreted and applied in China have little to do with the basic principles by the three ancient Confucianists. The Chinese cultural history since the first emperor Qin Shi Huang (259–210 BC) until today can be characterized by how ancient Confucianism is interpreted, admired, applied, criticized, and neglected subject to constant surveillance of the emperors with varied personalities and benefits/costs under heterogeneous socioeconomic conditions. Mencius' assumption of human nature being good was accepted by some emperors. Xun Zi's doctrine on human nature being evil was not advocated by any emperor. An emperor would not like the idea that he is nobody but born with evil nature and the fortune. A scholar might lose his life if he interprets ancient Confucianism in a way deviated from the emperor's personal interests. During Mao's period, the matter is quite simple—all the books of ancient Confucius were forbidden. During the Cultural Revolution, the entire nation criticized and mocked Confucius without even knowing what he said. The movement and the passion of the Chinese people during the national movement against Confucius make the younger generation of Chinese to doubt about whether the nation during the Cultural Revolution could be called a human society.

Like the Bible and Karl Marx, there is no convergence of interpretations of ancient Confucianism. Among the Confucian regions, Confucianism is applied as national value systems with diverse interpretations. Japanese Confucianism focuses on loyalty, while the Qing dynasty Confucianism emphasized the "rote" learning. In the Qing dynasty scholars who could survive the talented emperors' strict surveillance had to be practically smart as well. About two decades ago, top leaders, who are far better educated than the Mao generation top leaders, in China have begun to quote Confucius and sayings from other Confucian scholars with their own purposes and interpretations. Over 400 Confucius Institutions under the Ministry of Education are distributed globally in the name of Confucius, for better or for worse. The number varies annually as some countries close them while some others open new ones.

Ancient Confucianism was created when the area of contemporary China was composed of many smaller states. Like Europe in the nineteenth century (Western cultures did not create interesting thinkers for quite a long time after WWII), Chinese golden period in creation of thinkers is characterized by competition among states and relative freedom for scholars to travel among the states. Confucius' political thought was concentrated on harmonious co-existence of states with humanity and cultural differences. Their ideas were constructed when there was not a unified country. Like in Europe, the area now called China consisted of multiple cultures which communicated with, learnt from, and emulated each other. The three ancient Confucianist masters had life experiences in miscellaneous cultures and serve many governments.

They did not consider a world ruled by a single man or government or a universal idea/ideology/religion. They were not born into rich families. They earned their living like modern international professors, providing educational services to many states with knowledge.

A national value system is maintained due to inner mechanisms for the collective need of emotion and fairness, creation, distribution and continuation of power and wealth, reproductivity and collective survival, especially, the interests of the power group. When Confucianism was officially applied, China was either controlled by the emperor or the foreign invader. The emperors used Confucianism to solidify their power. The foreign invaders until the Opium War had neither a sophisticated rational thought system nor an acceptable religion proper for managing China.

We now list the main (ethical, political, and economic) principles commonly held by the main schools of Confucianism. I encapsulate these principles in Zhang (1999, 2003).

1. Free will and rationality

> Like Confucius of old, I am so absorbed in the wonder of the earth and the life upon it, that I cannot think of heaven and the angels.
>
> Pearl S. Buck (1892–1973)

In *The Religion of China: Confucianism and Taoism*, Max Weber (1864–1920, 1951) , German sociologist and philosopher, explains rationality of Confucianism as follows:

> In the absence of all metaphysics and almost all residues of religious anchorage, Confucianism is rationalist to such a far-going extent that it stands at the extreme boundary of what one might possibly call a 'religious' ethic. At the same time, Confucianism is more rationalist and sober, in the sense of the absence and the rejection of all non-utilitarian yardsticks, than any other ethical system, with the possible exception of J. Bentham's.

Confucius argues that each person has his own will and "I want you to be everything that's you, deep at the center of your being." Confucian rationality is concerned with the sense of justice (Schwartz 1972). It builds an ethical basis with its complex structure based on reciprocity, education, and rituals of ancestor worship. It values order, hierarchy, and tradition, and assigns the central role of maintaining social control and regulation to the extended family. Xun Zi (1: 3) avers: "The gentleman by birth is not different from other men; he is just good at employing external things." Xun Zi (1: 5) also remarks: "The coming of honor or disgrace must be a reflection of one's inner power." Xun Zi (10: 12) argues: "The ancient Kings and sages knew that if, in creating the position of ruler and superior, they did not refine and adorn him, he would prove inadequate to the task of unifying the people; that if he were not made rich and generous, he would be inadequate to act as the pitch pipe for his subordinates; and if he were not made majestic and powerful, he would prove inadequate to proscribe the violent and overcome the cruel. ... They caused the various classes of people of the world to realize that what they desired and longed for was to be found with them, and this is why their incentives work. They caused them to know that what they dreaded feared lay with them, and this is the reason their penalties inspired awe. When incentives work and penalties inspire awe, promotion of the worthy can be effected, retirement of the unworthy accomplished, and giving office to the more able and the less able according to their ability can succeed. ... Goods and commodities will come as easily as water bubbling from an inexhaustible spring."

2. Natural equality and social inequality

Natural equality among men is "hypothesized" in ancient Confucianism. Men being born equal is not questioned in Confucianism. Confucius (17: 2) says: "By nature, men are nearly alike; by practice, they get to be wide apart." Confucianism has faith in human equality, which is the basis for social mobility from low status upwards and vice versa. Mencius (11: 6) explains: "It is said in the Book of Poetry: 'Heaven in producing mankind, gave them their various facilities and relations with their specific laws. These are the invariable rules of nature for all to hold." Individuals are alike. There is no assumed greater intrinsic worth due to birth and heritage. Confucianism does not have conflicts with democratic principles such as popular sovereignty, the right of the people to choose and hold accountable those who rule them, and the inalienable nature of human rights in principles. Confucianism emphasizes the role of the sage in society; everyone can become sage, not through birth or power, but through self-improvement and virtue.

Social and economic environment has important impact on formation of human capital. Mencius (11: 7) reveals the relation: "In good years, the children of the people are most of them good, while in bad years the most of them abandon themselves to evil. It is not owing to their natural powers conferred by Heaven that they are thus different. The abandonment is owing to the circumstances through which they allow their minds to be ensnared and drowned in evil. … The sage and we are the same in kind." Xun Zi (2: 5) argues that man is human because of his human capital rather than social status or birth: "If a person cultivates his will and sense of purpose, he can take more pride in them than in riches and eminence. If he gives due weight to the Way and what is congruent with it, he will have slight regard for kings and dukes. Absorbed in the examination of his inner self, he will scorn mere external things. A tradition expresses this: The gentleman works external things; the petty man works for external things. Do whatever causes the mind to be serene though it gives the body toil, and whatever causes one's sense for what is right to develop, though it diminishes the concern for profit."

Confucianism does not lay any barrier to social status as human capital determines one's position and value in society. "If men of virtue and ability be not confided in," argued Mencius (14: 13), "a state will become empty and void. Without the rules of propriety and distinctions of right, the high and the low will be thrown into confusion. Without the great principles of government and their various business,—there will not be wealth sufficient for the expenditure." One is entitled the gentleman only if one lives up to the high moral standards, regardless of whether one was is noble or base by birth. With regard to the principles of a king, Xun Zi instructs: "Those lacking inner power shall be without honored status, those without ability shall be without office, those who lack accomplishment shall go unrewarded, and those who do not transgress shall not be rebuked. In the loyal court, none shall occupy positions out of mere good fortune. Among the people, none shall gain a living by mere good fortune."

If an uneducated man without any virtue except self-interest is put to the top position, he might easily shame country and harm the country in the name of national securities and welfare. Mencius says: "There are persons who serve the prince; they serve the prince, that is, for the sake of his countenance and favor. There are ministers who seek the tranquility of the state and find their pleasure in securing that tranquility. There are those who are the people of Heaven. They judge that, if they were in office, they could carry out their principles throughout the empire, proceed so to carry them out. There are those who are great men. They rectify themselves and others are rectified." The talented should be employed in more important positions. This classification is for the betterment of society. The Confucianists consider human inequality of capacity and the necessity of institutional efficiency with capable men as officials. Confucianism emphasizes inequality in social status due to talent rather than inequality of income and wealth. Officials should be well educated. Xun Zi (10: 13) is against equalitarianism: "If the methods of the Mohists are thoroughly carried out, then although the principle of frugality has been raised up, the world will have ever-increasing poverty; although combat has been condemned the world will daily be embroiled in strife; although the people toil away at bitter tasks, wearing themselves out and suffering from fatigue, they will increasingly be without accomplishment; although ruefully suffering and enduring hardship in condemning music each day, they will be less harmonious."

3. Cultivation through education and equal opportunity in education

Confucius (16: 9) emphasizes learning as indicator of humanity: "Those who are born with the possession of knowledge are the highest class of men. Those who learn, and so readily, get possession of knowledge, are the next. Those who learn after they meet with difficulties are another class next to these. As to those who meet with difficulties and yet do not learn—they are the lowest of the people." He taught that one should learn from others, regardless of their social positions: "When I walk along with two others, they may serve me as my teachers. I will select their good qualities and follow them, their bad qualities and avoid them." Confucius (7: 17) emphasizes lifetime learning: "Learning as if you could not reach your object and were always fearing also you should lose it." Confucius (15: 39) advocates that equal opportunity in education: "There being instruction, there will be no distinction of classes." This value is important for people to receive education. As social status is practically determined by education, education enables anyone to be successful through learning.

People may pursue learning not for the sake of learning. "It is not easy to find a man who has learned for three years without thinking of becoming an official." (Confucius, 8: 12). As education is offered for one's future, Confucius (7: 7) does not offer free education: "From the man bringing his bundle of dried flesh for my teaching upwards, I have never refused instruction." Rather than spreading a religion to serve a God, Confucius enables students to have ability to earn a living. Students ought to pay his services. He earned his living through teaching. Today Chinese get quickly educated with relatively low government costs. Families invest heavily on children's education, even though adults are not interested in learning. Nevertheless, in Chinese adult world, virtue and knowledge are seldom useful in ubiquitous *guanxi* networks. Like a room never cleaned, Chinese *guanxi* networks are connected with any kind of human relations. They have become wrong-dong sources of Chinese adult worlds.

Confucius established the first private school in China's history. Free market in education was basically established in ancient China. Confucius proposes equal opportunity of education for all: "There being instruction, there will be no distinction of classes." Both knowledge and virtue are accumulated through education and life experiences. As far as human life is concerned, nothing is so important as to learn and to constantly make self-improvement. In *The Doctrine of the Mean*, Confucius says: "To be fond of learning is to be near to knowledge. To practice with vigor is to be near to magnanimity. To possess the feeling of shame is to be near to energy. He who knows these three things, knows how to cultivate his own character. Knowing how to cultivate his own character, he knows how to govern other men. Knowing how to govern other men, he knows how to govern the empire with all its States and families. All who have the government of the Empire with its States and families have nine standard rules to follow—viz., the cultivation of their own characters; the honoring of men of virtue and talents; affection towards their relatives; respect towards the great ministers; kind and considerate treatment of the whole body of officers; dealing with the mass of the people as children; encouraging the resort of all classes of artisans; indulgent treatment of men from a distance; and kindly cherishing of the princes of the States."

Confucius emphasizes the efficiency of teaching. He considers it a waste of time if pupils were shallow in understanding and have no incentive to learn. The communication of knowledge should be conducted based on the capacity of understanding. The highest subjects will be discussed among those whose talent is above mediocrity. To those who are below mediocrity, the highest subjects may not be announced. Confucius has no intension to brain wash believers and simply maximize the number of followers. Some may obtain knowledge easily, while others may learn with great costs. Knowledge has miscellaneous effects on personality. He holds that the ancient poetry arouses the mind, the rules of propriety helps one to establish the character and music is to make man perfect. Although natural talents may vary, the most important factor for knowledge accumulation seems to be one's own efforts. He maintains that men are naturally not so much different from each other, but practice move them far apart. A simple, spontaneous humanity was not enough. Confucius says: "There is the love of benevolence without the love of learning; the beclouding here leads to a foolish simplicity. There is the love of knowing without the love of learning; the beclouding here leads to dissipation of mind. There is the love of being sincere without the love of learning; the beclouding here leads to an injurious disregard of consequences. There is the love of straight-forwardness without the love of learning; the beclouding here leads to rudeness. There is the love of boldness without the love of learning; the beclouding here leads to insubordination. There is the love of firmness without the love of learning; the beclouding here leads to extravagant conduct."

4. The state of the people, for the people, and by the moral and educated

The ancient Confucianists are concern with material living conditions of people. They justify self-interested economic pursuit. The three ancient Confucianists were all born into common families and they had to support themselves through working in fields, teaching, lecturing, and offering services to governments. None of them had a secured income. They do not neglect economic issues in their social thinking as they surely know that first is to survive as a bio-existence, rather than spiritual dreamer. They are born neither into the rich so that they could have unlimited sympathy for the poverty nor into a privileged group so that they could easily condescend others as slaves.

"If your Majesty loves wealth, let the people be able to gratify the same feeling, and what difficulty will there be in your attaining the Imperial sway?", Mencius argues that the people should be free in purchasing wealth. The main goal of society is to secure all the members' welfare. Xun Zi (27: 72) expresses the significance of people's welfare: "Heaven did not create the people for the sake of the lord; Heaven established the lord for the sake of the people." In Confucianism, the people's welfare is the sole reason for the existence of government and social ranks are arranged to serve the people rather than any other purpose. Their ideas are formed when there are free trade and free movement of people between different states. After multiple states is united under one emperor, the free spirit of intellectuals is losing as a scholar first has to justify the existence of a single monopoly who is empowered by Heaven through birth, even the rest should be selected by examinations.

5. A hierarchical social structure supported by talent and merit

Confucius conceives that individuals represent the articulation of the order into a hierarchy of parts and wholes. According to Xun Zi (9: 19), "Why can man form a society? I say it is due to the division of society into classes. How can social divisions be transformed into behavior? I say it is because of humans' sense of morality and justice. Thus, if the sense of morality and justice is used to divide society into classes, concord will result." The Confucian ideal society is hierarchical; this hierarchical system is socially mobile according to principles of morality and justice, rather than birth. A society is to be guided by morality and controlled by ceremony. He accepts natural differences in men as politically fundamental. The character of these differences necessitates a variety of kinds and functions among men in society.

Confucius' social order is built upon a basic assumption that men are educable. Confucius conceives of individuals and the state as an organic whole. It is only when the whole is healthy that it is possible for people to perform their functions and dwell in an efficient and secure state. Confucius teaches that every individual has strict duties: a subject must respect his ruler and a wife must respect her husband. There is a strict division of labor in Confucius' system. One should not interfere in others' official affairs. If one is not associated with any office, one should have nothing to do with plans for the administration of its duties. One should examine oneself to judge whether one is worthy of one's place: "A man should say, I am not concerned that I have no place; I am concerned how I may fit myself for one. I am not concerned that I am not known; I seek to be worthy to be known." Xun Zi argues that society should locate the important position to capacity disregarding birth: "Do not regard seniority but advance the worthy and able, dismiss the incompetent and incapable without delay;... develop the common people without waiting to compel them by laws.... Yet, although a man be the descendant of a king, duke, prefect, or office, if he does not observe the rules of proper conduct and justice, he must be relegated to the common ranks."

The most talented man with virtue would better society if he is endowed with power. According to Confucius (4: 8), different subjects of learning play varied roles on the mind: "It is by the Odes that the mind is aroused. It is by the Rules of Propriety that the character is established. It is from Music that the finished is received." According to Confucius, both learning and thinking are significant for cultivation and problem solving: "Learning without thought is labor lost; thought without learning is perilous." Confucius (13: 5) emphasizes applications of what one learns: "Though a man may be able to recite the three hundred Odes, yet if, when entrusted with a governmental charge, he knows not how to act, or if, when sent to any quarter on a mission, he cannot give his replies unassisted, notwithstanding the extent of his learning, of what practical use is it?" Xun Zi advocates the necessity for social inequalities: "Where the classes of society are equally ranked, there is no proper arrangement of society; where authority is evenly distributed, there is no unity; and where everyone is of like status, none would be willing to serve the other. ... Two men of equal eminence cannot attain each other; two men of the same low status cannot command each other—such is the norm of Heaven. When power and positions are equally distributed and likes and dislikes are identical, and material goods are inadequate to satisfy all, there is certain to become contention. Such contention is bound to produce civil disorder, and this disorder will result in poverty. ... There is equality insofar as they are not equal." Xun Zi (7: 4) says: "Being the worthiest of men, they are able to help the unworthy. Being the strongest of men, they are able to be magnanimous toward the weak. Certainly they are capable of placing others in mortal peril, but they would be ashamed to engage in conflict. With calm solemnity they perfect the arts of civilization and display them to the whole world so that violent states will become peaceful and transform themselves. Only when this has been done and yet some persist in occasioning calamitous portents or remain perversely twisted do they apply the death penalty."

6. Reliance on mutual obligation rather than law

> It is possible for one never to transgress a single law and still be a bastard.
>
> Hermann Hesse (1877–1962)

In Confucianism, ritual, propriety, self-cultivation and moral over codified law are the primary means of an effective and orderly society. Confucius considers that the virtue is more important than law in maintaining a harmonious society. For him, if the people improve themselves and have a sense of shame, the law would never need to be invoked. Confucius says: "In hearing litigations, I am like any other body. What is necessary is to cause the people to have no litigations. If the people be led by the laws, and uniformity sought to be given them by punishments, they will try to avoid the punishment, but have no sense of shame. If they be led by virtue, and uniformity sought to be given by the rules of propriety, they will have the sense of shame, and moreover will become good." This view is essential for understanding the Confucian cultures built on rice fields. It should be noted that Xun Zi favors law more strongly than Mencius.

7. The rectification of names

> There is no evil to which the mean man, dwelling retired, will not proceed, but when he sees a superior man, he instantly tries to distinguish himself, concealing his evil, and displaying what is good.
>
> *The Great Learning* (505–436 BC)

In the Confucian social system, men are ranked as in the following way: "Those who are born with the possession of knowledge are the highest class of man. Those who learn, and so, readily, get possession of knowledge, are the next. Those who learn after they meet with difficulties are another class next to these. As to those who meet with difficulties and yet do not learn; they are the lowest of the people." Confucius classifies people based on knowledge. Fan Chi asks Confucius about benevolence. Confucius replies: "It is to love all men". He then asks about knowledge. Confucius says: "It is to know all men." Fan Chi wonders what Confucius means by these answers. Confucius further explains: "Employ the upright and put aside all the crooked—in this way, the crooked can be made to be upright." Xun Zi (9: 1) applies the doctrine of the rectification of names: "Although they be the descendants of kings and dukes or knights and grand officers, if they are incapable of devotedly observing the requirements of ritual and moral principles, they should be relegated to the position of commoners. Although they be the descendants of commoners, if they accumulate culture and study, rectify their character and conduct, and are capable of devotedly observing the requirements of ritual principles and justice, they should be brought to the ranks of a prime minister, knight, or grand officer." The rectification of names and education work together to prevent biased news for the people to properly understand functions of the society, as Xun Zi (6:3) puts: "Some men indulge their inborn nature and emotions, are content with unrestrained passion and an overbearing manner, and behave like animals. They are unfit for employment to put usages in conformity with good form or bring success to government. Nonetheless, some of what they advocate has a rational basis, and their statements have perfect logic, enough indeed to deceive and mislead the ignorant masses."

8. Market mechanisms in education and proper wealth distribution

Confucius (8: 13) holds that profit is justified if it is obtained through proper way. Whether wealth and social products should be equally or unequally distributed among the population and what political economic mechanism should be accepted to determine income and property distributions are important in determining the division of labor and the division of consumption. One is paid according to the merit. In *The Doctrine of the Mean*, Confucius says: "Having great such virtue, it could not but be that he should obtain the throne, that he should obtain those riches, that he should obtain his fame, and that he should attain to his long life." Knowledge accumulation is positively related to diligence and learning efficiency may be individually varied. As individual ability is different, income may be varied. Confucius does not decry concern for profits as the mark of an inferior person (Chen 1911; Chen 1990; Brook and Blue 1999; Zhang 2000). Under just social and economic systems, one's income is related to one's labor. If the society is governed by virtue, it is a shameful matter to be poor. He says: "When a country is well governed, poverty and a mean condition are things to be ashamed of. When a country is ill governed, riches and honor are things to be ashamed of." Confucius' point is whether or not the profit is gained by one's ability and with virtue: "Riches and honors are what men desire. If they cannot be obtained in the proper way, they should not be held. Poverty and meanness are what men dislike. If they cannot be avoided in the proper way, they should not be avoided." For Confucius, the pursuit of knowledge is either socially useful or has its own utility. People learn with miscellaneous purposes: "In ancient times, men learned with a view to their own improvement. Nowadays, men learn with a view to the approbation of others." He values the pleasure from learning and emphasizes the personal cultivation from learning: "They who know the truth are not equal to those who love it, and they who love it are not equal to those who find pleasure in it."

Knowledge comes from thinking, learning, and practicing. Confucius holds that one should not concentrate solely on learning or thought alone. One may waste time if learning without thought; one may be faced with serious problems if thinking without learning. Knowledge should be used to solve practical (social) problems. He points out that even if a man be able to recite the three hundred Odes, if he does not know how to act when entrusted with a governmental duty, his learning is practically useless.

Xun Zi (10: 17) backs that taking less from people would reduce burdens on the government and better society: "A policy of 'not benefiting the people yet taking benefits from them' provides fewer benefits than that of 'benefiting from the people only after first having benefited them.' A policy of 'using the people but not loving them' results in fewer achievements than that of 'using the people only after having demonstrated love for them.' A policy of 'benefiting the people and only then receiving benefits from them' produces fewer benefits than that of 'benefiting the people but receiving no benefits from them.' A policy of 'using the people only after having bestowed love on them' results in less benefit than that of 'loving the people but making no use of them.' One who 'provides benefits but does not take them' and who 'loves but does not use them' will capture the world. One who 'benefits the people and only then receives benefits from them' and who 'uses the people only after having first bestowed love on them' will protect his altars of soil and grain. One who 'does not benefit the people yet takes benefits from them' and who 'uses them but does not love them' will imperil his nation." Xun Zi (9: 5) points out that heavy tax is to destroy country: "One who attends merely to collecting taxes is following a way that invites bandits, fattens his enemies, dooms his own country, and threatens his own survival. Accordingly, the intelligent lord does not treat this path." According to Xun Zi (10: 4), "If one taxes lightly the cultivated fields and outlying districts, imposes excises uniformly at the border stations and in the marketplace, keeps statistical records to reduce the number of merchants and traders, initiates only rarely projects requiring the labor of the people, and does not take the farmers from their fields except in the off-season, the state will be wealthy. This may be described as 'allowing the people a generous living through the exercise of government'."

9. Love with varied degrees of intensity

Confucius' thought is much concerned with moral duties, priorities, the purpose and destiny of man and his position in society. He considers that the natural affection existing between relatives within one family is the cornerstone of social morality. Zigong once asks, 'Is there one word which may serve as a rule of practice for all one's life?' Confucius says: "Is not RECIPROCITY such a word? What you do not want done to yourself, do not do to others. Hold faithfulness and sincerity as first principles. Have no friends not equal to yourself. When you have faults, do not fear to abandon them." It is when the natural human affection found within the family is extended without animosity beyond the confines of the family that human nature reaches perfection and the social order is appropriately maintained.

10. Diligence and frugality equipped with education

Confucius says: "The expectations of life depend upon diligence; the mechanic that world perfect his work must first sharpen his tools." Common man gets disciplined and works diligently, not but nature, but for survival and profits. The traits of hard work and frugality are the result of culture. When Confucius (13: 9) went to Wei, he observed, "How numerous are the people!" His disciple asked him what more should be done for the people. Confucius said: "Enrich them." When he was further asked what should be done after the people had become enriched, The master replied: "Teach them." Confucius (13: 29–30) emphasizes discipline in wars: "Let a good man teach the people seven years, and they may then likewise be employed in war. ... To lead an uninstructed people to war is to throw them away."

China's traditional education is not the same with modern education in contents, scope, and scale. The traditional education is concentrated on Confucian classics and is mainly for selecting officials at different levels of the state. As early as in 165 B.C., written examinations are conducted by the emperor for selecting officials. In 124 B.C. fifty students were selected to study in the Supreme School. Students of the school completed a course of study before they could take examinations before entering the bureaucracy. Before the end of the Sui dynasty (581–618), the Supreme School was turned to the Imperial College. The new institution lasted until the final years of the Qing dynasty. The Han examinations include practical knowledge for running the government. The contents are gradually replaced by the Confucian classics. The Han dynasty builds the tradition of the relationship between bureaucratic appointment, examinations, and the Confucian classics. The system as the main means of recruiting public officials are accepted from the Tang dynasty (618–907 AD) until the end of the Qing dynasty. In the Tang dynasty, the examinations include subjects in law, calligraphy, mathematics, and history. During the Sung dynasty (960–1279), candidates who pass the Board of Rites examination are directly appointed to the bureaucracy. Tests at the local level are also institutionalized in the same pattern as in the capital. The examination system become insignificant during the Mongol Yuan dynasty, when most important offices are non-Chinese. The examination system is revived during the Ming dynasty (1368–1644). In 1905, the Qing court abolishes the traditional examination system. Schools and universities are framed after Western models from that date until 1949.

11. Justified rebellion against corrupt and incapable governments

The ruler's duty is to work for the welfare of the people. Confucius proposed five methods—respecting people's business, sincerity, loving people, taxing properly, and operating economically. The government should follow these five methods so that it will be trusted by the people. The people are contented and not rebellious. When being inquired about governing, Xun Zi (9: 1) replies: "Promote the worthy and capable without regard to seniority; dismiss the unfit and incapable without hesitation; execute the principal evildoers without trying first to instruct them; and transform the common lot men without trying first to rectify them." There is a consistent emphasis on promoting capable men to important position for the benefit of society in Confucianism. According to ancient Confucianism, if the ruler fails to behave in fair way toward the people, the ruler's authority should be rejected. Rebellion is justified in Chinese tradition.

Xun Zi's Orderly Society Constructed on Evil Nature of Man

> Capitalism is the astounding belief that the most wickedest of men will do the most wickedest of things for the greatest good of everyone.
>
> John Maynard Keynes (1883–1946)

Great thought is interesting as it is often interpreted either positively or negatively, depending upon the interpreter. The above saying allegedly by Keynes tells that social order and benefits of individuals can be maintained by individuals who have not genuine interest in doing good to others. This is similar with what Adam Smith (1776 [1976]) argues about in the *Wealth of Nations*. An orderly and effective society is sustained by men with evil nature is not what we intuitively like to believe. This thought is held in a school of Confucianism more than two thousand years ago. The school is almost neglected in China until modern times.

Xun Zi is one of the three most important ancient Confucianists. If one chooses only one China's thinker to interpret modern Western civilization, Xun Zi is perhaps the one. Xun Zi maintains that: "The inborn nature of man is certainly that of the petty man. If he is without a teacher and lacks the model, he will see things solely in terms of benefit to himself. As the nature of man is assuredly that of the petty man, if the age in which he lives is chaotic, he will require its chaotic customs. For this reason, he will use the small to redouble what is small and use the chaotic to begat more chaos. If the gentleman does not use the power inherent in his circumstances to control them, then he will have no means to develop their inherent possibilities." He argues: "A person is born with a liking for profit". Adam Smith argues for self-interested human behavior: "It is not from the benevolence of the butcher, the brewer, or the baker that we expect our dinner, but from their regard to their own interest." Xun Zi (1: 1) discusses profits and virtue within an integrate system: "In broadening his learning, the gentleman each day examines himself so that his awareness will be discerning and his actions without excess." Xun Zi (1: 10) distinguishes the gentleman and the small man: "today people undertake learning for the sake of others. The learning of the gentleman is used to refine his character. The learning of the petty man is used like ceremonial offerings of birds and calves."

He believes that human nature is evil, but man can be educated and become a sage. "Human nature is evil, and goodness is caused by intentional activity." Xun Zi values the role of law more than Confucius: "A man who has no laws at all is lost and guideless. A man who has laws but does not understand their meaning is timid and inconsistent. Only if a man abides by laws and the same time comprehends their wider significance and applicability can he become truly liberal and compassionate." Evil nature leads to crime if not properly educated: "A person is born with feelings of envy and hate. If he gives way to them, they will lead him to violence and crime, and any sense of loyalty and good faith will be abandoned." He instructs about how to become a good person: "A person should be first changed by a teacher's instructions and guided by principles and ritual. Only then can he observe the rules of courtesy and humility, obey the conventions and rules of society, and achieve order." "I say that human nature is the original beginning and the raw material, and deliberate effort is what makes it patterned, ordered, and exalted." Unlike Adam Smith who allows the Law to limit what man cannot do, Xun Zi argues: "Human nature and deliberate effort must unite, and then the reputation of the sage and the work of unifying all under Heaven are thereupon brought to completion."

Confucianism as Cultural Capital

> ... [I]t was the Confucius in me, the faint voice I often heard when I was alone, that the only meaningful life is a life of learning.
>
> Qi Cui (D. C. Tsui, 1939–, China-born-American Nobel Prize in Physics 1998)

> Imagine for yourself a character, a model personality, whose example you determine to follow, in private as well as in public.
>
> Epictetus

Daniel Chee Tsui (Qi Cui in pinyin, 1939–) is a Chinese-born American researcher. He was awarded the Nobel Prize in Physics for his contributions to the discovery of the fractional quantum Hall effect in 1998. He shared the prize with other two physicists. He was born into a poor family in Fanzhuang village in Henan Province in the Second Sino-Japanese War. His village was filled with the years of drought, flood, and war. His parents never learned how to read and write. They gave him much love. His parent decided to provide him educational opportunity. He studied Chinese classics in a school in village. In 1951, his parent sent him for further education to Hong Kong. He spent his school years in Hong Kong and graduated in 1957. In 1958, he attended university in the United States, receiving a full scholarship. After graduating from university in 1961, he continued to study physics at the University of Chicago, where he received Ph.D. in physics in 1967. In 1968, he joined Bell Laboratories, where made the discovery which earned him the Nobel Prize 1982. Shortly after his discovery, he was appointed a professor at Princeton University in 1982. His colleagues and friends asked him why he had left Bell Laboratories and chosen to work at Princeton University. He did not know the answer with any degree of certainty. He reflected in his biography published in the *Nobel Lectures*, "Perhaps it was the Confucius in me, the faint voice I often heard when I was alone, that the only meaningful life is a life of learning. What better way is there to learn than through teaching!" This cultural trait in respecting learning is reflected by the degrees held by (overseas) Chinese top politicians in Taiwan, Singapore, and Hong Kong.

No education is not entitled to govern a human society is a practical implication of Confucianism. Rather than a heritage or born into a specified castle, ideal Confucian system is based on the examination performance. Although he did not receive proper higher education during the Cultural Revolution, Mr. Xi Jinping now holds a few honorable Ph.D. degrees from many places. Many top officials hold Ph.D. degrees in China. Some of them were criticized by the public as they might not even have time to do research and write, even though they are given degrees by universities. A man, how high the position he might hold, lacks something in his public image, if he has not substantiated the ability to pass examinations which are viewed as a signal of trustfulness and respectability in Chinese cultural environment. This is not the same with America, where practical abilities (and color of skin) are the main determinants. In Japan, Ph.D. degrees have almost nothing to do with the top positions in politics. As mainland Chinese universities are not very trustful as educational institutions, many Chinese are studying abroad to receive degrees. Million Chinese have returned to China with degrees from many parts of the world. The emphasis on educational degrees is a key factor that China has quickly absorbed global knowledge in almost all fields.

Confucianism shapes the social fabric, forged status consciousness, and provides the system of role enforcement before New China (e.g., Armes and Hall 1997; Bauer and Bell 1999; Berthrong 1998). Modernization of China is to 'modernize' manifestations of the Confucian principles according to changed economic and global conditions. In learning, educated man goes upwards, a learning mind tends to converge towards the popular opinion, and uneducated man tends to go downwards. Although the Confucian principles by the ancient Confucianists are not varied over history, its applications changed over history.

Ancient Confucianism is created in an environment when scholars freely travel among countries and cultures and they do not serve a single state in open societies. It is developed in an international open environment with co-existence of multiple states with varied cultural traditions and institutional structures. Nevertheless, what we know about Confucianism in practice is when Confucianism is applied to rice-based economies under political monopoly for a culturally isolated country. Applications in China distort the essence of ancient Confucianism with regards to freedom and individualism.

Tocqueville (1948: 346) observes: "Two things are astonishing, the changeableness of most human behavior and the strange stability of certain principles. Men are constantly on the move, but the spirit of humanity seems almost unmoved." Respect of education and measurement of being human according to education is a lasting character of Chinese culture. Over centuries Han Chinese people spend on their energies and resources on maintaining the Great Wall and education. Dating from the Manchus conquest of China in1644, the Great Wall lost its role for national security as the Manchus extended China's territory far beyond the Wall. However, the Manchus continue Confucian education, paying their loyalty to and respect for Chinese tradition and relying on talent and merit for administration. Moreover, the Manchu emperor has the power to kill any scholar who has courage to publicly criticize the Manchu authority. The Manchus succeed in ruling China by respecting Chinese values on education. The Chinese servility was deepened during the nomadic-farmer Manchus. The party now dominated by Han Chinese is far more "benevolent", if there is such a word to describe China, than the country controlled by the Manchus.

East Asia experienced rapid economic progresses after WWII. Japan embarked on its modernization much earlier. Unlike China, Japan did not attack Confucianism in principles when it was confronted with Western influences. Japan adapted Confucian principles to the changing international environment (Zhang 2010). Overseas Chinese societies in Taiwan, Singapore, and Hong Kong have also adapted their behavior according to a changing environment, modernizing Confucian manifestations. Governments in Taiwan and Singapore explicitly admitted positive roles of Confucianism.

Change is one thing. However, it is quite another thing to sustain temporary change. Mao could have made and sustained his changes according to his will till his death because he ruled the country by the barrel of a gun, destroyed higher education, isolated China from Western influences, and forbade Confucianism. The conditions left by Mao made it possible for China to make dramatic changes in almost any direction without further damages. As China is a society closely connected from the top to the bottom, the top person's values and characteristics have a decisive influence on how the nation operates. Mao and Deng might use their abilities and learn strategic skills to become influential and powerful. However, their influences on society are merely transitory at best. It is idea that changes historical path of a society. A monkey does not create ideas even though it is a master of movement. A monkey can do it but cannot "understand" it. Similarly, few successful businessmen have any intellectually interesting ideas about economics, management, or strategies, even though they can create great wealth and companies. Some politicians, perhaps even with barbarian mindsets, do not have solid ideas about political theory in any systematical sense even though they successfully govern or rule a nation. Neither Mao nor Deng could make any lasting impact on ways of Chinese thinking, even though they both altered the historical path of China significantly.

The Chinese *Yin-Yang* Vision Built in the *Yi Jing*

> The more humanity advances, the more it is degraded.
>
> Gustave Flaubert (1821–1880)

Joseph Needham (1900–1995), a British sinologist, evaluated the *Yi Jing* and noted: "Binary arithmetic, stumbled upon by Shao Yung in his arrangements of the sixty-four hexagrams of the *I Ching* and brought to consciousness by Leibniz (Mungello 1977), might be said in a real sense to have been built into the mammalian nervous system long before it was found convenient for the great computing machines of modern man." Almost anything Chinese, philosophy, politics, gender relations, medicine, and food are related to the *yin-yang* dynamic vision. Taoism and Confucianism cannot be properly understood without studying this book. Alfred North Whitehead judges: "The safest general characterization of the European philosophical tradition is that it consists of a series of footnotes to Plato." With regards Chinese thought, it is a series of manifestations of the *Yi Jing* (Fung 1952, 1953; Chan 1973). With regards to Chinese ethics, it is a series of footnotes of Confucius.

The *Yi Jing* is perhaps the most important work in China before Confucius. It was originally a manual of divination, and from it evolved a system of philosophy. It represents certain patterns of change, and thus can be used to provide a comprehensive method of viewing our world and the universe as an organized whole. It has been used in China as a source of wisdom for over 3000 years by scholars and the masses alike. It is based on trigrams, three-line symbols built of an unbroken line that stands for *yang*, the universal force of being, man, positive forces, progress, clarity, strength, and light; and a broken line that represents *yin*, the universal force of non-being, woman, negative forces, decline, obscurity, weakness, and darkness. Together, *yin* and *yang* are used to express the two extremes or poles of universal phenomena.

Change, rather than the composition of concrete objects and the physical laws that govern them, is the basis of this ancient attempt to grasp the essence of the world. From the opposite or complementary poles of *yin* and *yang*, the *Yi Jing* portrays basic stages in the cycle of change. Change takes place in the universe because of the complementary interaction of two fundamental principles. Change is conceived of partly as the continuous transformation of one force into another, and partly as a cycle of complexes of phenomena. Change is subject to the universal law, the way, or *Tao*. A human being is the joint product of the two poles, man, and woman. The universe is created by two prime principles, the universal force of being and the universal force of non-being. Any concept implies its negation. The negation of capitalism is communism—neither extreme is higher than the other, in the abstract sense. Without its negation, a concept cannot exist. Affirmation and negation are different ways of looking at the same thing.

The eight trigrams that can be formed by numerous combinations of the broken and unbroken lines reveal the progression of, basically, anything, from one extreme state to its opposite. by varied combinations of the eight trigrams, ancient Chinese thinkers attempted to explain man, society, and nature. The trigrams can further be combined in pairs, and that allows for sixty-four hexagrams. Each component of the Sixty-four Hexagrams has been assigned some meaning by which miscellaneous, yet typical situations or patterns can be determined. In the Chinese mind, everything in the universe is in a state of flux. Everything is in the process of changing into something else. Changes follow one another in both regular and irregular patterns. Every end is also a beginning. Change does not necessarily occur in every variable between two hexagrams. All things are in a state of flux; but they can only change in a certain way. Since there exists some way controlling changes, it is possible to predict (only certain) future events. It has helped the Confucian civilization to sustain the belief in man's ability to account for natural phenomena by rational means. We now find a few *yin-yang* pairs to see how the *Yi Jing* might provide a bridge to miscellaneous opinions in modern thought within a single framework (Fig 3.1).

Fig. 3.1 Interactions between the *Yin* and *Yang* (*Source* https://ja.wikipedia.org/wiki/%E9%99%B0%E9%99%BD)

Human Nature Being Evils versus Being Good

> Human Nature is the only science of man; and yet has been hitherto the most neglected.
>
> David Hume

Human nature is a key issue in Confucianism. As mentioned before, Xun Zi assumes human nature being evil, while Mencius assumes human nature being good. Over history, Chinese thinkers assume various "distributions" between the *yin* and the *yang*. The master, Confucius, does not even fix anything on human nature. In modern ethics self-interest and sympathy are the two poles. Adam Smith has two important books, one is *The Wealth of Nations*, constructed with the self-interest assumption; and the other one is *The Theory of Sentiments*, built on sentiments and sympathy. Why he did not write a book focused on interdependence between the contents of the two books is still a puzzle. I do think the job impossible for Adam Smith (1759 [1982], 1776 [1976]) due to the way he constructed the world and the scientific tools with which he was equipped.

Introversion versus Extraversion

> There is no such thing as a pure introvert or extrovert. Such a person would be in the lunatic asylum.
>
> Carl Jung (1875–1961)

The two poles are well discussed in modern psychology. The terms were popularized by Carl Jung (1987–1961), a Swiss psychiatrist and psychoanalyst. He was greatly interested in the *yin-yang* philosophy. Jung (1965, 1989) called a person introvert type if the person's behavior is "characterized by orientation in life through subjective psychic contents", while extravert type if "characterized by concentration of interest on the external object." Roughly, introversion is referred to as character exemplified by one exhibiting reserved and solitary behavior, while extraversion is referred to as being exemplified by outgoing, talkative, and energetic behavior. No person has been empirically identified as a pure type of either of the two poles. It is popularly accepted that some people are introverts while others are extroverts. There are unlimited types of persons between the two poles.

Perfect Competition versus Monopoly

> There is nothing either good or bad but thinking makes it so.
>
> Shakespeare

When studying market economy, we have two extreme markets. The two poles are perfect competition and monopoly. Perfect competition exists if some market conditions are satisfied. They include: a large number of buyers, a large number of sellers, perfect information of producers and consumers, both producers and consumers being price takers, perfect factor mobility, no barriers to entry or exit, profit-maximizing producers, and rational consumers. There are also no externalities, zero transaction costs, no network effects, and non-increasing returns to scale. These conditions are required to be satisfied at the same time. The requirements are rarely satisfied. The other pole is monopoly which means that there is only one supplier of a product. Both perfect competition and monopoly are rare what one observes in economic reality. Between the two poles, economists have unlimited market structures, such as imperfect competition, duopoly, oligopoly, monopolistic competition, and unlimited types of games. This also implies that between the *yin* and *yang*, there are unlimited types, like in personal types in psychology. It is interesting to note that Adam Smith wrote two great books, one about national wealth, and another about morality. He separated two important topics in separated theoretical frameworks. A reason for this separation is perhaps that there is no certain connection between the two. There is one pair of *yin* and *yang* in economics, there is another pair of *yin* and *yang* in moral sentiments. According to the *Yi Jing*, dynamic interactions between the two pairs will lead to complicated social and economic phenomena.

Capitalism Versus Communism and Democracy versus Dictatorship

> Democracy passes into despotism.
>
> Plato (423–347 BC)

Capitalism basically refers to the private ownership of the means of production. It is characterized by profit-maximization, private property, voluntary exchange, capital accumulation, wage labor, price determination by competitive markets. Communism fundamentally refers to the common ownership of the means of production. Almost all economies are between the two poles. In politics, the two poles are democracy and dictatorship. There are unlimited types between the *yin* and *yang*, like the US, British, Russian, Swedish, Japanese, and Chinese political systems. In the long term no country is purely democratic, and no country is purely dictator. China is moving towards "more democratic" (depending on how to measure national degree of democracy) and America is deviating steadily and slowly from its democratic ideal since the end of the cold war (Bell 1978, 1996).

Femininity versus Masculinity

> I've used my femininity and my sexuality as a weapon and a tool… but that's just natural.
>
> Dolly Parton

The two poles do not imply biological sex in the Chinese *yin-yang* vision. It refers to certain behavior or behavioral patterns. They are not necessarily descriptions of sexual orientation. Like introversion and extraversion, there are rare purely feminine or masculine extreme types of persons. Woman or man may have miscellaneous combinations of femininity and masculinity. A person adopts multifarious aspects of femininity and masculinity, consciously or unconsciously, depending on the society, environment, life stage, biology, and the like. In East Asia, man has been becoming more "feminine" in the last two decades. Some men apply makeup and skincare and exhibit some stereotyped feminine activities. As China has become enriched and socially freer, woman has become more masculine, while man has become more feminine, as the *yin-yang* vision implies.

Stability versus Instability

> Stability is when the U.K. and U.S. invade a country and impose the regime of their choice.
>
> Noam Chomsky

In social sciences and economic sustainability is a key concept for describing long-term perspectives of social and economic development. Sustainability is related to the concept of stability in dynamical systems. Stability versus instability is another pair for us to grasp in our analysis of behavior of dynamical systems. Humor is often the result of a turning point from stability (predictability) to instability (unpredictability). Stocks markets are structurally unstable, while German cars are notably stable. Whether a system is stable or unstable is important for understanding behavior of the system.

These polar contrasts are not mutually exclusive. They co-exist as a harmonious whole. Niels Bohr (1885–1962), a Danish physicist who received the Nobel Prize in Physics in 1922, characterizes quantum phenomena as both wave and particle at once. He considers his influential notion of complementarity similar with the *yin-yang* vision. There are many other pairs, such as rationality versus irrationality, object versus subject, order versus disorder, social harmony versus social chaos, law versus rite, which are essential for understanding social and economic behavior in individual levels as well as collective levels. My recent book *The General Economic Theory* (Zhang 2020) is to build a nonlinear dynamic system similar with the *Yi Jing* system. "This book develops a general economic theory, not only integrating ideas and theories from Adam Smith till Nobel prize laureates in economics, but also establishing important relations among economic variables unrecognized in the literature of rigorous economic analysis."

The Europe's *Yin-Yang* Attitudes Towards Confucianism

> We believe there is no fundamental structural changes in the young-adult market. There are, of course, fashion changes, and the success of each brand depends on the accuracy with which it predicts those changes.
>
> Richard Hayne (1947–)

Great thought, like anything meaningful in life, embodies *yin-yang* dynamics. Democracy can lead one country to freedom and greatness, while the same rule of social game may lead another country from freedom to mediocrity or even to dictatorship. This is dependent upon interaction between man and society. Keynes is well-known for emphasizing the equilibrium point of an individual life: in the long term we all die. In the long term, society will vanish, though not so quick like an individual. No man can stop the *yin-yang* socioeconomic dynamics as the man who has accumulated capacity and wisdom will die and younger generation re-constructs its own world in its own way. There is nothing new under the sun, but every generation creates its own meanings of life, which are drifting like a cloud.

Ancient Confucianism experienced many cycles of the *yin-yang* dynamics throughout China's history. Confucianism also contains self-destructive dynamics. While it valued talent and encouraged education, the emperor often used it to build a prosperous and strong state. The emperor's concentration of power often resulted in killing the creative brightest. Historically, Christianity has also experienced dynamics of acceptance, rejection, and diffusion in China since the religion was brought to China in the sixteenth century. The religion was first brought to China in the seventh century during the Tang dynasty but did not take root till it was reintroduced almost 1000 years late. Confucianism experienced admiration, criticism, and negligence in Europe. Its admiration is due to its power to enlighten Europeans and its essence to help Europeans to be liberated from religion. Its criticism is that its manifestations do not fit European styles of competition and survival. It was neglected as Europeans had absorbed its positive powers, had weakened its religious power, and seemingly had nothing do with it again. Mencius (14: 21) illustrates the falling and rising of a doctrine as follows: "There are the foot-paths, along the hills—if suddenly they are used, they become roads; and if as suddenly they are not used, the wild grass fills them up."

A doctrine may be interpreted variously by various people and manifest in miscellaneous forms in different times (the same culture) or spaces (heterogeneous cultures). This is like plants from the same (kind of) seed. They may manifest different forms in heterogeneous environments. A variety of societies might be formed under the same ideal. For instance, while traditional Korea, and China are claimed Confucian, their practical ethics, human relations, and behavioral patterns are varied. Similarly, many Western countries are democratic, but their institutional structures and voting processes are not the same. Stromberg (1996) concludes the non-existence of an authoritative history of democratic thought in Western civilization. Confucianism is interpreted both positively and negatively during different periods in China. Similarly, we can find two opposite views on Confucianism in the West.

In the age of the enlightenment, European thinkers were positive towards Confucianism. Matteo Ricchi (1552–1610) of Mazzarino in Italy translated the Confucian Four Books into Italian. The Confucian works first appeared in Europe. Soon the Confucian works were available in European languages. A great thinker of Western civilization, known as the last universal genius, Gottfried Wilhelm Leibniz (1646–1716), extensively studied things Chinese, such as philosophy, religion, history, geography, language, studies of flora and fauna, and technology. After reading the *Confucius Sinarum Philosophus*, he perceived himself as a follower of Confucianism. More than three hundred years ago Leibniz (1994) warned:

> It would be highly foolish and presumptuous on our part, having newly arrived compared with them [the Chinese]... to want to condemn such an ancient doctrine [Confucianism] simply because it does not appear to agree at first glance with our ordinary scholastic notions.

François Quesnay (1694–1774) was another Western giant who admires Confucius. Confucianism, which does not advocate hereditary aristocracy, was used as a weapon to attack against hereditary privilege in France and in England. Quesnay greatly admired the education system in China which helped the state to select talented people for public service through a rigorous program of study and a competitive examination system. The Chinese idea about government through merit and learning rather than through heredity is greatly attractive to him. In his lifetime Quesnay (Zhang 1998) is called "the Confucius of Europe." Voltaire (1694–1778) writes:

> The constitution of their [Chinese] empire is in truth the best that there is in the world... Four thousand years ago, when we did not know how to read, they knew everything essentially useful of which we boast today.

The *yang* and the *yin* changed their relative manifestations. Western intellectuals began to think that Chinese are not even able to think properly. Montesquieu (1689–1755) says, "It is impossible to find, in all the histories of this country, a single passage which discovers a free soul: we shall never see anything there but the heroism of slavery." More than 200 years ago, David Hume (1711–1776; 1994: 66) observes: "In CHINA, there seems to be a pretty considerable stock of politeness and science, which, in the course of so many centuries, might naturally be expected to ripen into something more perfect and finished, than what has yet arisen from them." In his 1859 *On Liberty*, Mill criticizes China without a little sign of respect. In association with the rise of Western civilization, Confucian practice in China had been criticized from a variety of perspectives in the West. None of these thinkers discussed the implications that China had been "colonized", from 1644 to 1912, by the nomadic Manchus who had almost no "high" culture and mainly applied the Chinese culture as a means to control the Chinese people. As the West was rising globally, China was declining under Manchu rule. Since then, scholars have tended to see possible negative consequences from the Confucian doctrine and deny and neglect it.

Lao Tzu for Cultural Building and Emotional Enrichment

> The goal of life is living in agreement with nature.
>
> Zeno of Citium (336–265 BC)

Genius are "boundary setters" of civilization in the sense that they settle possible intellectual and spiritual heights/depths. The lasting intellectual characters of a civilization are often shaped by its major philosophers either in intentional or unintentional way. In the West, for instance, great thinkers, such as Socrates, Plato, Aristotle, Descartes, Kant and Hume, give model expression to problems that remain with the Western civilization. Confucius and Lao Tzu had settled the concerns of traditional Chinese intellectuals. Taoism is as important as ancient Confucianism. The creator of Taoism is Lao Tzu. In a visionary sense, Confucius and Lao Tzu is a pair of the *yin-yang*. Confucianism and Taoism complement each other. These two trends of thought represent the opposite poles of Chinese philosophy. A Taoist tends to be a loner, seeking mountainous retreats instead of court or government service, and seeking cultivation and cessation of human conflicts in the simplicities of nature. The Confucian scholar was a commonsense gentleman, a good family man, a conscientious bureaucrat, and sober citizen. The spread of Taoism and Confucianism tend to be socially interdependent. They tend to nourish and decline in the same time. Confucianism provides social order on a large scale and Taoism colors the society on an individual level.

Little is known of the life of Lao Tzu. It was said that Lao Tzu retired from office as a keeper of the records because he saw how corrupt society had become. He put aside earthly ambition and retired from the world. Lao Tzu wrote a book, known as Tao Te Ching (The Classic of the Way and Its Virtue), which is often referred to as the Book of Five Thousand Characters. It laid the foundation of a philosophy called Taoism. No one can understand China without some knowledge of its contents for it has modified Chinese life and thought throughout history. The book has influenced Chinese philosophies, religion, government, art, medicine, as well as cooking. Taoist spirit has contributed largely to the proliferation of graphic arts and many crafts. In China, restraint and simplicity had been regarded as the hallmark of true greatness. This is well reflected in the best of Chinese poetry. The love of the simple and unassuming is much influenced by intuitive perception of the nature of the Tao. The poems of stillness inspired by Taoist love of nature convey the spirit of mountain-dwelling recluses. It is because of Taoist's insistence on the positive value of non-being that empty space has been utilized as a constructive factor in Chinese landscape painting.

Tao Te Ching has endured through the centuries and has been translated into many languages. The book was first introduced into the Western world in 1788, when a Latin translation was brought to the Royal Society in London. By 1844, there were complete translations of Tao Te Ching in both French and German. Some Western philosophers, for instance, Hegel, Schopenhauer, and Heidegger were interested in Tao Te Ching. Chang (1975) argues that Heidegger is the only Western philosopher who not only intellectually understands Tao but has intuitively experienced the essence of it as well.

Tao or the way is the key concept in Taoism. Lao Tzu says: "There is a thing confusedly formed, born before heaven and earth. Silent and void it stands alone and does not change, goes round and does not weary. It is capable of being the mother of the world. I know not its name, so I style it 'the way'." There is no name in the English that is applicable to the Tao. "Tao" is often left untranslated as it is regarded as indefinable. If it is translated, it is usually called the Way (Chan 1963). The meaning of Tao cannot be fully represented by words. "The way that can be spoken of is not the constant way; The name that can be named is not the constant name. The nameless was the beginning of heaven and earth; The named was the mother of the myriad creatures." (Lao Tzu). The "genuine truth" seems to be beyond ability of any existing language, such as music, mathematics, painting, and common languages, to manifest. Although the Tao is the "mother" and "ancestor" of all things, in no circumstances can Tao be thought of or used as "God". In the concept of Tao, the limitations of the finite human mind are realized, practically and sensibly. Due to Lao Tzu's (as well as Confucius') philosophy, the problem of the existence of God has never become a main intellectual issue. As in the *Yi Jing*, Lao Tzu does not deny the existence of natural laws. The Tao operates according to certain laws which are constant and regular. Lao Tzu says: "The way conceals itself in being nameless. It is the way alone that excels in bestowing and in accomplishing."

Lao Tzu holds that both being and non-being are of importance. They complement and produce each other. Non-being is not empty and devoid of everything. It is devoid of limitations but not devoid of definite characteristics. Tao as non-being is not only positive in character, but it is basic. This concept of non-being was new in Chinese thought. It provides the basic principle of the unity of multiplicity. Although being and non-being are both mentioned, through being the value of non-being is revealed. All forms, objects, and essences are inherent in the void, yet the Tao itself is indistinct and ineffable. Tao is the reality of all these things. Tao is neither chaotic nor unpredictable, for it is the essence which is very real and in it are evidences. Tao is "mysterious" only in the sense of subtlety and depth, not in the sense of irrationality. Lao Tzu says: "The way that can be spoken of is not the constant way; The name that can be named is not the constant name." Similarly, Albert Einstein remarks, "As far as the laws of mathematics refer to reality they are not certain, and as far as they are certain, they do not refer to reality." Heidegger (1971) says: "Tao could be the way that gives all ways, the very source of our power to think what reason, mind, meaning, logos properly mean to say.... Perhaps the mystery of mysteries of thoughtful Saying conceals itself in the word way, Tao, if only we let these names return to what they leave unspoken."

Taoism provides deep insight into the complexity of change and order. For Taoism the essence of life is change. When things obey Tao, all parts of the universe will form a harmonious whole and the universe will become an integrated organism. Lao Tzu holds that the dialectal world is a world of endless movement between conflicting forces. When one reaches one extreme and yet is free from it, one enters the realm of the unity of opposites, in which both extremes are immediately and spontaneously identified. Lao Tzu holds that the opposites of being and non-being or beauty and ugliness are mutually identified within themselves and not in any higher synthesis. Lao Tzu says: "The whole world recognizes the beautiful as the beautiful, yet this is only the ugly; the whole world recognizes the good as the good, yet this is only the bad. Thus something and nothing produce each other; the difficult and the easy complement each other; the long and the short off-set each other; the high and the low incline towards each other; note and sound harmonize with each other; before and after follow each other." Chan (1963) comments on Taoism: "Lao Tzu teaches us to 'benefit all things', to 'treat those who are good with goodness' and 'also to treat those who are not good with goodness', and to 'repay hatred with virtue'. He admonishes us not to have ulterior motives, to show or justify ourselves or to boast to be proud, to hoard things, or to be extravagant. He advises us to know the subtle and the eternal but when we do not know anything, know that we do not know." Lao Tzu emphasizes having no desires. Having no desires simply means having no impure or selfish desires, but not having no desires at all. While desires should be few, good ones are to be fulfilled. Ethically Tao stands for a simple life that is free from cunning and cleverness, is not devoted to the pursuit of profit or marked by hypocritical humanity and righteousness, but is characterized by plainness, tranquility, and purity.

Lao Tzu is concerned with life of common people. Lao Tzu says: "The people are hungry, it is because those in authority eat up too much in taxes that the people are hungry. The people are difficult to govern, it is because those in authority are too fond of action that the people are difficult to govern." The more any outside authority interferes with a man's use of life and the less the man uses it according to his own instinct and conscience, the worse for the man and the worse for the society. He argues: "Whoever takes the empire and wishes to do anything to it I see will have no respite. The empire is a sacred vessel and nothing should be done to it. Whoever does anything to it will ruin it; whoever lays hold of it will lose it. Hence some things lead and some follow; Some breathe gently and some breathe hard; Some are strong and some are weak; Some destroy and some are destroyed. Therefore, the sage avoids excess, extravagance, and arrogance." No action from authority is like Adam Smith's idea, but from miscellaneous perspectives. The government shall give free development to the spiritual life of each individual in the state. For Lao Tzu, to bring people together is to be humble toward them. Thus, harmony is achieved through humanity. Humanity is basic to the dissolution of hostility between opponents. Lao Tzu holds that the sage leads the people but does not master them; the sage does not seek to enlighten the people but makes them ignorant. Lao Tzu says that if the worthy is not exalted, the people will not compete; and if people have too much knowledge, they will be difficult to rule. Lao Tzu is against the talk of benevolence, filial piety and loyalty that was characteristic of Confucians, saying that insisting on the need for them is a sure sign of their being in decline (Zhang 2001). Laws, he felt, merely lead to an increase in the varieties of crime. Like Plato, he seems to have considered that until kings are philosophers, or philosophers are kings, cities will never cease from ill and that the study of economics, law, or finance are unnecessary qualifications for a legislator.

After some years spent on studying China's culture, in *The Religion of China: Confucianism and Taoism*, Max Weber (1864–1920; 1951: 248) concludes:

> The Chinese in all probability would be quite capable, probably more capable than the Japanese, of assimilating capitalism which has technically and economically been fully developed in the modern culture area.

After more than hundred years, China is substantiating that Weber might not be wrong. When he was writing, China's cultural stock was far richer than Japan's. China was similar with Japan in many other aspects. Weber had reasons to make his conclusion for China. Japan had many "fortunes" in modern development (Zhang 1999), while China had to deal away the Manchus as the single power over Han Chinese before its modernization (Zhang 2011). Timing, like in great success or disaster in person life, is a deterministic factor of national development, which is expounded by chaos theory (Zhang 1991). Chaos theory confirms that future development is not predictable as any trial events might change paths of historical development. A careful study of the cultural stock is important as it limits possibilities of the future.

References

Armes, R., & Hall, D. (1997). *Thinking Through Confucius*. New York, NY: SUNY Press.

Bauer, J. R., & Bell, D. A. (1999, edited). *The East Asian Challenge for Human Rights*. Cambridge: Cambridge University Press.

Bell, D. A. (1978). *The Cultural Contradictions of Capitalism*. New York, NY: Basic Books.

Bell, D. A. (1996). Afterword. In *The Cultural Contradictions of Capitalism*. New York, NY: Basic Books.

Berthrong, J. H. (1998). *Transformations of the Confucian Way*. Boulder, CO: Westview Press.

Brook, T., & Blue, G. (1999, edited). *China and Historical Capitalism—Genealogies of Sinological Knowledge*. Cambridge: Cambridge University Press.

Chan, W. T. (1963). *The Way of Lao Tzu*. New York, NY: The Bobbs-Merrill Company Inc.

Chan, W. T. (1973). *A Source Book in Chinese Philosophy* (translated and compiled). Princeton, NJ: Princeton University Press.

Chang, C. Y. (1975). *Tao: A New Way of Thinking*. New York, NY: Harper & Row, Publishers.

Chen, H. C. (1911). *The Economic Principles of Confucius and His School*. New York, NY: The Faculty of Political Science of Columbia University.

Chen, J. P. (1990). *Confucius as a Teacher—Philosophy of Confucius with Special Reference to Its Educational Implications*. Beijing: Foreign Languages Press.

de Tocqueville, A. (1948) *Democracy in America*, vols. I and II. New York, NY: Alfred A. Knopt.

Fung, Y. L. (1952). *A History of Chinese Philosophy* (Vol. I, translated from the Chinese origin by D. Bodde). Princeton, NJ: Princeton University Press.

Fung, Y. L. (1953). *A History of Chinese Philosophy* (Vol. II, translated from the Chinese origin by D. Bodde). Princeton, NJ: Princeton University Press.

Heidegger, M. (1971). *On the Way to Language* (translated by P. D. Hertz). New York, NY: Harper & Row.

Hume, D. (1994). *Political Essays* (edited by K. Haakonssen). Cambridge: Cambridge University Press.

Jung, C. G. (1965). *Introduction, Secret of the Golden Flower: A Chinese Book of Life* (translated by R. Wilhelm). New York, NY: Harcourt Brace Jovanovich, Inc.

Jung, C.G. (1989). *Psychological Types* (a revision by R. F. Hull of the translation by H. G. Baynes). London: Routledge.

Leibniz, G. W. (1994). *Writings on China* (translated by D. J. Cook and H. Rosemont). Chicago, IL: Open Court.

Mungello, D. E. (1977). *Leibniz and Confucianism—The Search for Accord*. Honolulu: The University Press of Hawaii.

Schwartz, B.I. (1972, edited). *Reflections on the May Fourth Movement.* Cambridge, MA: Harvard University Press.
Seldes, G. (1985). *The Great Thoughts.* New York: Ballantine Books.
Smith, A. (1759/1982). *The Theory of Moral Sentiments* (edited by D. D. Raphael and A. L. Macfie). Indianapolis, IN: Liberty Press.
Smith, A. (1776/1976). *An Inquiry into the Nature and Causes of the Wealth of Nations* (edited by E. Cannan). Chicago, IL: The University of Chicago Press.
Stromberg, R. N. (1996). *Democracy—A Short, Analytical History.* New York, NY: M.E. Sharpe.
Weber, M. (1951). *The Religion of China—Confucianism and Taoism* (translated from the German original by H. H. Gerth with an introduction by C. K. Yang). New York, NY: The Free Press.
Zhang, W. B. (1991). *Synergetic Economics.* Heidelberg: Springer-Verlag.
Zhang, W. B. (1998). *Japan versus China in the Industrial Race.* London: MacMillan.
Zhang, W. B. (1999). *Confucianism and Modernization.* London: MacMillan.
Zhang, W. B. (2000). *Adam Smith and Confucius—The Theory of Moral Sentiments and The Analects.* New York, NY: Nova Science.
Zhang, W. B. (2001). On Lao Tzu—His Impact on Chinese Thinking. In D. E. Andersson & J. P. H. Poon (Eds.), *Asia-Pacific Transition.* New York, NY: Palgrave.
Zhang, W. B. (2003). *The American Civilization Portrayed in Ancient Confucianism.* New York, NY: Algora.
Zhang, W. B. (2010). *Fukuzawa Yukichi: The Pioneer of East Asia's Westernization with Ancient Confucianism.* Frederick, MD: PublishAmerica.
Zhang, W. B. (2011). *The Rise and Fall of China's Last Dynasty: The Deepening of the Chinese Servility.* New York, NY: Nova Science.
Zhang, W. B. (2020). *The General Economic Theory: An Integrative Approach.* Switzerland: Springer International Publishing.

CHAPTER 4

Spread Education and Devouring Global Knowledge

> If I am walking with two other men, each of them will serve as my teacher. I will pick out the good points of the one and imitate them, and the bad points of the other and correct them in myself.
>
> Confucius

Mao left a poor and ignorant country in which learning was despised and higher education was neglected. Mao controlled the country with Western guns and Mongolian way of dealing with Han Chinese intellectuals. But like the Mongols and Manchus, he could not destroy Chinese cultural stocks in any essential sense because most of known Chinese cultural stocks were kept not only the mainland (especially in graves), but also in the world beyond Mao's control. The cultural stock would help Chinese people to quickly enhance domestic productivities and learn from world. Deng re-introduced higher (Western) education and market mechanisms to encourage people to effectively learn from miscellaneous sources. Millions of people of all ages began to absorb modern knowledge with great passions.

Napoleon (1769–1821) is allegedly said: "China? There is a sleeping giant. Let him sleep. For when he wakes, he will move the world." If he foretold so, we still have little idea why he did so. Indeed, it has taken about two hundred years for China to demonstrate possibilities of Napoleon's prevision. In age of economic globalization, the capacity of learning, innovation and applying knowledge is the most important

W.-B. Zhang, *The Butterfly Effect in China's Economic Growth*,
https://doi.org/10.1007/978-981-15-9889-0_4

resources for national development. Product from land has low share in national output in developed economies. Natural resources such as coal and oil can be transported to global ports with low costs per unit due to modern shipping technologies and scale economies. Labor with low skills are replaced by machines and cheaper labors are easily available in the world. Human capital and knowledge are main determinants of national economic advancement, at least in very near future, as they might be replaced by robots soon. Economies like Japan, Korea and Singapore have very high income per capita, even though they have almost no natural resources. Education is the basic way to enable poor nations to quickly accumulate human capital for development.

Education value is affected by the cultural capital and education provides the basic determinant for sustainable prosperity. China has a tradition of formal rational education over thousand years. The main determinant of social status in the Confucian value system is neither birth nor organization nor belonging to the church, but education. Except the emperor, many important positions in the government are determined, though not always absolutely, by passing the examinations. Another important feature was that education was privately financed, not by public funds or the church. Unlike religion-dominated Western civilization where education was basically free for the sake of diffusing religion, Confucianism educated people not only to learn for the sake of learning, but also to accumulate human capital to serve society in varied professions. This may explain why modern China's government has made little investment in education in comparison to the nation's educational achievements.

The Beneficiary of Global Knowledge Stock

> When our thousands of Chinese students abroad return home, you will see how China will transform itself.
>
> Deng Xiaoping

"Men make their own history", Karl Marx (Dickson 1997: 1) writes in *The Eighteenth Brumaire of Louis Bonaparte*, "but they do not make it just as they please. They do not make it under circumstances chosen by themselves, but under circumstances directly found, given and transmitted from the past." Deng launched the economic reform from the condition left by Mao in the Confucian cultural soil. Chinese people began to accumulate wealth and knowledge with almost same conditions in terms of human capital and wealth among themselves with social order guaranteed by the party. It is a rare condition for market mechanisms to function so effectively.

No country, like China, has learned so much from the world in almost all fields only in the four decades. The world had created and accumulated huge knowledge and know-how stocks in mathematics, philosophy, history, believes, ideologies, ideas and thought, social sciences, natural sciences, technologies, literature, arts, sports, recipes, fashions, and the like by 1980. An important character of most of these stocks is "purely public" in the sense that they are both non-exclusive and non-rivalrous. A typical industry is TV programs. Almost all once most popular TV programs, in US, UK, Japan, and the four little tigers appeared in Chinese TV channels with mainland Chinese language and Chinese styles reformed by learning and imitation (subject to the Chinese government surveillance). Theories by, for instance, Newton, Adam Smith, are learned freely by millions of Chinese people. Some ideas or methods which might be learned and freely applied to China are not strictly public. A recipe in Singapore may become popular in China. This kind of imitation might not cause much moral concerns but might make owners of some restaurants in Singapore lose consumers. Much of knowledge in the world is obtainable either freely or through purchasing books and articles. Some countries might be pleased to allow other countries to learn their cultural knowledge and methods. Millions of Chinese students have travelled and studied in many cultures since the onset of the economic reform. Certain knowledge is publicly inaccessible or very costly. Public media reported cases that Chinese companies stole foreign companies' techs. Picasso knows the art of artists: "Good artists copy, great artists steal." In high techs, sciences, and mathematics, like in arts, boundaries between creativity, imitation, learning, and stealing need experts to judge. In intellectual worlds, only most talented know what are going on within the field. Mediocre and masses judge according to the media and their own emotion and bias.

The seed is a main determinant of a plant. The soil may become futile if the same seed is repeatedly farmed in the same place over generations. Max Weber observes: "It is not true that good can only follow good and evil only from evil, but that often the opposite is true." Traditional Confucian education systems turned out to be what Bertrand Russell says about education: "Men are born ignorant, not stupid. They are made stupid by education." Societies may be addicted to its traditions and values, like persons addicted to drugs, without accepting new ideas and making essential changes. Respect for education and measurement of being human according to education is a lasting character of Chinese culture. A main reason that the Manchus controlled China almost 300 years with the Manchu population less than 1 percent of China's population is that the Manchus respected education even more than the past dynasties in China. The Confucian education in the last hundred years of the Qing dynasty partly explains why China was ignorant about Western progresses and lost opportunity to become an industrial economy. The destructive Cultural Revolution almost expunged the elite class (if there was one). It is understandable that an easy way for a man like Mao without a formal education to secure his power was to destroy China's cultural value of respecting for learning. Since the reform, social environment has changed in association with influxes of foreign things and ideas. the Chinese cultural value of respecting education manifests in many fields of social and economic development.

No country has learnt so rapidly and so much within such a short period of time like China. A young man who can learn quickly is mostly due to passions for learning, educational opportunity, strong motivations for knowledge, family and public supports, and other conditions. The Cultural Revolution had laid a condition for swift national learning as the setout point is so low. Many intellectuals suffered and lost lives during the Mao's time, but the consequences also "cleaned" ways to straightforwardly introduce Western ideas, sciences, and technologies. There was a reservoir of global knowledge for lowly-educated Chinese people to learn and apply. When Deng was rising to the top power, many Chinese craved knowing and aspired to receiving education to make changes. Excellence in education is regarded as the only key for children's success in Chinese culture. Although this tradition was broken during the Cultural Revolution, the rooted-cultural value came back soon as the economic reform was launched. Chinese parents who never received any higher education, were willing to make every possible effort to make their children to get better education. Millions of students have annually graduated from college and universities since 2000. This passion for education explains why China has made great progresses in almost fields related to knowledge and technologies through learning, imitating, copying, as well as stealing in multifarious ways and heterogeneous forms.

Over the four decades landscape, people's behavior, knowledge, human capital, concepts about meanings of life, visions, clothes, and food have experienced dramatic changes in China. A determinant of all these agile changes is due to Deng's policy of opening door. Once the door was opened, there has almost no way for anyone or the party to close China again. Deng emphasized science and technology. He made efforts to speed up progress in professional knowledge. Ethics and education on morality on freedom and individualism are largely neglected in Chinese education system. Over-emphasis on economic expansion and individual profit in education might explain, at least partly, that many poor children from countryside, who learned diligently in youth and worked hard in middle age, are ending their careers as corrupt officials or criminals. Schopenhauer reasons: "Money is human happiness in the abstract; he, then, who is no longer capable of enjoying human happiness in the concrete devotes himself utterly to money."

Modernizing Education as the Growth Tool

> When a country is on the verge of a great florescence, it is certain to prize its teachers and give great importance to breadth of learning. If it does this, then laws and standards will be preserved. When a country is on the verge of decay, then it is sure to show contempt for teachers and slight masters. If it does this, then its people will be smug. If the people are smugly self-satisfied, then laws and standards will be allowed to go to ruin.
>
> Xun Zi (298–238 BC, 27: 97)

One of the most famous TV series *River Elegy* in China (Barmé and Jaivin 1992: 155) shocked China in the earlier years of the economic reform, when Chinese society had little knowledge yet to properly appreciate positive energies in Confucianism. It blames Confucian cultures as follows:

> Confucian culture may contain all sorts of venerable and perfected 'treasures,' but for some two thousand years it has completely failed to create a spirit of progress among the Chinese or any mechanism for the renewal of the state's legal system and culture. On the contrary, in its progress toward collapse it has evolved a suicidal mechanism: It constantly thwarts and destroys talent, murders the life-giving elements within itself, and asphyxiates the best and brightest of every generation.

Confucianism is created more than two thousand years ago. China was either under the emperor's monopoly, or under foreign control, or in chaotic periods for searching a unified empire. There is almost no possibility for free spirit to sustain in long term under the centralized personal control. Free spirits and positive energies in ancient Confucianism had been seldom explored in China's history till the death of Mao. China had been so effectively isolated that there was almost no way for Chinese to immigrate to any other societies with higher cultures before the West forced China to open door. The examination system plus effective national control explain why China killed the best and brightest of every generation or made them obedient to the emperor or hide in mountains.

Four decades ago, Deng told the nation: "China will not become a modernized country just by talking about a grand vision: it must cultivate the necessary expertise and talent to make that vision a reality." One of most important reforms is the change in syllabuses. Traditional education during the Qing dynasty (1644–1912) under the Manchus, like in other dynasties especially from the Song, is focused on the Confucian classics. Confucianism is interpreted subject to the emperor's will. Since the New China is established, China interprets communism in way that the party needs. The contents of social sciences are under government's strict surveillance. As the party is a sole designer of education, the contents of education in social sciences are especially subject to political checking: "In deposit states each house is a separate government. As education therefore consists chiefly in social converse, it must be here very limited; all it does is to strike the heart with fear, and to imprint the understanding of a very simple notion of a few principles. ... Here therefore education is in some measure needless; to give something one must take away everything; and begin with making a bad subject in order to make a good slave." (Montesquieu, 1689–1755, 1748: 124). Nevertheless, there is freedom in contents of China's education in fields of natural sciences, engineering, and mathematics. Moreover, most of important Western and Chinese books in philosophies and social sciences are available in China's book markets. Criticisms against the party and issues related to some religious issues, Hong Kong, and Taiwan are under strict surveillance.

The Chinese education system is exam-oriented and highly selective. Basic education in China consists of primary school (Grades 1–6), middle school (Grades 7–9), and high school (Grades 10–12) education. The Compulsory Education Law of 1986 stipulates that all children must receive primary and middle education. The Law also decentralizes financing and administration of basic education, municipal governments taking the primary responsibility for basic education. The primary school and junior high school are compulsory. The policy has great effects on the spread of education. The change of literacy rate in the period 1984–2016 is illustrated in Fig. 4.1. Junior high school graduates can choose high school or vocational high school and take entrance exams. High school graduates are eligible for the college entrance exam, but in vocational school graduates cannot. There are limited places in higher education and a huge numbers of high school graduates who want to enter colleges and universities. There is a severe competition in entrance exams. The nation-wide college entrance which usually takes place three days in June. The competition makes schools and families to emphasize skills and abilities to pass examinations. Almost half of the three years in high school is spent on preparing the college entrance exams. High school students spend whole school life on exam-oriented questions and techniques, especially in the last one year, almost without any weekend and holiday. Teachers and students are rewarded according to students' performances in the exams.

The level of public education spending in China is low (Yuan and Zhang 2015). Households pay tuition and miscellaneous fees set by municipal governments to supplement school costs. Schools often make extra charges over student families for multifarious purposes. Increases in public spending on basic education are positively related to reductions in household private tutoring spending in urban China. Higher education

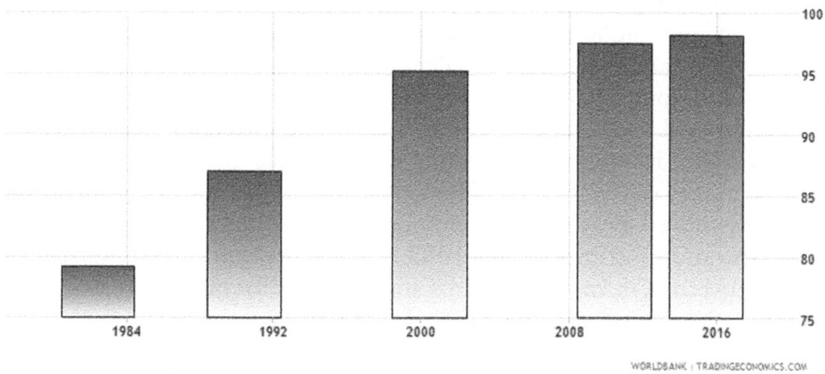

Fig. 4.1 China's literacy rate over the period 1984 to 2016 (*Source* https://www.china-mike.com/facts-about-china/facts-chinese-education/)

focuses on training specialists for economic development. Universities, colleges, and institutes offer four- or five-year undergraduate programs. After they complete a first degree, students may apply for graduate schools and then Ph.D. programs. The education system experiences reforms over years. There are visible progresses in secondary vocational education and senior middle-school education. The on-the-job training and continuous education are also rapidly developed. Chinese education is still characterized by rote learning. Chinese parents tell their children to study diligent. Children are trained to pass examinations, but not allow to develop the mindset towards what Confucius says: the highest is to enjoy in what you do. The educational problem is well recognized. The government needs a large of obedient administrators and markets require more flexible and creative minds. People make educational choice and different types of educational institutions also adopt their syllabuses and teachers' characters. Each year millions of students are receiving Western education in Western countries to enhance human capital.

Fast Spread and Enhancement of Education

> Human nature is such that people are born with a love of profit…, they will struggle and snatch from each other.
>
> Xun Zi (298–238 BC)

Since 1978, the government has treated education as a key for economic expansion and modernization. University recruitment has been determined by entrance examination. The merit-based recruitment encourages families and young people to have traditional dreams for changing their lives and social status through study. In universities faculty members have been required to upgrade their skills and academic qualifications through domestic or overseas training. From the early 1980s, the government has gradually moved away from a centralized style with detailed operations of high education institutions. In 1983, the *Decision on Education Reform* by the government showed its aims and methods for improving efficiency, quality, and equity. The decision also included releasing resources for developing and enhancing education at lower levels. Universities could also decide, partly, contents and methods of teaching. They were partly permitted to admit students outside the state plan if they were financed by enterprise or were self-financing. In 1993, the State Council and the CCP jointly made the *Guidelines for Development and the Reform of China's Education System*. It outlined the strategy reforming the Chinese higher education system for enhancing China's competitive position in the world: "Whoever receives education that is oriented toward the twenty-first century will gain the strategic initiative in international competition during the twenty-first century." The document decided to: (a) increase required specialists for modernization and for development of socialist market economy; (b) enhance teachers' higher social status, improve work and living conditions; and (c) develop 100 key universities and several key courses of study. The document emphasized decentralization for achieving these goals. Soon after, educational institutions were freer, the system of college enrollment was improved, and job markets for graduates were enlarged, and channels of funds for teaching and research were diversified.

During the period from 1977 to 1985, there were more than 230 new education institutions were established. The government also formally recognized numerous high-quality primary, middle, and high schools. Families and young people competed fiercely for these educational resources. Between 1978 and 1994, the number of regular public universities and colleges rose from 598 to 1080, while the number of staff in the institutions changed from 0.5 to 1.04 million and the number of students from 0.86 to 2.8 million. Seventy-one percent of the total students was state-sponsored, seventeen percent was enterprise-financed 17%, and twelve percent was self-financed 12%. The entrance rates were risen gradually. By 1990, only 2% of the population aged 25 and above had postsecondary education in China; while 11% in Hong Kong, 14% in Korea, 21% in Japan. In 1990, only 5.6 scientists and engineers engaged in research and development per 10,000 persons in the work force in China, compared to 30 in Singapore, 38 in Taiwan, 37 in Korea, and 75 in Japan. By 2003, the regional and central government had 1552 colleges and universities with 750,000 professors and 11 million students. In 2015, the primary and lower secondary schools supported by the government had 28.8 million students.

The Compulsory Education Law requires that residence estates are divided into designated school districts with regards to public elementary and junior middle schools, and children living in a school district can enroll in the school without selection. The policy is made to provide equal access to public educational resources and fairness in the enrollment processes. It is especially tended to allow low-income families by replacing selective enrollment fees with the relatively fixed locations of residence estates. Children enroll in the designated correspondence school. The policy appears to eliminate school selection. It soon originated the school district housing fever in the districts corresponding to reputed primary and middle schools with capable teachers and good learning environment. A typical case in Shanghai was quoted by Zhou (2018). In October 2017, sales price averaged ¥113,000/m^2 in Quandong neighborhood as it was located within the corresponding enrollment area of a reputed primary school, while the average sales price of apartments in the neighborhood area was only ¥69,800/m^2. There was only one block between the two residential areas. The only determinant for the prices difference was the correspondence to schools. This disparity resulted from the lack of high-quality public educational resources and uneven distribution of resources. The enrollment policy initially did not create so huge disparity as in recent years because income and wealth inequalities have recently enlarged. China's real estate industry nation-widely encouraged the school district housing fever. From 2009 to 2013, the industry was expanded at annul rate 22%, of which second-hand sales of school district estates was more than 13%. The policy has created a great inequality in educational opportunities among girls and boys. Children from poor families can no longer equally receive public resources for education due to unaffordable housing prices. They will be kept at the bottom of society in China as quality education play a crucial role in determining one's future. A variety of policies have been introduced in many regions in China to deal with the problems associated with the policy.

During the period from 1991 to 2003, China's Public Educational System experienced industrialization. The government's decision on the Acceleration of the Development of the Tertiary Industry of 1992 catalogues education as a part of tertiary industry. Education is a part of services in economic systems, rather than a component of the "superstructure". This rule enabled the governments of different levels and educational units to prioritize educational outcome to educational fairness. The scale and capacity of the educational system were rapidly expanded. In 1999, private institutions for basic education were legalized in 1999. Enrollment fees have been allowed to be collected by many institutions. Resource competition are severe. During the period from 1991 to the present, the government has re-emphasized fairness in public education.

The return to education from the 1980s and the 1990s in urban China was estimated to below, with one year of schooling increasing earnings by about 2–4 percent. The low return is pointed out partly due to that most of urban China was under a planned regime. As the reform had deepened, the return was enhanced, from 4 percent in 1988 to 10 percent in 2001. Nevertheless, it is pointed out that return to high school education was low, while returns to college and vocational education were high (Li, et al. 2012). There are now great educational inequalities. The wealthy afford admission fees for their kids to get into better schools. As analyzed by Mendoza (2018) and Golley and Kong (2018), there is a great inequality in educational opportunity. This inequality stems primarily from the divisive *hukou* system, father's education, birth cohort, province, parents' Communist Party membership, gender, family size and ethnicity. Timely supply of educated labor force results in a phenomenon that people are overeducated for their jobs. There is wage penalty of overeducation. The overeducated have lower abilities in comparison to the well-matched. "After all, the human capital per head in China is only a fifth of the United States and a quarter of Canada" (Wu and Wang 2018: 216).

Educational inequalities between rural and urban areas, between regions, gender, ethnicity. Individuals are faced with varied circumstances which they have no control, such as gender, parents' social and economic status, and birthplace. As far as China's educational opportunity is concerned, the *hukou* system is the greatest obstacle. "In the absence of any compelling evidence that there are inherent differences in the innate abilities of rural and urban children, any differences in their educational outcomes can reasonably be attributed to the circumstances they find themselves born into rural and urban—and thus reflect a lack of equal opportunity between the two." (Golley and Kong 2018: 120). Golley and Kong identify that the inequality educational opportunity was determined by factors such as father's education, the *hukou* status at the age 12, birth cohort, province, parents' Communist Party membership, gender, family size and ethnicity. In recent years, this inequality has been sped up due to the *hukou system* and the educated staying in cities. Intergenerational gaps between rural and urban are enlarged (Bhattachrya et al. 2018). The most typical Chinese factor is the *hukou* status. This single factor itself makes an additional three-year gift on national level. This substantial educational gift is playing an even increasing important role in one's life welfare as spatial equalities in educational opportunity, environment, wages, rents, and pensions are rapidly enlarged. The *hukou* system's impact on every aspect of life becomes increasingly more serious as China is further developed. For instance, in 2015 Beijing made rules to force rural immigrants to return their home villages and thus robbed the good educational opportunity of children. The unfair treatment of rural people caused much domestic and international attention.

China has now the world largest education system. The number of tertiary students surged sixfold from 7.4 million in 2000 to 45 million in 2018. Figure 4.2 plots the number of students admitted to universities over the period 1977 to 2018.

Many students purchased education in foreign countries. From 1998 to 2017, the number of Chinese students enrolled abroad rose by 590 percent to 900,000 (Gu et al. 2019). Figure 4.3 plots the dynamics of number of students abroad over the period 2000–2017. The return rate is quite high now. There are many reasons to stay abroad for young people. China has been the largest sending country of international students among countries. China has a great impact on global higher education. Most of students now return to China after completing education. China has now more Ph.D. students than the U.S. China has now 514,000 educational institutions and 270 million students enrolled at all levels of education. Chinese higher education institutions produce annually 8

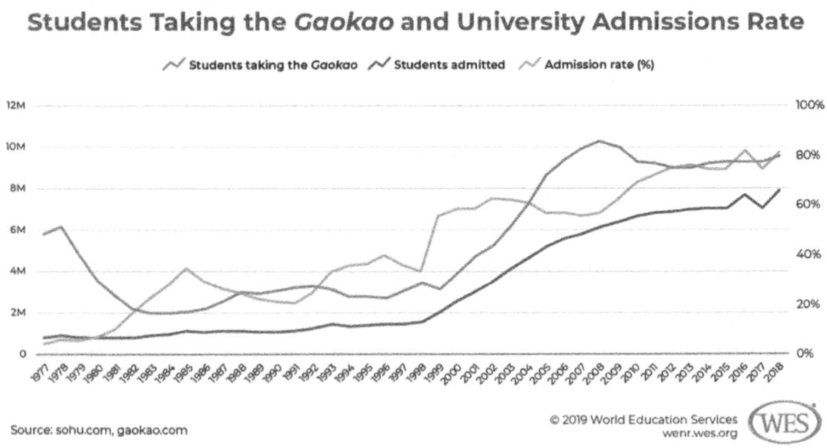

Fig. 4.2 The number of students admitted to universities over years (*Source* https://wenr.wes.org/2019/12/education-in-china-3)

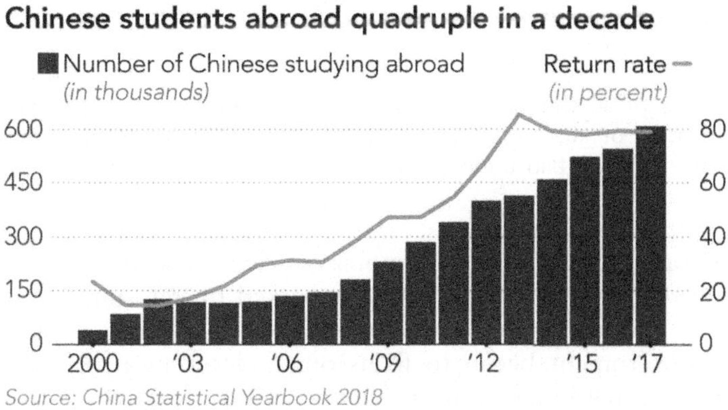

Fig. 4.3 Dynamics of chinese students abroad (*Source* https://asia.nikkei.com/Spotlight/The-Big-Story/Chinese-students-and-US-universities-become-pawns-in-the-trade-war)

million graduates. The number is expected to grow 300 percent until 2030.

Free choice of professionals and profit opportunities in markets guaranteed by the economic reform have encouraged people to accumulate heterogeneous types of human capital and apply their human capital in miscellaneous ways (Li and Wang 2018). Human capital accumulated through education or through practicing enhance productivities. Some studies verify that the productivity growth rate is highest in the late 1990s and then gradually falling. In enhancing productivity in creativity-learning field, what Einstein says is insightful: "To raise new questions, new possibilities, to regard old problems from a new angle, requires creative imagination and marks real advance in science." Since China was opened to advanced economies, unlimited number of new problems, new possibilities, and new necessities have been presented to Chinese people. Through solving their problems in production and consumption, Chinese people have accumulated human capital quickly as reflected in varieties of products and enhanced incomes.

Development of Science and Technology

> Ignorance of all things is an evil neither terrible nor excessive, nor yet the greatest of all; but great cleverness and much learning, if they be accompanied by a bad training, are a much greater misfortune.
>
> Plato (423–347 BC)

Deng Xiaoping was a strong promoter of science and technology. Once returning to power, he immediately embarked on reforming the system of science and technology built on the Soviet model. By 1979, the Central Government began to focus on modernization of science and technology. Intellectuals were encouraged to do research, even though the party has continued to control intellectual expression. The government established a group of scientific and technological management organs, scientific research institutes and academies. The State Science & Technology Commission (SSC) and local science and technology commissions were restored. New science and technology development plans were completed across the country. In 1981, the state decided that science and technology should be developed in association with economic and social development. The State Council established a leading group of science & technology to macro-control the work in the country. The same policy was applied to various levels in provinces and units. The country sped up trial reform of scientific and technological systems. The state opened-up technological market, emphasized protection of intellectual property rights, improved scientific award system, built experimental facility supporting system, and encouraged non-governmental science and technology institutes. The state strategy for science and technology in 1986 was made to serve national social and economic development, to create high technology and related industry, and to advance basic research. The state established six big programs. Among the programs, the 86–3 Program was approved by Deng Xiaoping in March 1986 for the development of new and hi-tech researches. The program made breakthroughs in key technologies. Deng's idea on developing high technology to realize industrialization has been the basis for China to commercialize, industrialize, and globalize new and hi-tech achievements. In May 1995, the CPC Central Committee promulgated the Decision on Speeding up Science and Technology Progress which initiated the strategy to quicken scientific and technological progress. Science and technology were considered as a main productive force of economic proliferation and modernization. Academic institutions, universities, and firms were encouraged to carry out research. Researchers became more mobile and were paid according to their performances. Seniority became less important. Intellectual property rights were mentioned and asked to be respected. Competition and open bidding on projects were introduced.

Science and technology have developed rapidly since the 1990s after China had a relative solid basis due to large numbers of students graduated from higher educational institutes. The government has provided research funds and carried out institutional reforms. Researchers' social status were also enhanced. Science and technology have increasingly enjoyed freedom in choosing research directions. There has been a rapid growth of investment in research and development. There were 1.5 million science and engineering students graduated from Chinese universities in 2006. In 2017, China surpassed the U.S. in the number of scientific publications (Toffefson 2018). China now spends more on research and development than the countries in the European Union. It is expected to exceed the U.S. in research expenditures soon.

The Chinese economy has increased R&D to have more advanced technology for producing higher value-added products (Mah and Yeo 2014). China published about one-quarter of all academic articles around the world in material sciences and chemistry and 17 percent in physics between 2004 and 2014. Due to lack of arable land and water, China needs new technology to enhance agricultural output. China bought millions of foreign breeder animal and large amount of semen and livestock embryos to improve the genetics of Chinese livestock. Problems such as overuse of pesticides are causing public concerns. Research in aquaculture has made contribution to sustainable advancement of aquaculture. China has also made essential technological changes in deep sea exploration. Technological changes have important implications for deep sea mining. There were dramatic developments in electronics, telecommunication, internet, software industries. China has increasingly targeting indigenous innovation. In the last 15 years China has developed innovation infrastructures. Many of Chinese companies are now strong competitors in domestic markets and increasingly in global markets.

To access foreign technologies, in the early 1980s China asked foreign companies to transfer technology by licensing agreements and sales of equipment. In the late 1980s many multinational corporations made transferring for entering joint ventures with Chinese companies to access

Chinese markets. Technology transfer was important when China was making catch up with advanced economies. In the 1990s China introduced more regulations for the same purpose. The entry of China into the WTO in 2001 required the regulations to be stopped. Once China was in a position in competition in cutting edge technologies, the practice was not so helpful. China has also increasingly attracted multinational corporations to build R&D centers in China by using Chinese talents. In 2010 1200 such R&D centers existed in China. These foreign R&D activities provide a role model for Chinese government and companies to develop Chinese R&D. The practice also benefited the foreign corporations as they could develop products for the huge Chinese market and employ Chinese engineers and scientists.

The government has well recognized that the nation lacks indigenous innovation capacities Between 2003 and 2012 China increased its expenditure on R&D from 1.13% to 1.97% of GDP. China's number of engineers and scientists reached to 1.59 million by 2008. *The Medium and Long-Term Plan for the Development of Science and Technology* (2006–2020) planed 2.5% of GDP on R&D by 2020. In 2015 China spent 5.1% of total research spending on basic research. It was planned the rate rise to 15% by 2020. and functional systems of technological intellectual property protection. The government has made a series of projects for promoting innovation, such as The Strategic Emerging Industries initiative, the Internet Plus initiative, and the Made in China 2025 Program. The government prioritizes industries and protects and guides their developments. The government encourages firms to replace foreign technology with indigenous technology. Foreign companies are provided incentives to transfer technologies to Chinese companies and to move R&D to China. The percentage of the number per 1000 population was still very low. The *13th Five-Year Plan for the National Economy and Social Development* (2016–2020) planned to embark on the *Scientific and Technological Innovation 2030 Project*. It targeted areas such as quantum communication and quantum computers, brain sciences, robots, and space-terrestrial information network.

Necessity Is the Mother of Invention

> In England, an inventor is regarded almost as a crazy man, and in too many instances, invention ends in disappointment and poverty. In America, an inventor is honoured, help is forthcoming, and exercise of ingenuity, the application of science to the work of man, is there the shortest road to wealth.
>
> Oscar Wilde (1854–1900)

Someone—often alleged to Darwin—says: "It is not the strongest of the species that survives, nor the most intelligent that survives. It is the one that is most adaptable to change." China's economic reform is a great achievement by adapting to its internal and international environment. It has modernized its national economic structure by assembling, imitating, and leaning to make innovation in grand scales. As a country with little natural resources per capita, China must if it further enhances per capita income in a long-term perspective. Possible advantages from cheap labor have been explored already domestically and internationally. There are many people in the world who would work even for lower wages than Chinese.

China had a long history of creativity and innovation. But it does not yet have a modern Western legal system to protect results of creativity and innovation. In modern economies, high value-added products are mostly due to innovations and their markets under protection of. To enter and survive in globally competitive and high value-added markets for goods and services China must make innovative breakthroughs in science and technology. In recent years, China has emphasized innovation. In 2006, it planned 20 large megaprojects in areas such as aircraft, high-end generic microchips, and new drugs. It also began to learn the Silicon Valley approach with small start-ups, venture capital, and cooperation between industry and academic research institutions. The government has encouraged the acquisition of intellectual property as part of its efforts to enhance the level of technology innovation. Patenting is commonly considered as the most measure of national innovation performance. The 12th Five-Year Plan of Science and Technology Development for the period from 2011 to 2015 made a target for patents: its target is to increase the number of invention patents in force per 10,000 people from 1.7 in 2010 to 3.3 in 2015. The government at all levels soon introduced incentives to encourage patent applications. China soon became the top in the world in the number of patent applications filed with the State Intellectual Property Office in 2011. The application number is affected by factors, such as technological sophistication and over-confidence and ignorance about patenting. To execute plans such as this, Chinese government at different levels introduced incentives to promote patent applications. Hu et al. (2017) verify that most of increase of the patenting surge come from firms that did not apply for patents in the past. Their research concludes that non-innovation related motives for acquiring patents might have played an important role in the increase of application number. In recent years China's economic expansion has slackened. The working age population is no more increasing. Returns to investment have fallen. It is necessary to have indigenous innovations for maintaining fast advancement. It is increasingly difficult to rely on foreign technology. China has emphasized building national innovation capacity. Shi and Wu (2017) verify that Chinese innovative firms tend to be old, large, exporters, and state-owned.

China has made progresses in education, high-tech manufacturing, academic publishing, infrastructure, patents, and commercial applications. In some fields China has even become a global leader. In 2017 the Chinese State Council made the national plans to make China the global leader in artificial intelligence by 2030. China is now the leader in drone technology, the first country to produce large scale transport drones, an amphibious drone, and flying taxi drone. Some regions in South China have labor shortage problems. Wages are risen rapidly. Fast proliferation of industrial robots expeditiously replaces workers. By 2017, China is the largest producer and user of robotics technology. The Chinese software industry in 2010 shared 15% of the world's software and information service market. China is now one of main leading pioneers in the fields. In 2017 53% of the population was internet users. The number of mobile internet users was 724 million. There were 1.36 billion mobile subscribers. The e-commerce market is today the largest in the world. In 2017, the e-commerce market was worth US$ 1.132 trillion, the triple of the US market. China is rapidly adopting 5G network nationwide. China is determined to lead the global deployment of the next-generation mobile technology.

China has many shortcomings in innovation systems. It has little cultural stocks in comprehensively and systematically carrying out large research projects in modern science and technology. In the earlier years of the economic reform, Chinese government had no experiences in helping firms to apply new ideas of science and technology to get profits for privates as well as the public. It still lacks a solid mechanism of optimally allocating national funding to grow science and technology. China has been effective in making small, innovative improvements to existing designs. Firms are good at making current designs, often initiated in foreign economies, less expensive and more energy efficient. Through making improvements, Chinese also learned about how to make new products. By the 2010s, Chinese economy was becoming increasingly innovative. China made efforts in transforming from "Made in China" to "Designed in China" and creating companies with brand names. By 2019 China surpassed the US as the top source of international patent applications filed with the Geneva-based World Intellectual Property Organization. By 2019, China overtook UK in highly cited researchers and ranks second after the US. Supercomputing in China has developed quickly. The technology affects multifarious fields of research. In 2017, China had 202 of the 500 greatest supercomputers in the world, while the US was the second with 143. Over some years the top two most powerful supercomputers had changed hands between the US and China. Chinese Tianhe-1 was in 2010 and 2011 the world's fastest supercomputer, Tianhe-2 in 2013; Sunway TaihuLight in 2016. China is making great progresses in chip-making technology. China is also creating much more powerful large-scale distributed supercomputing by connecting its supercomputer centers.

Some industries with heavy government intervention do not perform well. China's semiconductor industry has received extensive government support. The industry has relatively slow in creating new designs. A reason is that local governments tend to support outdated technologies. There lacks a well-organized management system for resources. Poor protection of intellectual property and geographically scattered locations of the industry also make contributions to unproductive development of the industry.

There are also more research-directed strategies on utilization of resources. Return of students from many parts of the world accelerates positive role of scale and scope economies in national development. China also explores multifarious sources of energies. Coal has been the main power source. China is now a world leader in clean coal technology. China has made huge investments in renewable energy technologies. Nuclear power is rapidly expanding with international cooperation. Special attention is now paid to environmentally clean technologies.

China has been accused of not protecting foreign intellectual property, allowing technologies to be copied, and of facilitating transfers of foreign technological intellectual property from corporations to Chinese companies.

References

Barmé, G., & Jaivin, L. (1992). *New Ghosts, Old Dreams*. New York, NY: Times Books.

Bhattachrya, P., Palacio-Torralba, J., & Li, X. (2018). On Income Inequality Within China's Provinces. *Chinese Studies, 7,* 174–182.

Dickson, B. J. (1997). *Democratization in China and Taiwan—The Adaptability of Leninist Parties*. Oxford: Oxford University Press.

Golley, J., & Kong, S. T. (2018). Inequality of Opportunity in China's Educational Outcomes. *China Economic Review, 51,* 116–128.

Gu, M., Michael, R., Zheng, C., & Trines, S. (2019, December 17). *Education in China*. https://wenr.wes.org/2019/12/education-in-china-3.

Hu, A. G. Z., Zhang, P., & Zhao, L. J. (2017, January). China as Number One? Evidence from China's Most Recent Patenting Surge. *Journal of Developmental Economics, 124,* 107–119.

Li, H. B., Liu, P. W., & Zhang, J. S. (2012, May). Estimating Returns to Education Using Twins in Urban China. *Journal of Developmental Economics, 97,* 494–504.

Li, T. T., & Wang, Y. (2018, October). Growth Channels of Human Capital: A Chinese Data Study. *China Economic Review, 51,* 309–322.

Mah, J. S., & Yeo, M. (2014). The Role of the Government in R&D Promotion and the Development of Technology—Intensive Industries in China. *China Report, 50*(2), 91–107.

Mendoza, O. M. V. (2018, October). Heterogeneous Determinants of Educational Achievement and Inequality Across Urban China. *China Economic Review, 51,* 129–148.

Montesquieu, C. (1748). *The Spirit of Laws* (edited with an introduction by D. W. Carrithers). Berkeley, CA: University of California Press.

Shi, X., & Wu, Y. R. (2017, December). The Effect of Internal and External Factors on Innovative Behaviour of Chinese Manufacturing Firms. *China Economic Review, 46,* S50–S64.

Toffefson, J. (2018). China Declared World's Largest Producer of Scientific Articles. *Nature, 553,* 390.

Wu, N., & Wang, Q. Y. (2018, August). Wage Penalty of Overeducation: New Micro-Evidence from China. *China Economic Review, 50,* 206–217.

Yuan, G., & Zhang, L. (2015). Public Education Spending and Private Substitution in Urban China. *Journal of Developmental Economics, 115,* 124–139.

Zhou, T. C. (2018). Capitalization of Public School Quality into Housing Prices: An Empirical Analysis Based on School District Housing for Public Primary Schools in Shanghai. *Chinese Studies, 7*(4), 287–327.

CHAPTER 5

Economic Growth from Hunger with Animal Spirits

Introduction

> [M]ere social contact begets in most industries an emulation and a stimulation of the animal spirits that heightens the efficiency of each individual workman.
>
> Karl Marx

China's national butterfly effect is observable from the onset of Deng's economic reform. There are numerous butterfly effects with varied scales in multifarious fields of China from 1978. It has been an epoch of, positive and negative, butterfly effects. Deng embarked national rags-to-riches stories of different levels. Ma Yun's rags-to-riches process is a typical story among many thousands of Chinese in miscellaneous fields. China had potentially huge markets for internet due to Deng's grand policy and the development of the business in the US economy. Due to technological and market structural characteristics of the internet business, they should be a few super-rich in that business. Mu Yuan, who had little technological knowledge and even has not a proper brain to pass simple entrance exams for higher education, initiated the butterfly effect in the business by grasping the opportunity with the prepared human capital. He triggered off the butterfly effect due to his searching internet first time in America. The economic conditions in the 1990s, rapid proliferation in internet business and technologies mainly in America, China's

W.-B. Zhang, *The Butterfly Effect in China's Economic Growth*,
https://doi.org/10.1007/978-981-15-9889-0_5

economic structure, and the timing were synthesized together to result in his fortune which mirrors the epoch of Chinese dream—dream-like results which never appear in dreams.

Ma Yun is a well-known household name and very influential motivational name for youth not only because of his wealth and business, but also because of his lack of any resources (such as wealth, social status, power, or *guanxi*, physical attractiveness, degrees of education or family background) or even professional knowledge. He was born in poor family. He has an older brother and a younger sister. One often hears his admirations for Steve Jobes as a man who changed the world and the life on the earth with his personality. Ma Yun's human capital is not the same as the American hero. Both Deng and Ma Yun grew in Chinese cultural and social soils. Mao provided the preconditions for their achievements. It is neither formal educational nor professional knowledge, but human capital accumulated through experience and the personality that are the keys to their amusing stories.

Ma Yuan is well known for being kind in helping others and cooperative, which is perhaps a condition for team building, especially for him as he had neither wealth nor professional knowledge. He had a great passion for learning English from childhood. His love of English enabled him to know modern ways of expressions and basic management skills in dealing with human relations. His influential speeches in Chinese reminds one of Western businessmen, while his English expressions have much Chinese contents. He had little opportunities to learn English in his teenage years. After Nixon visited his home city in 1972, Hangzhou became a tourist mecca. The flood of Western tourists made him aware of the English as the source of income. The city's West Lake is now a UNESCO world heritage site. He used to visit international hotels to chat in English with tourists in Hangzhou. He publicly mentioned that he learned English by giving tourists free guides around the city. The reality is perhaps that he might earn the tips from generous English-speaking tourists more than a worker (monthly wage in China was then a few USA dollars). If this is the case, it proves his talent, dutifulness, responsibility, and personal character to use limited resources to make personal growth as well as living for family as a dutiful man. Strong duty for family survival is the common character of many fortunate Chinese men and women, except high officials and their children, in that generation. He had practiced "free" guide for nine years. He improved not only English but also learned from tourists different from what he might be unable to study about the West at a Chinese school in that time. His failures from primary school, middle school and colleges and his unstopped trials were astonishing stories in China. He failed to pass the College Entrance Examination two times before he entered a then unknown college with easy entrance. His passion and perseverance in getting education inspirits many young people. He graduated in 1988 with a B.A. in English. He late expressed his admiration for Bill Gate, who was born in rich and received best education opportunity on the earth without fully using it. He was rejected many times in applying for unskilled jobs. He applied 30 jobs and was rejected by all. He applied for Harvard 10 times and was rejected 10 times. He was only one rejected among 24 applicants in applying a KFC job in his home city. He was hired as an English teacher at a local university with salary US$12 per month which should be much lower than his free guide job. He had many stories of fails to battle with life. But like many of fortunate people, he never stopped trying new things.

In 1995, he went to America. During the trip, for the first time he used the internet. He made a searching for "beer" and found no result related to China. Then he made another searching for "China" and no result. The experience inspirited him to develop internet in China. The seed for the most successful website in China was thus sown. He came back to Hangzhou to found Alibaba.com, a China-based B2B marketplace site, in his apartment with his team of 17 friends and students in 1995. Alibaba now evolved into a multinational technology conglomerate. In his speech at Davos in 2015, he said, "Life is like a box of chocolates because you never known what you are going to get." He was the 14th richest in the world, with a net worth of US$42 billion in 2017. He is kind to help others—important personality and basic skill for human networking for exploring scale and scope economies. He is a very influential businessman and a philanthropist. He is a typical case of the Chinese dream realized before making the dream. He provided a Chinese confirmation about what Einstein says: "Everybody is a genius. But if you judge a fish by its ability to climb a tree, it will live its whole life believing that it is stupid." In 2018, Ma Yun told the public that he would retire from Alibaba and continue his favorite teaching and pursue other meaningful causes. His story to great fortune with the spirit of trying and learning has been inspiriting millions of Chinese youth. The story of Ma Yun is structurally, not only individual. The founders of many giant companies and fortunate entrepreneurs have experienced typical fortunate path of many Chinese entrepreneurs—from hungry childhood to the rich. They persistently make efforts and try in all possible directions with all possible methods with high spirits. There are great fortunes in almost fields of economy, from raising chickens, fish, pigs, planting mash rooms, investing in property markets, and establishing giant e-related companies. Ma Yun's life itself is an example of China's butterfly effects. It was first time dreamed of in a bar in America where he had the idea of initiating internet business in China. Many fortunate stories of escape from poverty are repeatedly told to younger generations in China. The CEO of Huawei was born into an even poorer family and in far less developed area than Ma Yun's. Figure 5.1 illustrates an aggregated story of the national escape from poverty.

It is perhaps more difficult to convincingly explain why poor countries remain poor than to tell why rich countries are rich. It is quite challenging to explain why and how a poor country with the largest population in entire human history could have become (relatively) rich within a short span of time. China's aggregated economic advancement association with reduction of poverty in the last four decades is no doubt the great economic achievement of mankind—it is a showcase of what modern science and technology can bring about to human life in large, and to a country in special.

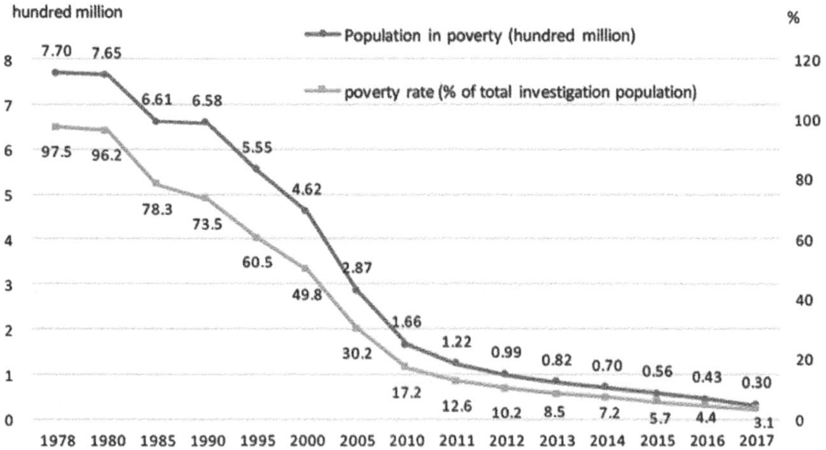

Fig. 5.1 China's national story of escaping from poverty (*Source* Fang et al. [2018])

Economic Reform and Structural Change Under Deng's Political Stability

An institution or reform movement that is not selfish, must originate in the recognition of some evil that is adding to the sum of human suffering, or diminishing the sum of happiness.

Clara Barton (1821–1912)

China's rapid economic progress took place when the former socialist economies of the Soviet Union and Eastern Europe (which had perhaps much less rational cultural stocks than China) were in ruins and other high-flying Asian economies experienced severe setbacks. Socialist countries were aware long time ago that there were serious problems in planning economies. Some planning economies had carried out reforms earlier than China. A main difference from other socialist countries is that China did not believe in the so-called "big bang approach" to carrying out socialist reform. The big bang approach, which was advocated by some well-known Western academic economists, basically holds that change from a planned economy to a market-based economy should take place, socially, politically, and economically, abruptly. Moreover, such a swift transformation would bring about improved economic performances. The belief has no solid theoretical support but had been practiced in some countries with little positive consequences. The reason for this mis-leading advocate is that traditional theoretical economics has a very simplified world view and over-simplified analytical structures. It is thus rational for the rational economist of traditional economics to believe in the big bag approach as traditional theoretical economics provides only a linear and unique equilibrium view on economic development. When the reality does not fit the assumed linearly changing world and economists believed in the validity of the linearized world view, the big bang approach to structural transformation reasonably led to political instabilities and low economic efficiencies for these socialist countries. Balances between economic proliferation and social and political order are not durable in the sense that swift big movement in either side may lead to catastrophes. China reformed the economy with most of social and political structures ossified.

Stability is a key factor for structural transformation. Each society has special factors for social stability during its initial stages of industrialization. To illustrate the complexity, we reflect on what Landes (1998: 38) describes: "... Christianity, craving imperial tolerance early made the distinction between God and Caesar. … In the end, it was the Church, and this meant yielding to Caesar what was Caesar's and then a good part of what was God's. Among the things that gave, homogeneous orthodoxy: where authority is divided, dissent flourishes." Landes points out that this division of the powers sustains a social and cultural environment proper for the spirit and popular initiatives, perhaps not good for certainty and conformity. The British built a modern sophisticated economic system with relative social stability partly because the empire sent so many energetic people to many foreign countries, colonized such a large of the world, and enslaved so many peoples. Colonization played an important role for social stabilities during some periods in European modern developments. The conflicts among European economies led to the two world wars—an undesirable but perhaps necessary way to solve economic, social, and political instabilities among countries. So many countries paid costs for European modern economic expansion—there were potential benefits as well. Similarly, the rise of the United States with relatively social and political stabilities was associated with domestic slave system and extensive discrimination and exporting social "negative energies" to other countries. Japan's modern development before WWII was associated with colonizing. Its development after WWII was under control and protection of the world superpower. The so-called four little tigers had experienced fast proliferation with social and political stabilities under protection of the superpower and threats of communist enemies.

China experienced its modern economic expansion, neither colonizing others nor being protected by external powers. The centralized authority kept its social and political stabilities without political freedom and democracy. Chinese people were not fairly and equally treated, especially, through the *hukou* system. But in comparison with early stages of capitalism in currently developed economies, peasants, and workers in China's earlier stage of the reform were perhaps better protected by the socialist government. This is culturally understandable as well. The Chinese tolerated any government unfairness if the emperor could maintain the Great Wall secured. The emperor within the Great Wall domestically brutely treated his people and globally smiled and provided gifts. It is easy to identify this approach in the New China. Minorities within China got "nicer" treatments than Han Chinese, in the West it is often the opposite. Monkey society has different institutions, values, and social relations from wolf society or lion society. Each kind of mammal society is "domestically" interlinked with different principles and mechanisms. Globalization implies convergence of social and economic structures among human societies which were geographically separated in human history.

Economic development is a consequence of complicated interdependence between population change, wealth accumulation, productivity improvement, market structures, economic structure, preference change, changes of incentive mechanisms with economic reforms, miscellaneous policies over time and space, not to mention international relations. Each culture has its own path of modern development, following its traditional rules and values, utilizing resources (including knowledge, institutions, values, and the like) available, and taking advantages of opportunities. Development is path-dependent and is constantly confronted with bifurcations into lower or higher branches of development. Deng Xiaoping's basic idea on speed of economic reform was that China should slowly but steadily conduct economic reform under the conditions that political and social stabilities were guaranteed.

In 1978, China's bureaucracy was poorly educated. Uneducated and poverty-stricken members appeared to be loyal to the party and were obedient. Any deviation from the party line defined by a few in the top was "effectively" forbidden. Officials' career achievement and promotion had little to do with economic expertise and professional knowledge. Since he rose to the power, Deng embarked on building bureaucracy on education and merits. China recruited officials through examination and made merit-based promotion at all levels of the bureaucracy. As early as first-generation university students were graduated from universities in 1982, the state immediately recruited them to replace the uneducated generations in the system in association with introducing a mandatory retirement system for officials. It did not take many years for China to build a state sustained by meritocracy. After Deng retired, top party leaders were mostly college-educated. As official promotion in all the levels of the government was closely related to GDP growth performance, officials made efforts in promoting economic development and poverty reduction. They were eager to get project funds and develop the projects for economic development. These projects brought about economic benefits to their jurisdictions as well as to their own advantages for future promotion and material awards.

The economic reform was decided in the Third Plenum of the Eleventh Central Committee in December 1978. The consequence of the reform demonstrates to the world with its scale, scope, and speed of economic expansion unprecedented in human history. The foundation for this fast progress is Mao's dictatorship, widely spread poverty, low education of the population, obedient or/and depressed masses, discarded Confucianism, and international isolation. All these features which might appear to hinder China's economic progress played a positive role in China's economic dynamics. The Third Plenum officially closed the campaign to discredit the ousted leadership and officially ended the era of class struggles. Under Deng's leadership, China changed almost every institution from farms to factories, rural markets to urban stores, schools to universities, and military units to committees in personal structure and operation. All sectors, except the political one which would be filled with obedient and smart interpreters of the master, have been opened to market mechanisms.

The leadership has claimed to build a socialist market economy. The hybrid system has been designed to create benefits of a competitive free market environment in a setting in which the government retains a significant residual degree of planning authority. On the other hand, the government has not provided a clear and practical vision of the future economic structure. As the entire economy has been targeted at enhancing economic productivities and incomes with market mechanism, heterogeneous sectors, many industries, and heterogeneous households in many regions have witnessed multifarious changes from 1978. The government has changed the ways in which goods are allocated, people employed, wages and prices determined, policies adopted, leaders and officials selected, students educated, soldiers trained, and foreign trade conducted. The government has used profit incentives and bonuses rather than ideological slogans to encourage people to work hard and more effectively.

People's communes in Mao's period were replaced by a responsibility system soon after the onset of the economic reform. Peasants were given greater decision-making power over agricultural production and distribution. Factory managers were granted the flexibility to negotiate with both domestic and foreign counterparts over matters previously decided by the state planners. The social mobility was enhanced in many ways. For instance, rural reform released surplus labor over 200 million by the late 1990s. The people provided labor supply for rural industries and urban development. Foreign investments employed 17.5 million people. They were paid relatively higher and worked in better conditions. People could freely swap jobs. Many people studied and worked in foreign countries.

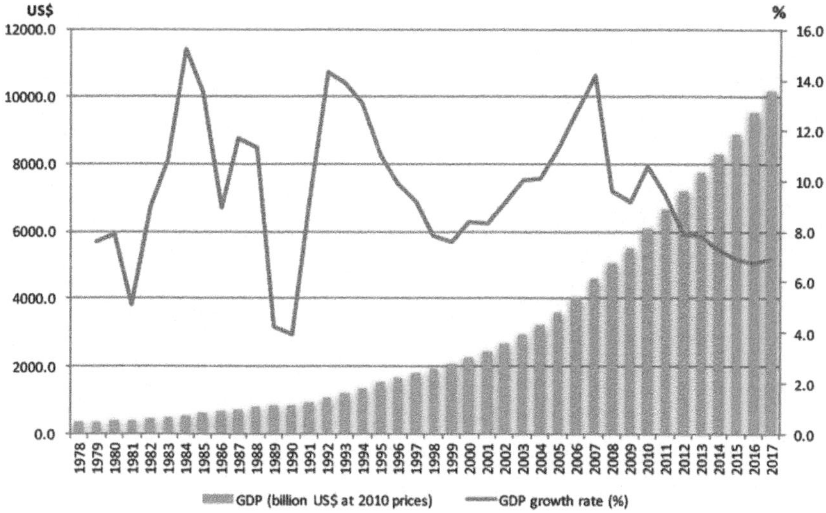

Fig. 5.2 China's GDP and growth rate, 1978–2017 (*Source* Fang et al. [2018])

As demonstrated in Fig. 5.2, these reforms led to fast proliferation of the economy.

China's GDP has experienced dramatic expansion. The onset condition of the economic reform was an average GDP per capita 180 US$ (based on the official exchange rate). It now reaches over 10,000 US$. Figure 5.2 shows the changes and the change rates over the period 1978 to 2017. The World Bank reported that the poverty rate in China fell from 88.3% in 1981 to 1.85% in 2013 with 1.90 US$ per day poverty line (Wan et al. 2018). Figure 5.3 shows that China's GDP per capita increased over years.

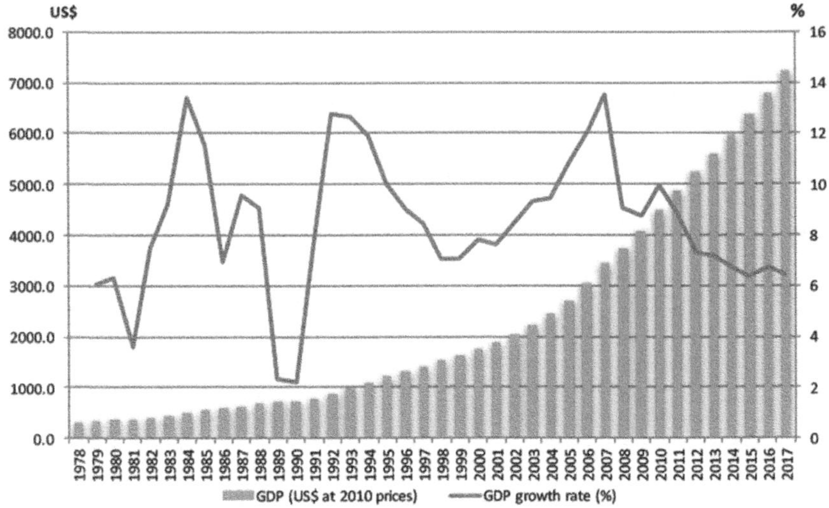

Fig. 5.3 China's GDP per capita and growth rate, 1978–2017 (*Source* Fang et al. [2018])

Market Mechanism Was Spread from Countryside

> There is nothing more difficult to take in hand, more perilous to conduct, or more uncertain in its success, than to take the lead in the introduction of a new order of things.
>
> Niccolo Machiavelli (1469–1527)

The party got monopolistic power over China by motivating Chinese peasants to attack urban areas from countryside. The so-called Mao's strategy in the domestic war against Jiang's army hints on why Deng launched economic reform from countryside rather than in urban areas. As Napoleon judged himself, "I am sometimes a fox and sometimes a lion. The whole secret of government lies in knowing when to be the one or the other." Deng knew that industrial sector and modern urban life were complicated for people who experienced only traditional agricultural economies. Introduction of changes from urban areas might easily cause the national system into disorder. On the other hand, peasants could be easily manipulated by short-run promises. Deng was familiar with

Mao's strategy of motivating peasants to conquer cities. Politically experienced Deng launched the economic reform from countryside in 1978, keeping large cities such as Beijing and Shanghai almost no changed. This strategy partly explains the occurrence of the Tiananmen Square Incident in 1989. The Beijing and Shanghai "citizens" had "superiority" over people in other cities and peasants. Chinese immobility had been solidified by the *hukou* system. Chinese people, from cities, countryside or returned students, have little concerns about democracy, demonstrated after 1989. The fast economic advancement of countryside made urban people very upset as peasants got their awards from their diligence while urban residents were lowly paid with fixed wage rates. Urban adult people, except young students, who have always genuine passions for something, violated in streets in the name of democracy and freedom. Deng settled the urban people's heart simply by allowing them to freely earn money without disturbing the political system after his successes in countryside. As entire countries' energies were turned to profit-hunting, democracy and freedom largely neglected, at least until today. Now urban people have little concerns about corruption even though corruption has been far more widely spread than in the early 1990s.

The agricultural sector is composed of farming, forestry, animal husbandry, and fisheries. Each component has its own segments and its segment has its own complicated units and processes of production over time and space. In national aggregated level, the annual real growth rate in the gross value of agricultural output is 6.1% during the period of 1978–2015 (Gong 2018). There were several waves of institutional reforms and market deregulations in the supply side. These changes helped the sector to enhance productivity and reshape agricultural processes of production. In association with national economic prosperity, national demand for miscellaneous goods and services are further diversified. There are accordingly structural changes within the agricultural sector. With regards to the development of the agricultural sector since the 1978 economic reform, China's reform period is divided into six periods as in Gong. (1) The period of 1978–84 is the transition from the collective system to a household-based farming system. The government carried out decollectivization and decentralization by implementing the household responsibility system (HRS). It was established to endow farmers with the right to control their own production after meeting government procurement quotas. By the end 1983, 98% of the production teams joined HRS. The reform brought fast proliferation in the agricultural sector. The period is generally considered as great achievements in the reform. (2) The period of 1985–89 introduced a two-tier system, liberalizing agricultural pricing and marketing systems with more products, except some strategic products like grain and cotton, traded in market. Some inputs were also exchanged through market mechanism. Problems of misallocation of resources were partly solved. Nevertheless, the associated rises in input costs and unpredictable changes in policies caused output growth to fall. The reform efficiency on growth was so not high as in the previous period. In contrast to the productivity enhancement rate of 8.1% in the previous period, the rate was 2.4% in the period. It was argued that the decollectivization of farms in the previous period provided a one-time productivity gain, which made it difficult to maintain a high rate in the period. Another reason was that the government did not carry much market liberalization after 1984. (3) During the period of 1990–93, the government further reformed the sector. More market mechanisms were introduced and governmental inference in marketing was reduced. By the end of 1993, over 90% of all agricultural products were traded at market-determined prices. The reform was not fully carried out yet as there were segmentations between regional markets and the isolation of domestic markets. Resources of labor, land and capital were quickly moved away from agriculture to the rest of the economy. (4) The period of 1994–97 experienced national tax system reform. The government raised procurement prices for grain to secure and increase agricultural production. The government also extended land contracts. The farmers were encouraged to invest more in land by raising the awareness of their use rights. The self-sufficient policies were implemented in regional levels, asking some regions to produce enough food for themselves. (5) The period of 1998–2003 experienced the integration of rural development with the overall economic reforms. The government wanted to reduce the financial burden of the grain support program. China entered WTO in 2001. This forced China to reduce protection policies. The quota procurement system was abolished in 2001. China had to focus more on quality in the agricultural sector to face competition in global markets. By 2004 the free grain market was allowed in most regions in China had. (6) From 2004 to the present, the national focus was on the issues of agriculture, farmers, and the countryside. In 2004, China changed from trade surplus in agricultural commodities to deficit. The food security became a national issue. A national land policy was adopted to preserve at least 126 million hectares of arable land. This resulted in supply of agricultural products from low productive and less competitive farmers. This explains partly why the average productivity was not much improved. The government made efforts to raise agricultural production capacities and farmers' income. In 2006 agricultural taxes were abolished. The rural reforms were more complicated in recent years. Although more land and fertilizer inputs were increased in the period, the productivity did not experience much enhancement.

Investment in Physical Infrastructures

> For years, American officials visiting China marvelled at how Chinese leaders could push through infrastructure projects and sweeping legislative changes without the complications of opposition and the niceties of voting.
>
> Evan Osnos (1976–)

The Great Wall demonstrates how China could have mobilized national human and financial resources to build national projects since the very day that China had the first emperor. Over centuries Chinese people could tolerate any cruelty, forced labor, and heavy tax to build and maintain the Great Wall of many thousand miles. The Great Wall divided the nomadic and agricultural societies. As far as the number of people mobilized over such long time periods is concerned, no contemporary national project can be called grand when one thinks of the Great Wall. From the onset of the economic reform, China has succeeded in completing numerous national projects.

Infrastructures, such as roads, railways, airports, telecommunication servers, and cables, directly or indirectly affect productivities and welfare. Indirect effects of infrastructures on national economy are through agglomeration and scale and scope economies. Modern economies, which are characterized by close connectivity, rapid information, low-cost and rapid access to markets, cannot effectively function without sophisticated infrastructures for networking economies. Scale and scope economies are explored with support of infrastructure. Infrastructure and innovation are closely interrelated. Wang et al. (1918) examine how the road density affects firm innovation, using China's data for the early 2000s. A rise of 10% improvement in road density brought about the average number of approved patents per firm by 0.71%. The better is the road system, the stronger are the effects on innovation due to enlarged market sizes and sped-up knowledge spillover. Infrastructure projects can be financed by agents, such as private investors, governments at many levels, public-private partnership, and so on (Wan and Zhang 2018). National productivity's enhanced by scope and scale economies. IT industry cannot quickly develop without supports of physical infrastructures. Scale and scope economies exhibit their powers through trade within cities, between regions, and between nations. Trade takes place over infrastructures. A modern economy can hardly become effective and advanced if without proper nationwide well-developed infrastructures. Even an only resource-dependent economy needs reliable infrastructures to export resources. All developed economies have well-developed infrastructures. In recent years, in comparison with China US economy is behind in development of railway and highway infrastructures. India is an example which has a lot talent but not a well-developed infrastructure system. As the Indian national economy is not well physically effectively connected, the Indian economy has difficulties to catch up China in terms of GDP and per capita income.

Socialist market economy implies a hybrid of centralized planning and market mechanism. As China has adopted a strategy of steadily introducing market mechanisms into China's economy, the planned share in national economy remains large. China has a lot of potentials to explore scale economies due to infrastructures by state planning. Mao left China to be covered with modern transport networks over land, water, and sky. The rapid expansion of economy also provides the centralized government to have effective power and resources to build national networks in air, over sea, and cross land. All these infrastructure developments enable private sectors to effectively explore scale and scope economies. The infrastructure development provides a solid physical foundation is partly explains why China could have maintained its economic development, at least so far. The combination of scale economy and state planning is reflected in the development of high-speed rail (HSR) in China. The population size implies possible enhancement of productivity due to scale economies and the government's power provides huge human capital and materials resources needed for building a nationwide network without local barriers for the whole system. It is an example about the government's role in enhancing national living standard and aggregated efficiency of the society. Economic theories by popular or well-known economists in the West have little insight into modern economies as their analytical results are mostly suitable farming-like money-based worlds.

The High-speed Rail (HSR) in China is a network of passenger-dedicated railways designed for speeds of 250–350 km/h. Even by 1993, commercial train service in China was average 48 km/h. In 1978, Deng Xiaoping visited Japan. He was deeply impressed by the then world's first high speed rail, Shinkansen. He had a dream for building China's high-speed rail. State planning for China's current HSR network was introduced in the early 1990s. In 1990, the Ministry of Railway proposed to build a high-speed railway between Beijing and Shanghai. In 1995, the government announced that preparatory work on the line would begin in the 9th Five Year Plan (1996–2000). But the construction was completed in the first decade of the next century. By the beginning of 2011, China had the world's longest HSR network with 8358 km of routes capable for at least 200 km/h in service including 2197 km of 350 km/h. The government spent US$108 billion in railway construction in 2010. The trend has been continued till today.

The HRS network is now the longest HSR network in the world. The network is the most extensively used on the earth. China's HRS accounts for two-thirds of the world's total-speed railway networks. In 2019, China already tested a magnetic levitation prototype train with speed of 600 km/h. The network run 35,000 km in total length. It is planned to reach 38,000 km by 2025. Almost all HSR trains, track and service are owned and operated by the China Railway Corporation under the brand China Railway High-Speed. The network has been developed rapidly in the last 15 years with substantial funding from the central government. The early technologies were imported mainly from Germany and Japan. Chinese engineers have recently built indigenous trains manufactured by the state-owned companies. The network has greatly reduced travel time and has played a significant role in transforming Chinese society and economy. Its attractiveness due to comfort, convenience, safety, and punctuality explains why it is used by a broad range of travelers of heterogeneous income levels. The highly capital-intensive HSR construction projects are mainly government-financed. About 40–50% is financed by state-owned banks and financial institutions, another 40% by the bonds issued by the Ministry of Railway, and the remaining 10–20% by provincial and local governments. The Ministry of Railway issued US$150 billion (in 2010 dollars) to finance HRS construction from 2006 to 2010, for instance.

As in many fields of Chinese economy where officials and huge money are involved there exist corruption in scale and scope unbelievable in a modern human society. Market economy with Chinese character and the size of Chinese population has resulted in corruption unparalleled in history. In February 2011, Railway Minister Liu Zhijun, a key proponent of HSR expansion, was removed from office due to corruption. It was estimated that he accepted US$152 million in bribe in connection with railway construction projects. Another top official in the Railway Ministry, Zhang Shuguang, lost office for misappropriating to his personal overseas accounts the equivalent of US$2.8 billion. Behind each socially glory project in China, there may be dirtiest stories.

Another example about development of national infrastructures is highway development. Before the economic reform, freight and passenger transport activities were mainly carried out by rail transport. In 1978, rail transport accounted for 54.4% of the total freight movement, while road transport only for 2.8%. Since the early 1980s, China has constructed an integrated system of national and provincial-level expressways. The expressway network was initiated with the construction of Shenyang-Dalian Expressway on 7 June 1984, opened by 1988. By then, there was no expressway in China. The first modern at-grade China National Highways is the Shanghai-Jiading Expressway opened in 1988. By the end of 2019, China built 14,900 km' expressway network, the largest expressway system by length in the world. It overpassed the American Interstate Highway System in 2011. The major expressways parallel routes of the older China National Highways. By 1997, road transport accounted for 13.8% of freight movement while rail transport for 34.3%. By 1997, road's share of passenger transport was 53.3%. While the railway's share was 35.4%. The structural change was due to the development of the expressway network. In 2013, the Ministry of Transport announced the National Highway Network Planning, covering both the national highway system and the national expressway system to 2030. The national road network will reach 400,000 km, including 265,000 km of common national highways and 118,000 km of expressways. The total costs of the national expressway network are estimated some 300 billion US dollars as rate in 2016. It should be noted that the data on expressways are from "Expressways of China" in the Wiki. The construction fund comes from vehicle purchase tax, fees and taxes collected by local governments, state bonds, and domestic and foreign investments.

China also embarked on a grand plan to interact with many parts of the world. When visiting Nazarbayer University, President Xi mentioned the vision of the Silk Road Economic Belt on September 7, 2007. He announced the vision of New Maritime Silk Road when visiting Indonesia one October 3, 2013. These two visions consist of the One Belt One Road initiative. It is a grand plan for China's economic integration with many parts of the world. The project was aimed at connecting China, Central Asia, Russia, Central and Eastern Europe, and Western Europe, linking China with the Persian Gulf and Mediterranean Sea through Central Sia and Western Asia, and joining China with Southeast Asia, South Asia and the Indian Ocean. The maritime road covers a vast sea area, linking China's coast with East Africa and Europe via South China Sea and Indian Ocean, and connecting South Pacific via South China Sea. Since the project was initiated, China's overseas direct investment was increased dramatically in the belt-road countries, especially along the continental route. It connects 60 emerging market economies and relates total population of 4 billion. The project has constructed infrastructure, such as ports, roads, airways, and railways. China's state-controlled acquirers were main investors in infrastructure sectors, while the non-state-controlled acquirers were actively involved in non-infrastructure sectors (Du and Zhang 2018). Through connecting the Eurasian continent and its African neighborhood, the government aimed to explore development potentials (Andornino 2017).

Improved Living Conditions and Consumption

They must often change, who wound be constant in happiness or wisdom.
Confucius (551–478 BC)

Consumption is a basic determinant of economic growth. National economic proliferation is driven by investment, exports, government spending, production as well as consumption. When China's economy is becoming more capital-intensive and covered with infrastructures, returns from domestic investments in physical capital and infrastructures tend to fall. China's economy has been strongly driven by exports. Nevertheless, the relative importance of export-oriented economy is weakening as other developing economies are also rapidly increasing their productivities, protectionism is becoming stronger, wage and other costs are domestically increasing, and trade restrictions among countries are increasing. China is now much less export-oriented than it was some years ago. China's share of exports to its GDP was 20% in 2018, while South Korea was 44% in the same year. In 2018, domestic consumption was 76% of its GDP, while in 2013 the number was only 50%. To stimulate economic growth, the government is moving towards stimulating consumption. China is more emphasizing personal consumption of goods and services. Chinese markets have been changed not only quantitively and qualitatively, but also swiftly in variety of goods and services. Before the economic reform, the state controlled nearly all aspects of what people produced and consumed. From everyday necessities to any cultural products, the state decided everything. Today luxury malls and hypermarkets filled with a multitude of products are everywhere in large cities. Like any society which experiences rapid economic expansion, China has been characterized a dynamic interdependence between consumption of necessities, consumption of housing, luxury goods, and tourism, happiness, pleasure, social status, and lifestyles. Figures 5.4 and 5.5 (Wang 2020) plot, respectively, annual growth rate of GDP and change of consumer spending proportion, and annual total retail sales and annual variation. Technological changes also encourage consumption. China has advanced systems of mobile payments and instant credit verification.

The average household income in China has experienced rapid growth. In association with changes in incomes, consumption and saving behavior also vary over time. The Chinese economy has become more market oriented. Nevertheless, expansion of market economy also implies more uncertainty about futures. For more people, there is no more secured job,

Fig. 5.4 Annual growth rate and change of consumer spending proportion

Fig. 5.5 Annual total retail sales and annual variation

certain future income, and guaranteed medical care. In association with improved living conditions and medical care, how long one might live become most uncertain in contemporary China.

China's national economic conditions and wealth distribution in earlier years of economic reform is characterized by ubiquitous poverty. Mao provided the situation under which whatever Deng would do, so far as he enabled some people to enhance national productivity, national economic conditions would be improved without making some, at least large group of, people worse off. China's reform in the 1980s and 1990s is often called Pareto-improving (Lau 2008). The concept is due to an Italian economist and political scientist Vilfredo Pareto (1984–1923). A Pareto improvement is an action that leads to an economic benefit without making someone worse off. With regards to China's political economy, if the economic reform enriches at least one individual without harming anyone else. The initial conditions in the late 1970s and 1980s China imply that China could easily find some economic Pareto improvements. China had reached economic conditions long time ago that Pareto improvements can hardly be made. Societies are full of potential conflicts rather than possibilities of Pareto improvement.

Spatial Unequal Development with Enlarging Income Gaps

This City is what it is because our citizens are what they are.

Plato (423–347 BC)

As a socialist market economy, every aspect of Chinese economy is strongly characterized by both state planning and market mechanism. This is also reflected in regional infrastructures and regional income gaps. In service- information-, and knowledge-based economies, spatial agglomeration brings about enhancement of productivity in multitudinous ways. It is associated with negative impact as well. Congestions, high rents, and pollutions in large cities are evident. In association with rapid national economic advancement, inequalities in all dimensions of the economy tend to be enlarged. To reduce regional gaps in economic development, the government has distributed more resources to less developed regions from 2003. The efforts have little impact on convergence between regional welfare, wealth, and income partly because interregional mobility of people is strongly limited by the *hukou* system. Limited national resources have been invested in a less competitive region. Nevertheless, this not efficient-based investment might improve less developed regions but cause spatial misallocation of resources.

The southeastern coastal areas have easy sea roads to global seaports. Low cost of shipping plus diligent and lowly paid workers explains why the region had experienced rapid expansion of export-oriented manufacturing. Workers in most other regions did not benefit directly much from the open policy as they were not allowed to freely work and live in the southeastern coastal areas. Initial gaps in income and economic scale and scope effects associated with spatial agglomeration have led to huge interregional gaps in income and wealth of households. The government has made attempts to have a balanced development by adopting strategies, such as the West Development Strategy, Northeast Area Revitalization Plan, and Rising of Central China Plan, to reduce regionals gaps. The government allowed beneficial allocation of construction land-use quotas, made direct fiscal transfers, supported construction of industrial parts and development zones, and made investment in infrastructures. Another measure of the central government is to use stricter standards to get urban *hukou* for slowing down formation and expansion of mega cities. Low labor mobility impedes human capital applications of individuals and thus reduces aggregated regional and national productivities.

Regional development can be divided into two stages (Liu et al. 2018). In the period of 1978–2003, the government focused on efficiency of resources utilization and introduction of market economy, paying not so much attention to possible rapid unbalanced development between regions. Certain groups and certain regions were encouraged by the government to develop first and fast with the assumption that poor people and underdeveloped regions could catch up. As almost all Chinese officials and people had never experienced agglomeration in a free and industrialized economy, people had little ideas about long-term implications of inequal regional policies. The nation conceived that the everyone could enjoy common prosperity in the long term. The coastal areas were opened to international capital and technology. Four special economic zones were established as early as in1979. In 1984, the government opened 14 coastal cities to foreign investment. Hainan was opened in 1988. These open areas enjoyed preferential policies and obtained opportunities to implement new styles of management. In 1985 the government abandoned the control of all agricultural products except grain and cotton and allowed them to be circulated and traded freely in the market. After 1985 urban and rural gaps were reduced some years before they increased again. From the 1990s to 2003, economic activities continued to be concentrated in coastal cities. There was also a great number of population inflows into these areas. As the *hukou* system was not much changed, interregional immigrants faced discrimination in employment and had difficulties in accessing public services and social security. Regions were varied in adopting methods for fostering industrial development and technological innovation. Officials modified national technology policy to fit local conditions. Local officials were competing for national resources in building up information industries a pillar industry of the regional economy. For instance, in the 1990s Beijing concentrated on developing small, hybrid enterprises, and Shanghai on large business groups. All these strategies were closely related to local conditions under the same national policy. Local governments had a high degree of freedom to influence ownership structures. In the early 1980s, local governments had power to recognize *minying* enterprises and create procedures for registering and regulating enterprises. Late, regional officials could helped collective enterprises to register as private or nongovernmental enterprises or private ones to register as collective. Local officials also dealt with formation of limited stock companies, the insurance of technology shares, and the listing of companies on domestic and foreign stock markets. All these influences or direct involvements by local governments affected patterns of industrial development, structures of the industry, incentives, cost sharing, and redistribution of profits.

In the period of 2003–2018, the economy was still increasingly concentrated in the coastal areas. The society began to be critical about enlarged inequalities not only between regions, but also other issues about income and wealth distribution. Some people wondered about how people of one region can have better lives than those of other regions under the same socialist system. The government has insisted on continuing the *hukou* system, especially in large cities, intact. One choice for the government to reduce regional disparity is through allocating resources, rather than free mobility, to inland China. At the same time, the *hukou* system is further changed to limit agglomeration in the mega cities. Spatial misallocation of production factors lowers the total national productivity. Administrative intervention in resource allocation is supposed to maintain a balanced development.

The Fiscal and Tax Reform

China has changed its fiscal and taxing systems over years. Gao (2018: 106) summarizes the 40 years fiscal and tax reform as follows: "China's fiscal and tax reform so far has followed a consistent path, which in essence is laying the groundwork for market reform by transformation into a 'public' fiscal and tax system and building the according mechanisms, and then laying the cornerstone for the modernization of state governance by building a modern public finance system." Gao (2018) provides a basic survey on China's fiscal and tax reform from 1978 to 2018. The fiscal and tax reform is divided from 1978 to 2018 into five phases. The first period (1978–1994) paved the way for overall reforms. The period is characterized by decentralizing power and transferring benefits to the relevant players for increasing productivities. Financial management power, fiscal revenue collection and distribution are decentralized. Local governments had more power in fiscal matters. There were many reforms, such as profit reservation, profit-to-tax, self-responsibility for profits and losses, and contracted managerial responsibility system. The government started to build a multi-tax system with multiple taxation procedures and multi-layer tax collection. China also began to build a tax system for foreign entities and income taxes for domestic enterprises and improved tariff system.

The government guaranteed huge resources for development of science and technology and education. All these measures played a significant role in steady implementation of overall reform plans. However, in net the government had less tax revenue and used more fiscal expenditure. The ratio of fiscal income to GDP fell from 31.1% in 1978 to 25.5% in 1980, 22.2% in 1985, 15.7% in 1990, and 22% in 1993. The ratio of central government's fiscal income to overall national fiscal income rose from 15.5 in 1978 to 24.5% in 1980, 38.4% in 1985, and fell to 33.8% in 1990, and 20% in 1993. Fiscal expenditure rose rapidly, from RMB112.2bn in 1978 and RMB464.2 in 1993 with annual growth rate of 21%. The reform was associated a lot of serious and widespread problems, such as illegal tax reduction and embezzlement of fiscal revenue. China's fiscal deficit also increased rapidly, RMB6.9bn in1981, RMB6.9bn in1981, and RMB14.9bn in 1990, and RMB29.3bn (RMB97.9bn with debt insurance income included) in 1993. China also began to take on foreign debt in 1979 and domestic debt through issuing treasure bonds in 1981. During the period, the state introduced bonds for key construction projects, fiscal bonds, inflation-protected bonds, national construction bonds, and the like. By 1993, the central government made its fiscal expenditure 50% from its debt issuance or borrowing.

During the period of 1994–1998, China implemented the policy of institutional innovation. The government soon recognized that the pervious reform of the decentralization and transferring benefits could not be continued. In 1994, China embarked on reforming the fiscal and tax system in a series of measures. The newly reformed turnover tax system was mainly based on value-added tax and supplemented by consumption tax and business tax. It included other measures such as expanding the scope of resource tax levies and levying a land value-added tax. The taxes were also divided into central taxes, local taxes, and taxes shared by the central government and local governments. This laid a foundation for a tax-sharing fiscal management regime. The corporate income tax rate for state-owned enterprises and the profit distribution system of state-owned enterprise were introduced. The government forbid overdrafts or borrowing from the central bank. The fiscal deficit was supposed to be bridged by issuing treasure bonds. The reform was to cut possible links between fiscal deficit and inflation. During the period of 1998–2003, China built an institutional system for public finance. By 1994 China had already made many institutional innovations through the fiscal and tax reforms. The government was still faced with numerous problems with government revenue and expenditure. Different government agents and regions self-made regulations on tax collection and fees. The government needed a system of the management of all government incomes. The government made reforms in effective structure of fiscal expenditure, the departmental budgetary system, the centralized revenue, and expenditure management system. The government recognized that sporadic and partial adjustments would no more be effective in the national management. In 1998, the government decided to establish China's basic public finance framework, which should include all important items, such as revenue, expenditure, management, and regulation as a connected whole.

During the period of 2003–2012, the government focused on improving the public finance system. China further improved its public finance system. In October 2003, the taxation system reform was further refined. The goals of the reforms included improving the public finance system, strengthening department budgetary management, clarifying the fiscal expenditure duties of governments at different levels, improving the transfer payment system, increasing fiscal support for central and middle and minority concentrated areas, separating management of government procurement from that of revenue and expenditure, and so on. Moreover, public finance was gradually available in rural areas. Fiscal expenditure was increasingly spent on education, health, social security, and housing. From 2010, the government has been focusing on building a modern public finance system. The government tried to connect the goals of fiscal and tax reform with modernization of state governance. The reform has been made to establish standardized, open, and transparent modern budget system.

Trade and Shifting Status in the Global Division of Labor

> To found a great empire for the sole purpose of raising up a people of customers, may at first sight appear a project fit only for a nation of shopkeepers. It is, however, a project altogether unfit for a nation of shopkeepers; but extremely fit for a nation whose Government is influenced by shopkeepers.
>
> Adam Smith (1776II: 129)

A butterfly effect is determined not only by a single flapping. The structure and current state of the system make the butterfly effect possible. When Deng rose to the power, Mao had already initiated relations with the superpower USA. Deng decided not only to domestically carry out economic reform, but also to more fully open China to the world.

In December 1978, the third Plenum of the 11th Central Committee decided a national policy towards modernization and open policy. So and Chu (2016: 55) give some possible determinants for China's open-door policy: "The fading of the Cold War, the rise of the neoliberal globalization project, and industrial relocation of the NIEs had provided the global precondition for the critical transition." China was at the right time in the right position to enter the America-dominated global market. The fast proliferation period has been fueled by export-oriented industrialization. In the early stage low labor costs were main advantages for China to absorb foreign direct investments. In recent years, risen labor costs and economic conditions have made foreign firms to leave China. Manufacturing capitals are leaving China. But China's large consumer markets and talented human resources increasingly attract foreign firms.

The reform policy brought about sharp increases in foreign trade, utilization of foreign funds, and direct foreign investment. Total trade (= exports + imports) grew from US$21.0 billion in 1978 to US$113.8 billion in 1990, an average growth rate 15%; exports grew from US$10.0 billion in 1978 to US$61.2 billion, an average growth rate 16%; imports grew from US$11.1 billion in 1978 to US$52.5 billion in 1990, an annual growth rate 14% (Cheng 1993). During the same period, world trade grew at an annual growth rate 8.6%. In 1978, the total value of China's imports and exports was less than 1% of world trade. Since 2009, China has been the largest export. In 2013, China became the largest trading nation of goods (Li and Jiang 2019). Figure 5.6 plots the changes of China's share of international trade over the period of 1980–2016.

From the onset of the economic reform, China has been the world factory, from initially producing simple cheap goods to gradually manufacturing more complex goods, without many highly value-added products belonging to China. Ju and Yu (2018) divide the open policy according to trade, foreign investment, and global product sharing. Economic changes and international trade relations are divided into four dimensions: (i) from a world assembly line to a world manufacturing powerhouse; (ii) a world capital receiver to a world investor; (iii) a world factor to a world market; and (iv) from the position of "made in China" to one of "innovated in China". China has been a global manufacturing center. Numerous plants assembled multifarious value-added parts of the products owned by developed economies into final products with very marginal profits. Figure 5.7 reveals that even today the share of qualified export goods in the total export is still low.

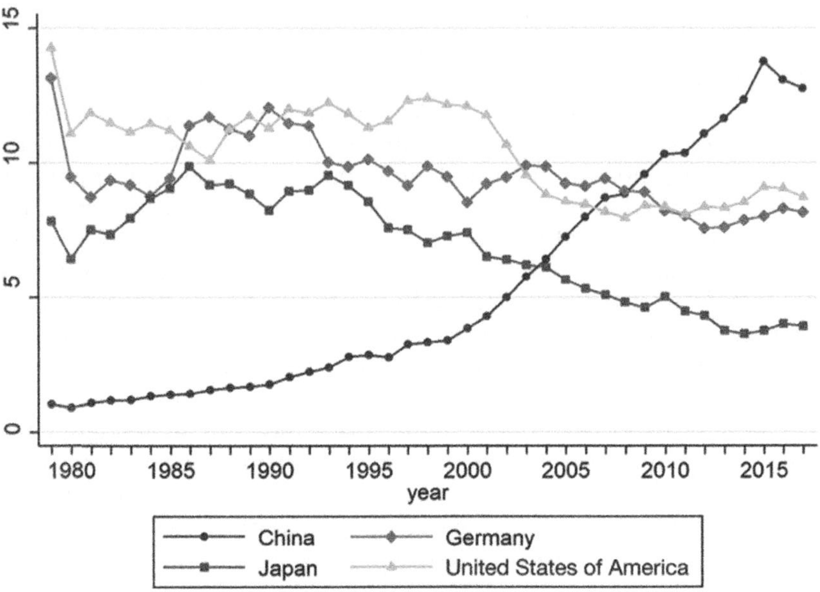

Fig. 5.6 China's share of world trade in terms of percentage (*Source* Li and Jiang [2019])

When analyzing trade in earlier stages of the reform, processing trade has been important for China. The processing trade basically involves business activities in which the firms import all or parts of the raw or ancillary materials, spare parts, and components and re-exports finished products after processing the imported materials. China has promoted processing trade since the 1980s to increase export. A study by Dai et al. (2016) verifies that processing exporters in China had a lower productivity than non-processing exporters and non-exporters. These firms did not have high profit. They paid lower wages, had smaller scales, lower capital intensity, and very little investment in R&D. The firms had relatively low fixed costs of exporting as the foreign buyer shared the exporting cost of distribution and marketing. The government encouraged processing exports by providing favorite conditions such as exemptions or reductions of input tariffs and corporate income tax rates. Nevertheless, these

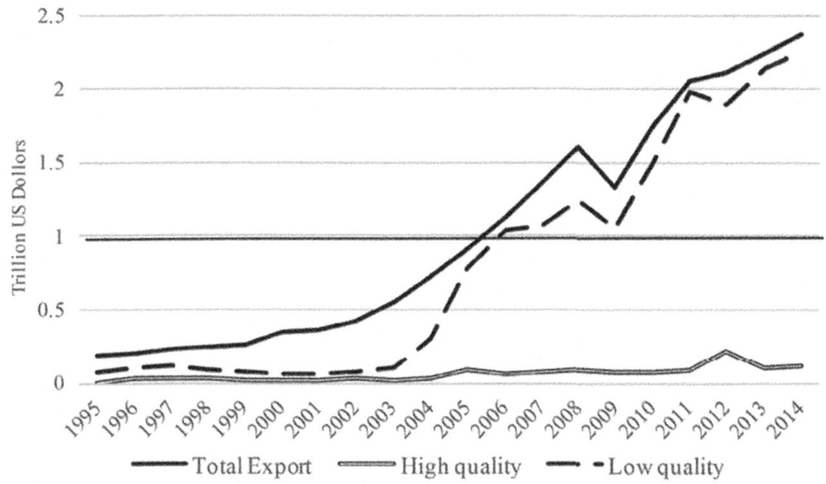

Fig. 5.7 Evolution of relative prices and quality of export products in China (*Source* Li and Jiang [2019])

firms had low share of profits as they were not engaged in high value-added processes. Firms with technologies and qualified labor force had other alternatives for higher profits.

At the onset of the reform in 1978, China had been isolated from the world for so long that its industry had little chance of reaching world levels without inviting in foreign manufacturers. China attracted foreign direct investment as a solution to the lack of funds for investment and the low level of technology. There were large inflows of foreign investment since the early 1980s. The government implemented policies to attract foreign investment. By the end of 2000, 23,870 foreign-funded enterprises were operating in China, while only 21 in 1980. During the periods, the government approved 367,500 foreign investment projects for a total value of US$681 billion. The government treated FDI as an effective means of transferring technology and managerial skills. The government adopted multifarious modes of FDI, including equity joint ventures, cooperative joint ventures, wholly foreign-owned enterprises, and joint development ventures (JDVs). As listed in Table 5.1 (Chadde and Qiu 2003: 109), overseas Chinese provided the major source of FDI in China during the period of 1979–2000. Behind the huge financial

Table 5.1 Sources of China's FDI, in US$ millions (share in percentage)

	1979–1986	*1987–1991*	*1992–2000*
Hong Kong, Macao, Taiwan	4645 (59.0)	10,170 (60.7)	185,623 (57)
U.S.	11,168 (14)	1562 (9.3)	27,333 (8.4)
Japan	1113 (14.1)	2216 (12.7)	24,561 (7.6)
Major European investors	637 (8)	513 (3)	17,884 (5.5)
Major Asian investors	5 (0.06)	351 (2.0)	32,190 (10)
Others	300 (3.8)	2209 (12)	37,506 (11.5)

Note 1 U.K., France, and Germany
Note 2 Singapore, Malaysia, Thailand, South Korea, and the Philippines

capital, they have managerial skills, technical know-how and global business networks. They influenced China's modernization through capital flow, importing ideas about management. Hong Kong was China's largest external investor. Chinese reformers sent many groups to study the experiences of overseas Chinese's economic successes. In earlier years of the reform Deng Xiaoping called on China to learn from Hong Kong and Singapore.

China has followed many market institutions that have been practiced in the overseas Chinese economies. Singapore and Taiwan (at least till the fall of the Jiang family) provided ideas about economic successes under the Chinese authoritarian governments. Oversea Chinese businessmen and firms provided models for mainland, especially southern, Chinese to imitate. The two stock exchanges in Shanghai and Shenzhen were set up after the mainland scrupulously examined the experiences of Hong Kong Stock Exchange. Many rules were directly borrowed from Hong Kong. Many overseas Chinese have directly involved in business management in China. Japan and the four little tigers have much to offer for China in physical capital, know-hows, and so on. In earlier years of the reform, Western societies had little direct impact on China's economic reform as oversea Chinese (still in the low position of global economic networking)

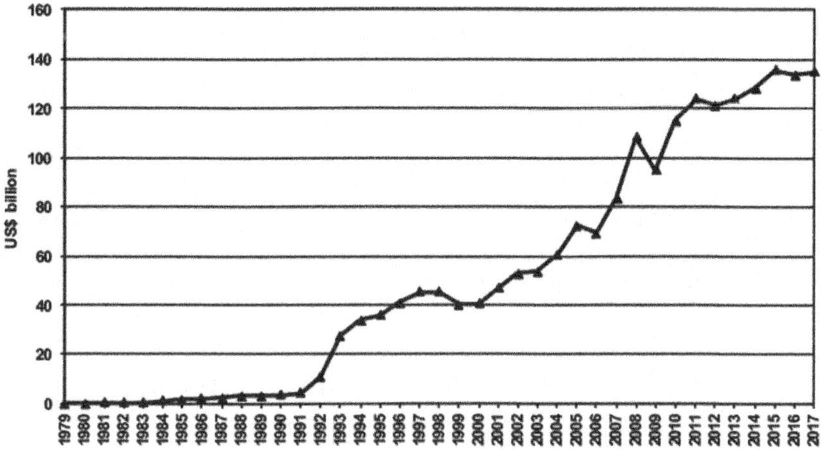

Fig. 5.8 FDI inflows into China, 1979–2017, in Current US$ (*Source* Chen [2019])

were advanced enough for China. As demonstrated in Fig. 5.8, China had increasingly absorbed more FDIs over the four decades.

China has been transited from a mandatory planning to a market-based international trade system (Du and Lu 2018). Stricter regulations and higher labor costs have impact on the international competitiveness of Chinese firms. Labor costs in China have been enhanced greatly in recent years. One of the reasons for the rise is due to the changes in minimum wage rate. From 2001 to 2012, average monthly minimum wage across China rose from 271 yuan to 717. This caused reduction in firms' profitability. It also affected outward FDI. China's FDI outward stock rose from 27.8 billion US dollars in 2000 to 1.01 trillion US dollars in 2015. By 2015 China has already become the third largest FDI outward country after the USA and Japan, according for 8.6% of the world's total FDI flows (Fana et al. 2018).

China's international trade has become very complicated in recent years. Its scope and scale have been spanned dramatically. A common computer sold in Japan is manufactured in Taiwan with involvement of global value chains spanning many countries with various stages of the production in heterogeneous cultural and political environment over times. An iPhone is finally assembled in Shenzhen, China, with its numerous components produced in Japan, USA, Germany, and other cities in China. There are complicated interactions between trade, productivity, and comparative advantages among countries. China's culture on education has enabled the national economy to make quick upgrading in almost all fields largely dependent on brain and diligence. Even in sports, Chinese, like Japanese and Koreas, are strong in the fields, such as figure skating, diving, table tennis, which require mental controlling and physical strength. China has "naturally" becoming stronger in the digital economy due to the Chinese socioeconomic structure and Chinese average IQ.

China as Low Value-Added Assembly Factory and Global Garbage Cane

> Some labor with their minds, and some labor with their strength. Those who labor with their minds govern others; those who labor with their strength are governed by others.... This is a principle universally recognized.
>
> Mencius (372–289 BC)

The New China before the 1990s could exist only in dreams or fake stories of young Chinese. Only 30 years ago, a common Beijing young worker needed to work 2 weeks to have a regular lunch in MacDonald's, when it was opened in Beijing in 1992. Pizza Hut and MaDonald's were opened in China in September and October 1990, respectively. For most of Chinese people in the early 1990s, McDonald's, if they knew the name at all, implied unaffordability and luxury consumption. The first-time consumption in the McDonald's by 1992 is still a lifetime memorable experience for many now old people. It was an emotional experience for many people. It meant being modern, successful, accessible to modern societies, and capable of consuming luxury goods. The first McDonald was opened in Shenzhen, not in the China's capital city, as the restaurant could get supplies from Hong Kong from 1990 to 1992. The first McDonald's in Beijing, the largest in the world then, was opened on April 23, 1992. The opening day was a global event. It was reported in many countries' important newspapers. The restaurant had 700 seats, 29 cash registers, and served over 40,000 on its opening day with its near

1000 employees fully occupied in the day. By 2019, there were over 2500 McDonald's in China. McDonald's has become only one of convenient, timesaving, and consumer-friendly, perhaps considered unhealthy by some Chinese, restaurant chains in China's metropolitans.

As Adam Smith argues, national wealth can be accumulated either by working hard with division of labor under law and/or by invading others and extending markets. Some of modern societies have become developed via both ways. In the early 1980s, the world was in peace in large, even though there were regional conflicts and wars. Colonization by the West was basically a history partly due to economic reasons. As China had neglected higher education for a long period of time, mainland Chinese "ought" to be economically governed by others in traditional Chinese way of thinking. One country's relative position in the global village is measured in terms of prices of traded goods and labor wages in global markets.

World economy has increasingly become a complicated networking system. An effective globalized economy may lose, at least temporary, its efficiency if any national economy already in the chain becomes socially unstable, politically uncertain, and legally unreliable. Countries are cautious in choosing with which countries they do business. Developed economies selected China as the main trade partner among all the poor populations in the world. The reason among all the reasons is due to the Chinese character of socialist market. China has been controlled by a well-organized and highly educated orderly government with a single party. Chinese people are obedient and disciplined with low wages. The orderly government guarantees profits of foreign investments and reliable supplies of goods. Ideological differences between the West and China have little impact on mutual trade over years as economic benefits were obviously there and national interests and businessmen followed profits. Moreover, ideological conflicts between the West and China are like blind date as the Chinese educated since Deng's reform has no real understanding and genuine concerns with any Western ideology. When China peered out through the strict control of the state for the first time, the regions, such as Japan and Korea, in the world which had stable social environments, reliable governments and (at least possibly) skilled labor forces had already become expensive. China had not only comparative advantage in lowly paid labor force, but also in reliable social environment guaranteed by the party. When foreign investments came to China, investment environment and associated profits were relatively harmonious and predictable. Even costs of corruption could be approximately assessable, especially for investments from large international companies, as charges were "rationalized" by officials. If bribes were demanded too high, officials might fail to attract investments and would have no political merit in severely competitive official markets. Moreover, corruption occurred mainly at certain stage(s) of transactions because the party is a well-defined hierarchical organization. Irrespective of China's human rights records and other issues, developed economies have continued to make huge investments in China over years. Money flows towards profits, especially predictable profits. The government had provided the predictable environment to do business for Western and oversea Chinese capitalists.

China, left by Chairman Mao, was not only a low-cost assembly plant for developed economies. It was the garbage can of these economies. Due to the existence of unlimited lowly paid labor force in China, the USA used China as a lowly paid servant through free trade. Under the single party system with premature capitalism, China was economically reasonable and socially orderly to conduct the global waste trade, importing waste from advanced capitalist economies where labor costs were high. People of developed democratic economies would not deal with their own garbage, while people of underdeveloped democratic economies had no opportunity to deal with garbage of the rich ones, due to the economic principle of division of labor as well as the human rights for strikes. Global waste, including toxic or hazardous wastes, was sent to China for further treatment, disposable, or recycling. China was once the largest importer of waste plastic, the United States, Japan, Germany, and the United Kingdom. It is estimated that Britain alone had exported garbage to fill up 10,000 Olympic-size swimming pools. Since 1992 to 2017, 106 million tons of plastic waste was imported into China. It accounted for half of the world's plastic waste imports. Only in 2016 the United States sent 16 million tons of waste to China. Disposable of waste caused environmental damages and health deterioration of workers. By 2017 China had handled nearly half of the world's recyclable waste for 25 years and had been the top importer of waste in the world.

The trade of waste brought job opportunities and many resources by recycling. During the 30 years of hard work, many poor men and women who had engaged in cleaning American garbage succeeded in bringing up and providing higher education to their children. Many of these children got degrees from American universities and would not follow their parents' career. Although China still had many lowly paid workers, it does not benefit the nation to continue the past practicing. China announced on August 2017 that it would stop the import of 24 kinds of solid waste from foreign countries. The policy was implemented on 1 January 2018. A tighter policy was implemented on 1 March 2018. The import of several types of waste, such as plastics, has been banned by China's government. As China had been the largest importer of waste plastics and processed them for some Western countries, the ban strongly affected spatial location of recycling industries. The ban symbolized a turning point in China's role in international division of labor and production. Trade wars between the USA and China has been intensified after the ban. It is also a turning point of China's economy—whether stay or even fall below a middle-income trap or continue to catch up the developed economies in terms of per capita income.

The USA as a Steppingstone of the East Asian Economic Miracles

> I have visited the laid-off factory workers and the communities crushed by our horrible and unfair trade deals. These are the forgotten men and women of our country.
> My big focus is China and OPEC and all of these countries that are just absolutely destroying the United States.
>
> Donald Trump (1946–)

Neither Japan nor successful Chinese societies in Asia deeply believe in the American value, even though these societies obediently follow the American mighty and learn effectively from the American business models. For East Asian people, if they are culturally educated both in Western and Confucian cultural values, they evaluate the Western values and behavior in the light of Confucian values as well. It is reasonable that the Western intellectuals forgot Confucian thought as non-religious Confucian thought is rationally competitive with modern rational Western thought. It is economical and trouble-saving for Westernized and West-educated East Asian intellectuals to be silence on ancient Confucianism.

China's economic reform was initiated with many favorable conditions for fast expansion. There is nothing so important for explaining China's sustained growth so far without mentioning three great "fortunes". One is the political and social fortune brought about by the rise of Deng Xiaoping after the Cultural Revolution. Confucianism is a cultural fortune provider. America is an international fortune for China's economic reform. The economic reform has been implemented with continued adaptive political and economic changes according to the domestic and international conditions in Chinese cultural soil. The international conditions, on which China could have hardly exerted significant influences in the earlier period of the reform due to its economic weakness and isolation policy, were adeptly explored under Deng's leadership. An ideology or religion is not only a national tool for organizing the society in order, but also an effective weapon for plundering and destroying others. The Japanese nationalism before the end of WWII, for instance, was introduced and solidified when the country was threatened by foreign invasions and faced with opportunities of plundering others. The nationalism as formed before WWII is almost impossible in contemporary Japan as it would bring harms to the country. Deng's non-ideology approach secured China's beneficial trade with the USA.

Japan, the four little tigers, and mainland China have effectively explored the international advantages basically created, controlled, maintained, and dominated by the Western powers. American and East Asian cultural characters, institutional traditions, resources, and market sizes explain why America has been a steppingstone of the East Asian economic miracles after WWII. Japan's agile growth was through taking advantage of open American markets and the Korea war. Rapid economic progresses of Taiwan and Korea enjoyed American protection and American wars in Vietnam and other areas. As Japan and the four tigers had become increasingly more expensive for American consumers, China was economically opened and gradually welcome by American markets with its stabilized supply of unlimited cheap products.

Keynes describes: "Americans are apt to be unduly interested in discovering what average opinion believes average opinion to be." America is the largest market in the world. America has the highest GDP, very high per capita GDP, heterogenous peoples with huge lowly income people, and high propensity to consume (and low propensity to save). Its high inequality in income and wealth and high propensity to consume implies high demand for cheap consumer goods. This American character is important for East Asian economies. East Asian people are collective, diligent, talented (highest IQ countries), and frugal. East Asian economies have been an effective "servant" of American people. After WWII, they experienced fast expansion period one after another with

America as the steppingstone in the sense that Americans consumed whatever they produced in large amount. Americans had confidence in that no country could technologically, politically, and culturally challenge their greatest country. The poverty-stricken and diligent East Asians could have quickly learned, imitated, and copied Western technologies once they have social order and conditions to secure their fruits of efforts and investment. America has provided not only markets for their goods, except China, but also military protection. These economies have enjoyed peaceful environment with low military expenditures and market-friendly global environment dominated by American existence. In the early 1960s and 1970s, Japan was a low-wage supplier in globalizing supply chains. South Korea, Taiwan, Hong Kong, and Singapore had steadily increased their shares in the core-periphery division of labor due to their labor cost advantages. "Low parts" of manufacturing activities had been shifted from the West to other parts of the world. When China was opened to the world, its poverty and almost non-educated population plus social and political stabilities had increased China's comparative advantage in global markets.

In the 1980s the world had a relatively stable international environment. People in the developed economies had become far more educated and were far more enriched than before the end of WWII. The world had also created a large reservoir of scientific knowledge. As countries had free access to much of the world knowledge reservoir, the world was providing developing economies good opportunities to join global economic games. There were also great opportunities for developing economies to enter markets of developed economies because peaceful relations between the developed economies had resulted in convergence of productivities, which created the need for underdeveloped economies' cheap goods. The American tastes and belief in free market implied that the American economy would swallow up almost any products by cheap mainland Chinese labor force under China's government control. Another important trade component between the two economies is international students (see Fig. 5.9). Chinese studied in the USA for obtaining degrees, learning knowledge, experiencing American life, and enjoying American freedom and liberty, pleasing parent's expectations, or immigration.

China has no national (state) religion like some other civilizations. Confucianism is the dominant value system. The distinguished character is its emphasis on the *yin-yang* dynamics, rationality, and learning. Confucius gives a positive attitude and an effective way of learning: "When

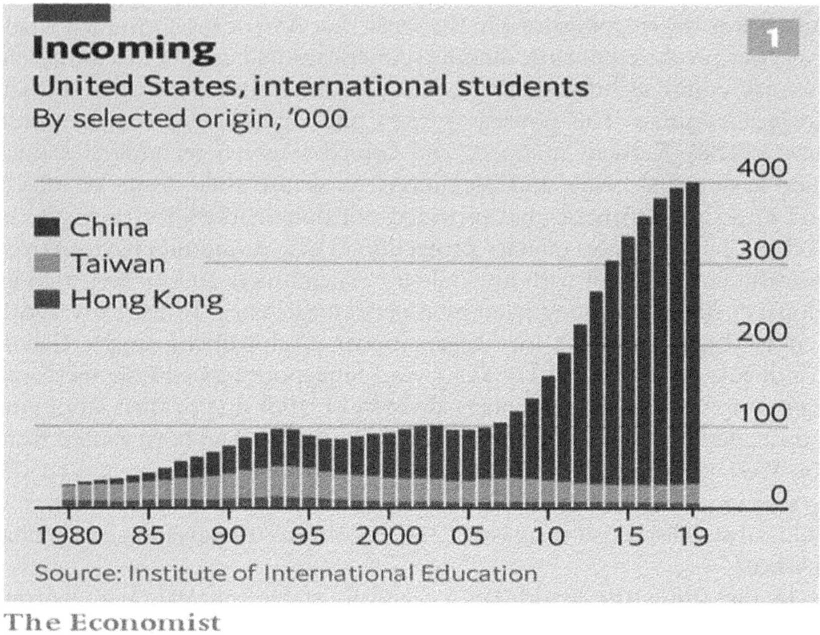

Fig. 5.9 Chinese students in the US from 1980 to 2019 (*Source The Economist* [2020])

we see persons of worth, we should think of equaling them; when we see persons of a contrary character, we should turn inwards and examine ourselves." In Confucian tradition one earns power, respect, and wealth by acting and learning, not due to heritage. The people should rebel against the ruler if he does not perform his duties to enrich and educate the people. Rebellions led by people educated in Confucianism are common in Chinese history. When Deng rose to the top power, the United States was in its golden time. By the 1980s, normalization of U.S.-China relations opened the doors to an explosive expanding exchange of ideas, people, and material goods. The basic principles of China's trade with the rest of the world are given by Deng. With regard to the theory of class struggle which had been penetrated into every corner of Chinese society at the end of the Cultural Revolution, Deng said: "In China, we intend to acquire advanced technology, science and management skills to serve our socialist production. And these things as such have no class character." He convinced Chinese no political conflicts between Marxism and leaning knowledge from the West. His political wisdom as the leader of a poor and lowly educated state is reflected in his following strategy: "Observe calmly; serve our position; cope with affairs calmly; hide our capacities and bide our time; be good at maintaining a low profile; and never claim leadership." This strategy enabled China to have peaceful relations with America, at least till the time when Xi got power over China.

The United States' relationship with the PRC and its over 1.3 billion Chinese in the last 4 decades has been too complex, varied, and fast changing to be reduced to a clear picture. Although China has also had complicated relations with other countries and regions, the United States has been perhaps most influential country on China. On 7th July 1979, Trade Relations Agreement was formally signed by the two governments. The agreement accorded each other Most Favored Nation treatment (MFN), which played the role of a cornerstone in trade expansion. Numerous agreements on some specific areas were made in the following years. China bought U.S. civil aircraft and U.S. agricultural products and imported chemical fertilizers, cotton, timber, paper, paper pulp, machinery equipment, computers, and medical apparatus. There were many U.S.-China joint venture companies.

China's WTO membership marked the final step in normalizing U.S.-China trade relations. The US supported China's WTO implementation to accelerate China's economic reform. It has made China more market-driven economy. Since joining the WTO in December 2001, China has taken important steps to improve market access, including lowering tariffs on a range of products important to U.S. exporters. China became the 143rd member of the WTO. The event was considered as a potential watershed for the reform process. Under the WTO, China had better access to FDI, increased industrial competitiveness, and improved the legal and regulatory framework necessary for a more open and free economy. The government made commitments to trade and investment liberalization to substantially open the Chinese economy to foreign firms. In addition to increasing market access, China agreed to undertake broad reforms that would foster greater transparency, providing for notice and comment on regulations, permitting judicial review, and applying laws uniformly. China changed many laws, institutions, and policies to be in conformity with international trade rules. Tariffs barriers, restrictions on foreign investment, inadequate protection of intellectual property rights,

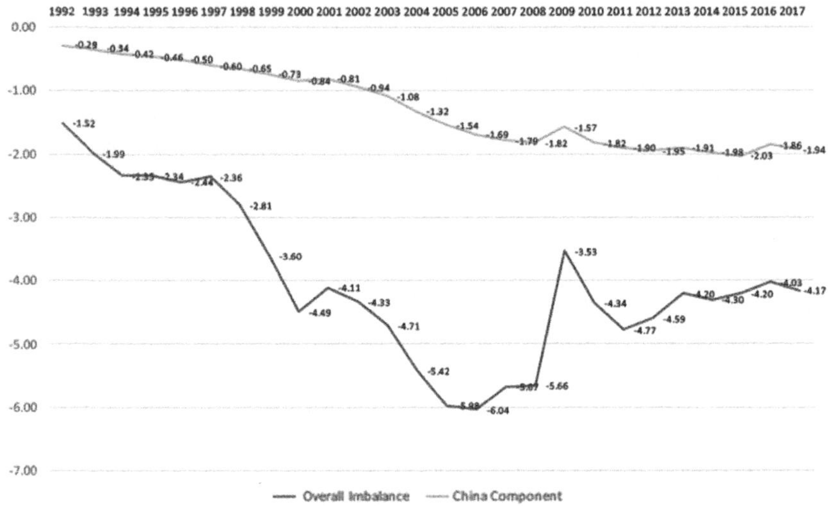

Fig. 5.10 US trade balance in goods (percentage of GDP) (*Source* Woo [2019])

and trade-distorting government subsidies were all important areas that China had to improve.

There are recently trade conflicts between the US and China. Figure 5.10 plots the overall US trade account balance and the bilateral US-China trade account balance over the period 1992–2017. The overall US trade deteriorated rapidly from 1.52% of GDP in 1992 to 4.17 in 2017. The US economy spends much and borrows from different countries to sustain its consumption. China's contribution to the US trade unbalance had been increasingly during the period. The plot hints on some reasons for trade wars between the two economies.

References

Andornino, G. B. (2017). The Belt and Road Initiative in China's Emerging Grand Strategy of Connective Leadership. *China & World Economy, 25*(5), 4–22.

Chadde, D. D., & Qiu, F. (2003). Recent Trends and Emerging Patterns of Foreign Direct Investment in China. In I. Alon (Ed.), *Chinese Culture,*

Organizational Behavior, and International Business Management. Westport: Praeger.
Chen, C. L. (2019). *The Liberalisation of FDI Policies and the Impacts of FDI on China's Economic Development*. Retrieved from https://press-files.anu.edu.au/downloads/press/n4267/html/ch29.xhtml?referer=&page=41.
Cheng, H. S. (1993). Foreign Trade. In W. Galenson (Ed.), *China's Economic Reform*. San Francisco: The 1990 Institute.
Dai, M., Maitra, M., & Yu, M. J. (2016, April). Unexceptional Exporter Performance in China? The Role of Processing Trade. *Journal of Development Economics, 121,* 177–189.
Du, J. L., & Zhang, Y. F. (2018, February). Does One Belt One Road Initiative Promote Overseas Direct Investments. *China Economic Review, 47,* 189–205.
Du, Y., & Lu, Y. (2018). The Great Opening Up and the Roadmap for the Future. *China and World Economy, 26*(2), 68–93.
Fana, H. C., Lin, F. Q., & Tang, L. X. (2018, November). Minimum Wage and Outward FDI from China. *Journal of Development Economics, 135,* 1–19.
Fang, C., Garnaut, R., & Song, L. (2018). 40 Years of China's Reform and Development: How Reform Captured China's Demographic Dividend. In R. Garnaut, L. Song, & C. Fang (Eds.), *China's 40 Years of Reform and Development 1978–2018*. Australia: ANU Press.
Gao, P. Y. (2018). China's 40 Years of Fiscal and Tax Reform: A Basic Trajectory. *China and World Economy, 26*(2), 94–106.
Gong, B. L. (2018, May). Agricultural Reforms and Production in China: Changes in Provincial Production Function and Productivity in 1978–2015. *Journal of Development Economics, 132,* 18–31.
Ju, J. D., & Yu, X. D. (2018). China's Opening Up After 40 Years: Standing at a Historic Turning Point. *China & World Economy, 26*(2), 23–49.
Landes, D. S. (1998). *The Wealth and Poverty of Nations: Why Some Are so Rich and Some so Poor*. New York: North & Company.
Lau, L. J. (2008). Thirty Years of Chinese Economic Reform: Reasons for Its Success and Future Directions. In C. Papadimitriou & S. Zhang (Eds.), *Internet and Network Economics* (Vol. 5385). Lecture Notes in Computer Science. Berlin: Springer.
Li, K. W., & Jiang, W. (2019). *China's Foreign Trade: Reform, Performance and Contribution to Economic Growth*. Retrieved from https://press-files.anu.edu.au/downloads/press/n4267/html/ch28.xhtml?referer=&page=40.
Liu, Y. L., Lu, M., & Xiang, K. H. (2018). Balance Through Agglomeration: A Race Between Geography and Policy in China's Regional Development. *China & World Economy, 26*(6), 72–96.
Smith, A. (1776/1976) *An Inquiry into the Nature and Causes of the Wealth of Nations* (E. Cannan, Ed.). Chicago: The University of Chicago Press.

So, A. Y., & Chu, Y. W. (2016). *The Global Rise of China*. Cambridge: Polity Press.

The Economist. (2020). Retrieved from https://www.google.com/search?rlz=1C1OKWM_jaJP857JP857&source=univ&tbm=isch&q=number+of+students+in+China&sa=X&ved=2ahUKEwik5q_95s7qAhXFzIsBHRIeBBMQsAR6BAgJEAE&biw=878&bih=380imgrc=gWbyGekODkaVNM.

Wan, G. H., Wang, C., Yin, H., & Zhang, Y. (2018). From Equality of Deprivation to Disparity of Prosperity: The Poverty-Growth-Inequality Triangle in Post-reform China. *China & World Economy, 26*(2), 50–67.

Wan, G. H., & Zhang, Y. (2018, June). The Direct and Indirect Effects of Infrastructure on Firm Productivity: Evidence from Chinese Manufacturing. *China Economic Review, 48*, 143–153.

Wang, C. (2020, March 4). *The Evolution of China's Consumer Market in the Past Decade*. Retrieved from https://food.chemlinked.com/news/food-news/the-evolution-of-chinas-consumer-market-in-the-past-decade.

Wang, X., Xie, Z., Zhang, X. B., & Huang, Y. P. (2018, June). Roads to Innovation: Firm-Level Evidence from People's Republic of China (PRC). *China Economic Review, 49*, 154–170.

Woo, W. T. (2019). *A US Perspective on China's External Economic Disputes in the Past 40 Years and in the Coming 40 Years*. Retrieved from https://press-files.anu.edu.au/downloads/press/n4267/html/ch31.xhtml?referer=&page=43.

CHAPTER 6

Uncertain China with Docilely Educated Population

> The fate of our times is characterized by rationalization and intellectualization and, above all, by the disenchantment of the world.
>
> Max Weber (1864–1920)

Fan Bingbing (1981–), once national superstar and the symbol of Chinese female beauty, is a shining example of changes in China. The fine of US$129 million only for tax evasion in 2018 for the female mega star whose parents' monthly wages had been a few hundred US dollars caused a ripple among the Chinese public. The national symbol of female sexuality equipped with beauty, wealth, and hobnobs with the rich and famous via intrigue human networks is a natural focus of national media and gossips. Fan was born into a common family in Qingdao. She was a female household name for her beauty, huge wealth accumulated over a short period, acting, and once for her huge tax-evasion and various sources of wealth. She graduated from an art college. She had been a superstar as actress, model, television producer, singer, a member of the Communist Part of China and philanthropist till she was fined US$129 million for tax evasion in 2018. She rose in 1998 with drama series *My Fair Princess*. From 2013 to 2016, she was the highest-paid celebrity listed in the Forbes China Celebrity. From 2006 to 2015, she was in the top in the same list. She received many domestic and international awards. As one of the highest-paid actresses in the world, she frequently appeared on the movie premieres and fashion shows in international stages. Gossips

W.-B. Zhang, *The Butterfly Effect in China's Economic Growth*,
https://doi.org/10.1007/978-981-15-9889-0_6

about scandals of wrong-way to get wealth and power and gender relations and sex-related topics travel quick and widely. Fang is only one case of many hundreds of scandals of wealthy people published by the Chinese government since Xi rose to the top power.

Most of important events, except age and eventual death, in life are not predictable. China is faced with more uncertainties than at any other stage of its modern life. No one could have imagined the economic prosperity and enhanced global status of China within such a short period. Any big change in society is a consequence of deterministic and random factors. China's economic achievements are not miracle in any intellectual sense as both ancient Chinese thinkers and British economists have long ago pointed out the direction how to organize an orderly society with the welfare of the people as the most important matter of the society. The Chinese failures and miserable past before 1978 were due to that the Chinese society had been organized in the social and economic principles contrast to what ancient Chinese thinkers advocated. China's changes since 1978 to the present in scale, scope, and speed, like a butterfly effect, may intrigue anyone who knows about China's past before 1978.

The economic reform is a great show period in China's history about how wealth, power, and sexuality can be created, distributed, and utilized in modern ways. There is nothing new under the sun, but everyone is a unique existence due to alternative combinations of the invariant elements. What Marx called negative aspects or evils associated with industrializing capitalism have gradually and steadily appeared in China with unstopped forces. Wealth, power, and sex (or sexual relations) are the three key connectors of human society which is maintained to satisfy the basic desires and needs of the social animal with unlimited dreams and desires for limited resources. Wealth markets, power markets, and markets of sexuality have their own mechanisms and possible varieties. They are now interlinked in the way that Chinese farmer-poet Mao was unable to dream of. But China is no exceptional in the sense that human society is, like human body, healthily maintained by the same combination of basic ideas and principles for a modern economically effective society. The ancient Greeks view a human society as a single organism. Over history many thinkers compare the roles of organizations in society and the functions of organs and circuits in the body. Confucius says: "The faults of men are characteristic of the class to which they belong. By observing a man's faults, we may learn what kind of man he is." This is similarly applicable to the contemporary world. No country is perfect; one country's good points are similar to others, but bad points are carried on in its own unique way.

Higher Dimensions of Consciousness and Sustainable Development

> The key to growth is the introduction of higher dimensions of consciousness into our awareness.
>
> Laozi (6th or 4th BC)

> The nature of peoples is first crude, then severe, then benign, then delicate, finally dissolute.
>
> Giambattista Vico (1668–1744)

A nation which has neither honesty nor courage to admit its past mistakes, is not strong enough to correct them and will not make sincerer efforts to make any essential progress as a decent human society. China's past economic development has explored different fortunes offered by the domestic and international environment. Its economic miracle in the past 40 years is often said an exception to the common pattern of modernization in the rest of the world. As China's current prosperity has been a transition from a trapped socialist equilibrium point toward a higher market-oriented state, the path is naturally exceptional as each transitory process has its singularity during structural changes. Leo Tolstoy starts *Anna Karenina* with "All happy families are alike; each unhappy family is unhappy in its own way." In this well-connected world all developed economies are alike (in a visionary and structural sense); each undeveloped economy is poor in its own way. A well-developed economy improves itself and swiftly adapts to its environment in a beneficial manner. In *Catastrophe Theory*, Vladimir Arnold (1992: 31–32), argues that good things tend to be fragile as a good system has simultaneously a number of qualities and it falls apart if one of these qualities fails: "… for systems belonging to the singular part of the stability boundary a small change of the parameters is more likely to send the system into the unstable region than into the stable region. This is a manifestation of a general principle stating that all good things (e.g. stability) more fragile than bad things. It seems that in good situations a number of requirements must hold simultaneously, while to call a situation bad even one failure suffices." There are limited structures or patterns of rationally civilized societies. The law of jungle does not sustain a highly civilized society with large number of people in an already highly educated, at least developed and middle-income economies, world. Aristotle (Aristotle 2009: Book 2) points: "Again, it is possible to fail in many ways (for evil belongs to the class of the unlimited, as the Pythagoreans conjectured, and good to that of the limited), while to succeed is possible only in one way (for which reason also one is easy and the other difficult—to miss the mark easy, to hit it difficult); for these reasons also, then, excess and defect are characteristic of vice, and the mean of virtue; For men are good in but one way, but bad in many."

China lacks freedom and social justice in many aspects. If China wants to become a properly educated global citizen, it has to make efforts to solve political problems as mentioned by Keynes: "The political problem of mankind is to combine three things: economic efficiency, social justice and individual liberty." Although China has made great improvement in economic efficiency, there are more issues related to social justice in association with hasty economic expansion. Individual liberty, at least in the Western sense, has never been an integrated part of Chinese culture since the first emperor unified many cultures in one China. Mencius emphasizes cultivation: "He who attends to his greater self becomes a great man, and he who attends to his smaller self becomes a small man." We read from the *Book of Rites*, "Through the perception of right produced by ceremony, come the degrees of the noble and the mean; through the union of culture arising from music, harmony between high and low. By the exhibition of what is to be liked and what is to be disliked, a distinction is made between the worthy and unworthy. When violence is prevented by punishments, and the worthy are raised to rank, the operation of government was made impartial. Then come benevolence in the love of the people, and righteousness in the correction of their errors; and in this way good government held its course." Confucianism holds that a party exists for the sake of the people, not the people live to feed a party. Mencius states: "The people are the most important element in a nation, the spirits of the land and grain are the next; the sovereign is the lightest." The duty of the state is not to order people to do what it desires, but to provide people what they desire. The government should behave in such a way that the people's welfare is increased. "There is a way", Mencius, points out, "to get the empire - get the people, and the empire is got. There is a way to get the people - get their hearts, and the people are got. There is a way to get their hearts - it is simply to collect for them what they like, and not to lay on them what they dislike." Democracy in modern times is to create and maintain such a government.

In his *Lectures on the Philosophy of World History*, Hegel argues that the dialectic of universal history reveals the development of consciousness of freedom and consequent realization of that freedom. Hegel holds that China lacked the essential consciousness of the idea of freedom and thus China was outside world history. China people were subsumed within the spirit of the family and could not achieve formal independence. Even Chinese law did not contain consciousness of wrong. According to Hegel (1827: 120), "Unconstrained morality, in practice and theory, heart, inward religion, science and art properly so called is alien to it [China]. The Emperor always speaks with majesty and paternal kindness and tenderness to the people; who however cherish the meanest opinion of themselves and believe that they are born only to drag the car of imperial power. The burden which presses them to the ground, seems to them to be their inevitable destiny; and it appears nothing to them to sell themselves as slaves, and to eat the bitter bread of slavery."

China has been fortunate in providing the basic material needs of the ubiquitously poor and homogenously educated population. Deng's famous saying: "It doesn't matter if a cat is black or white, so long as it catches mice" could have caused the butterfly effect because of the situation left by Mao. Deng succeeded in the condition where it would be sufficient to allow people to pursue their own material interests with the rest under the party's surveillance. As the people's basic material needs and basic desires for education are satisfied, China is faced with the challenge of what Lao Tzu calls "higher dimensions of consciousness". What Laozi says is described by Maslow. Maslow's hierarchy (or a pyramid with five levels) of needs theory holds that while people want to meet needs, these needs are successively ranked in a form of a pyramid as illustrated in Fig. 6.1 (Maslow 1943, 1987). The first four levels are called deficiency (D−) needs and the highest one growth or being (B−) needs. The D-needs motivate people when they are not met. People are motivated strongly especially if such needs are denied long. Individuals tend to satisfy lower level need before searching higher one(s). It is not necessary that lower need must be satisfied 100% before the next one appears. As the D-needs are met, people may be motivated towards meeting the next level

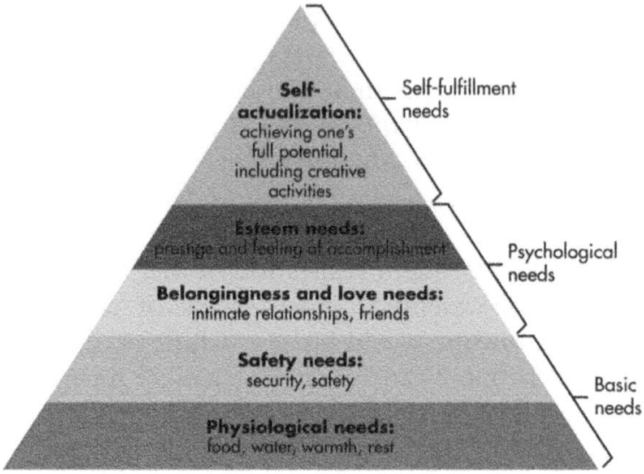

Fig. 6.1 Maslow's hierarchy of needs (*Source* McLeod [2018])

of needs. The B-needs may stem from a desire to grow as a person and to achieve self-actualization. Processes are personally varied. Some people may fluctuate between different needs without going to higher needs. Cultural dynamics is illustrated by the author Zhang (1998: 19): "Cultural dynamics are characterised not by a smoothly co-ordinated synergy of parts, a massive coalition of the whole, but by disjointed movements of first one part, and then the other. Some parts change very rapidly, while some others may be sluggish. Cultural changes do not always occur in order. They exhibit bifurcations and chaos. New orders are born from structural changes. Sometimes, cultural movement is well directed, while sometimes it may wander a long time before it is sure what to do. There is no simple progression from traditional to modern, but a twisting, spasmodic, unmethodical movement which turns as often toward repossessing the emotions of the past as disowning them."

Hasty economic expansion is associated with unequal growth of people with social status and economic income. In Beijing and Shanghai, unlike the 1990s, there are now almost no voice of democracy. The conspicuous consumption has become the dominant social phenomenon, rather than an increasing demand for freedom and democracy. In Chinese culture need for respect or reputation is subject to the government surveillance. It is the first time in China's history that a large percentage of people have enough food and access to higher education. The question is what will happen next after China has experienced rapid economic proliferation. "At once other (and "higher") needs emerge and these, rather than physiological hungers, dominate the organism. And when these in turn are satisfied, again new (and still "higher") needs emerge and so on. This is what we mean by saying that the basic human needs are organized into a hierarchy of relative prepotency" (Maslow 1943: 375). Maslow also recognized other needs such as cognitive needs (such as knowledge and understanding, exploration, meaning), aesthetic needs (such as appreciation and search for beauty), and transcendence needs (such as mystical experiences and religious faith). A person finds the meaning of life in self-actualization. People are not homogeneous and have their own needs in self-actualization. This implies that a government should have freedom for people to satisfy their varied higher needs. It is reasonable to argue that more people will have higher needs if China's economic development is sustainable. If the growth of self-actualization is a basic need for many Chinese people, China's government is not yet prepared or constructed to satisfy higher needs of the coming generations. There are few public debates in China about political freedom and liberal ideas. China is far from a modern society, irrespective of its rapidly increasing economic and military powers.

Hasty Economic Expansion and Widely Spread Corruption

> The petty thief is imprisoned but the big thief becomes a feudal lord.
>
> Zhuangzi (369–295 BC)

Public glory and internal evil are often the two sides of the same person or the same organization.

In 2016, the Chinese government announced its great achievement in having punished more than one million officials only in the past three years. Unfortunately, no one knows number of corrupt officials still in office or in retirement. Many not-yet-corrupt officials have not low probabilities of becoming corrupt due to the Chinese *guanxi* networking. To keep himself profitable and safe, the *guanxi* network implies that to keep himself safe and more profitable in the long term, a corrupt official has strong motivations to make other officials in his *guanxi* network or related positions corrupt. Money and power are co-operating in cycles of corruption of highly educated Chinese officials. An accountant described his enforced participation in webs of corruption in the following way: "In an accountant in a state-owned enterprise. To keep my job, I have to maintain good relations with my superiors or they'll just get someone else. My boss regularly brings in bills for ¥3000 for lunch for four, which I have to sign off on. We constantly rotate the bills through the different units so they aren't too obvious. Other accountants and I get together to exchange stories about how corrupt our bosses are, but there's nothing we can do about it. Even if you oppose it, all that happens is that you lose your job and nothing changes. I do things that make me sick. Sometimes I can't sleep at night. But I don't have any other choice." (Levy 2002: 47). Corruption allegations reached to the vice-minister or vice-governor levels. In Heber province, for instance, there was a collective embezzlement involved at least seven high-ranking officials, including the province's executive deputy governor, bureau chief of transportation, director of the taxation department, and the party secretary of a major city (*Hebei Ribao*, 21 November, 2000). One Politburo member, Chen Xitong, was convicted of corruption. Corruption allegations reached to the vice-minister or vice-governor levels. Tens of thousands of cases of corruption are reported and investigated each year. Corruption has been considered as a serious threat to China's political and economic systems. Throughout the 1990s, Transparency International evaluated China as one of the world's most corrupt countries (Levy 2002: 39).

Corruption is the abuse of political power for private ends. Economic causes and consequences of corruption are important and difficult issues. There are many theoretical studies on corruption and economic progress. There are also many empirical studies on corruption and economic advancement. Researchers emphasize different aspects of corruption. There is no general convergent conclusion on the role of corruption on economic prosperity. Chea (2015: 187) argues: "From the theoretical background and empirical evidence from various studies spread in various countries in the world using different methods over the years, there are mostly negative findings of economic growth. Nevertheless, there are also positive findings found on the effects of corruption on economic growth." Leff (1964) gives possible positive effects of corruption on economic expansion. Huntington (1968) argues that the "efficient corruption" in the form of bribery may help firms to get works completed in a political economic environment plagued by bureaucratic complexity. Myrdal (1968) holds that corruption leads to economic inefficiency as officials may delay permissions of projects to get bribes. Chinese corruption is pervasive also because the law does not function in society. The closely tied *guanxi* network system makes anyone hard to survive in a decent manner if he/she holds "profitable" official positions. Chinese official life in a "profitable" position can hardly be uncorrupt as the *guanxi* network will explore potential profit of the position as large as possible. If one in the profitable position is uncorrupt, the official would be moved away as no profit is added to the *guanxi* network. As China has become richer and more educated, corruption is increasingly sophisticated and complex in causes, forms, and connections.

The transition from a centrally planned economy to a more open and market-oriented system has been associated with pervasive corruption. From earlier years of economic reform, the government has been faced with problems of corruption. China still lacks a modern legal and judicial framework for a market economy. The government has problems with transparency and public accountability. Corruption speeds ups income and wealth inequality, mis-uses resources for environment protection, derives education opportunities for students from poor family, and undermines the legitimacy of the CCP. China has an anti-corruption system which consists of the Discipline Inspection Commission (DIC), the Ministry of Supervision and the People's Procuratorate. These three main agents have their branches at different local levels. The DICs are internal to the CCP. The Ministry of Supervision often have the same operations as those by the DIC. The DIC is the key player among the anti-corruption agents in China (Chan and Sun 2018). Since the 2012 campaign, many high-ranking government and military offices were sentenced due to corruption. High-rankings officials can use their power to put their children to the profitable positions. Children and relatives of political leaders have accumulated large personal wealth mainly due to political positions. Rapid enrichment of these people has led public complaints about the CCP. Officials spent fraudulently public money for their own interests. As some of officials have monopolistic power to grant licenses to local businessmen or other clients, they can get additional rents in form of bribes, illicit impositions, fees, and different other charges. Corruption is not necessarily in monetary form. Corruption may be conducted in form of, for instance, cronyism, clientelism, nepotism, and usurpation of official privilege.

Table 6.1 lists corruption perceptions for some selected countries and selected years. The index is an aggregated measure of graft, bribery,

Table 6.1 Corruption perceptions for selected countries and years

Country/Region	*Corruption index 2012*	*Corruption index 2014*	*Corruption index (rank) 2017*
China	36	39	41 (77)
South Korea	56	55	54 (51)
Taiwan	61	61	63 (29)
France	71	69	70 (23)
Japan	74	76	73 (20)
United States	73	74	75 (16)
Hong Kong	77	74	77 (13)
Germany	79	79	81 (12)
United Kingdom	74	78	82 (8)
Singapore	87	86	84 (6)
Switzerland	86	86	85 (3)

Source https://www.transparency.org/news/feature/corruption_perceptions_index_2017

embezzlement, backdoor deals, nepotism, patronage, and statistical falsification. The perceived levels of public sector corruption are given by experts and businesspeople with scale of 0–100, with 0 being highly corrupt and 100 very clean. In 2017, China's rank is in the 77th among the 180 countries and territories.

Problems in China's Market Economy

> Things joined by profit, when pressed by misfortune and danger, will cast each other aside.
>
> Zhuangzi (369 –295 BC)

In *Capitalism, Socialism and Democracy*, Schumpeter replies his own question: "Can capitalism survive? No. I do not think it can." Since Deng introduced capitalism to China's economy, China has been moving almost unidirectionally towards capitalism. The *yin-yang* theory seems valid for explaining dynamic paths of world economic evolution. China's economic growth has been sustained so far, at least, with regards to some macro indexes. This fast proliferation is due to the combination of the conditions left by Mao, Deng's switching to market economy at the right time, the cultural capital stocks and fortunes of overseas Chinese societies, spread education, diligence with animal spirits, simplified mindset of the population, proper policies, and so on. After having explored obvious growth opportunities, China is now confronted with complicated issues about continued advancement and sustainability.

Over years there were numerous—labor, rural, environmental, nationalist, ethnic minority, and so on—protects in China (Wright 2018). A Chinese professor describes the situation in China (Qin 2017): "In America, if you purposely falsify data, then your career in academia is over, … But in China, the cost of cheating is very low. They won't fire you. You might not get promoted immediately, but once people forget, then you might have a chance to move up." Baruch Spinoza (1632–1677) gives insights into Chinese academics under the government surveillance: "Academies that are founded at public expense are instituted not so much to cultivate men's natural abilities as to restrain them." Self-destruction is a process of human evolution. What appears great and beneficial in the short term often becomes mediocre and harmful in the long term. In 1919, Fu Sinian (Schwarcz 1986: 130) observes: "The other day I asked a man who trains dogs why he chose only foreign dogs. He answered: Chinese dogs are very smart; their sense of smell is sharper than that of foreign dogs. But they are incapable of single of single-mindedness. If you tell them to fetch something, midway they'll run into other dogs and forget their mission. So it's no use training them. … Chinese people are not unlike Chinese dogs. It's not that they're not smart; it's just that they lack a sense of responsibility."

There is no perfect law in society; there is disrespectable society in which the written law and rule are used to punish the honest and are manipulated by the dishonest. There is no perfect criterion of human right; there is barbarian society in which the human right written by the state is applied to sustain dictatorship rather than to protect the people to freely examine the meaning of life and justice in society. One might wonder whether contemporary Chinese practice is an effective way to build a modern human society as too many talented people are engaged in a corruptible sector (the government). Overconcentrated distribution of talented in one monopolistic sector will not create socially desirable results. But without the social stability controlled/maintained by the obedient and well-trained, what might have happened in China invites one to figure out different possibilities.

In 1978, there were not so many equally poor people as in China. Chinese people made the national economic miracle from the same poverty line. This uniform line was relatively suitable for perfect competition. Nowadays, there is not such an almost equal starting line for young people as resources and opportunities are highly unevenly distributed. Hopes for a better life among the poor are no more easily built and easily achieved (in comparison to the New China in the 1990s). Education resources and job opportunities are often unfairly taken away by the rich and the powerful. Moreover, capital misallocation has been pointed out to be a great factor for relatively low total factor productivity (TFP). It is estimated that capital misallocation alone may reduce national TFP by 20% in later 2000s (Wu 2018). In earlier periods of the reform, the TFP loss may be 30–50% due to resource allocation. A stylized fact on Chinese economy is that average marginal revenue product of capital differs greatly between firms of different ownership. This variation is often treated due to policy distortions, lagged legal and not-well performed auditing and contracting environment in in capital formation and allocation. Political connections and policy distortions lead to capital misallocation. China is composed of many provinces with heterogeneous climates and cultures. In most of the Mao period, the state emphasized the development of inland. China's open-door policy was first applied to special economic zones (SEZ) and gradually extended to coastal cities,, other coastal areas, and inland regions consecutively. Because of differences in policy, infrastructures, accessibility, FDI was mainly distributed over coastal regions. The biased policies have resulted in enlarged gaps between regions.

China's economic expansion has been accompanied by a rapid epidemiological transition from communicable to noncommunicable diseases, such as mental disorder. Qin et al. (2018) verify that the prevalence rate of depression is high—37.9% for depressive symptoms and 4.1% for depression. The rate is uneven across regions and populations. Over 100 million Chinese experience a variety of mental disorders during a year. The people who are likely to be depressed are women, older people, people in the central and western regions and rural areas. People with higher education and income levels are less likely to have mental diseases. The youth and immigrant families have an increasing tendency. Mental diseases decrease physical wellbeing, affect human capital accumulation, reduce productivities, lead to high health costs, and many other social problems.

Hasty economic expansion has been associated with development and diffusion of many negative consequences in society, such as issues related to drugs and environmental change. According to World Bank (2007), twelve of the twenty most polluted cities in the world were in China. Only 5.6 million of the 560 million urban dwellers in China could breathe safe air in the European Union standard. The total economic cost of China's air pollution was estimated about 4.1% of the GDP in 2002. The total economic cost of water and air pollution was almost 6.9% of the GDP in 2003. The government has made efforts to improve environment. The government designated 7.5 billion U.S. dollars to protect environment in 2017. Many polluting factories in heavily polluted cities were closed or removed. The government also rewarded and punished officials on basis of their environmental performances. This policy motivated local government officials to reach the goal of environmental protection (Chen et al. 2018).

The key task facing policymakers in China today is how to sustain economic development while improving welfare more widely across society. Mencius says: "When one by force subdues men, they do not submit to him in heart. They submit because their strength is not adequate to resist. When one subdues men by virtue, in their hearts' core they are pleased, and sincerely submit." Since a good government takes the welfare of its people as the main purpose, society under such a government should attract people abroad and make the people not to leave. Confucius gives a simple indicator for measuring the efficiency of government in open international environment: "Good government obtains when those who are near made happy, and those who are far off are attracted." In an open society, one's choice through feet is a way to enhance one's welfare. Many rich people are immigrating abroad due to heterogeneous factors. These people take their human capital and wealth away. It does not seem to cause any serious brain drain problems in China's economic development as China does not suffer from shortage of talented people. But the immigration with huge wealth causes social concerns.

Cheap labor, which has been a comparative advantage of China, is a key determinant for the made-in-China. The advantage is now faced with more challenges. Market forces cause many companies, especially SOEs, to lay off workers. Many industrial enterprises owned by the government are losing money. They are kept alive by government loans and subsidies. China is faced with challenges brought about by galloping regional inequalities and inequalities among social and economic groups. Chinese economic advancement has been achieved with formidable obstacles including inefficient state enterprises, ambiguous property rights, irrational prices, primitive transportation, outmoded banking and securities facilities, and pervasive corruption in sustained Chinese characteristics. These problems will be great obstacles for China's further development, especially, in enriching and enhancing social status of the poor.

Like many parts of the world, China is aging rapidly due to low fertility and low mortality rates. There are 13 older people (60 years and older) for every 100 people in China in 2012, whereas this figure will be raised to 34 in 2050. Those aged 80 years or over will be 22% of the total population by 2050. The old age support ratio is about 8 in 2012, whereas the figure becomes 2 by 2050 (Pan et al. 2018; Singh 2018). The demographic change is a great challenge. Factors such as formal or informal care from society or relatives, living condition, living location, income source, the presence of spouse, the number of children and grandchildren, are important for the elderly care.

After the 40-year economic reform Chinese people should have been aware of what Karl Marx's theory on class struggle implies. When Marxism was first spread over China, Chinese people had little idea about the Jewish man's theory. The Chinese race collectively and undiscerningly received Marx and was emotionally engaged in destroying the so-called Chinese capitalism which even did not exist in Marx's sense. The problems and evils associated with capitalism in Marx's theory on capitalism now begin to appear in China, but there is no national passion for revolution as many people taste the fruits of capitalism. Chinese people are fully engaged in enriching themselves to make the nation richer and technologically more advanced as Marx predicted. Poverty is a great challenge for China, as for any (genuine) capitalist economy. Many Chinese poor people have not benefited, especially in relative terms, from the capitalism-based economic proliferation, as Marx foresaw.

Political Stability and Conformity of the Elite with the Party

> Those who today are called 'scholar-officials' are base and reckless, given to villainy and anarchy, to self-indulgence and excesses of passion, and to sheer greed. They are offensive and insulting, and they lack any sense of ritual principle or moral duty, except when motivated by the desire for positions of power and influence.
>
> Xun Zi (298–238 BC, 6: 13)

Cunning ... is but the low mimic of wisdom.
Plato (423–347 BC)

Cultural genes are constantly changing appearances but slowly mutate. Montesquieu (1689–1755, 1748: 277) observes: "From hence it proceeds that liberty in Asia never increases; whilst in Europe it is enlarged or diminished according to particular circumstances." Europe's history is characterized by mutual killings among peoples among peoples with heterogeneous cultures. They made progresses together by mutual killing and learning. "There reigns in Asia a servile spirit..." Montesquieu (1748: 277) holds, "It is impossible to find, in all the histories of this country, a single passage which discovers a free soul: we shall never see anything there but the heroism of slavery." Montesquieu (1748: 221) describes the Chinese character: "It is determined by the laws of China, that whosoever shows any disrespect to the emperor is to be punished with death. As they do not mention what this disrespect consists in, everything may furnish a pretext to take away a man's life, and to exterminate any family whatsoever." In the light of modern knowledge on cultural geography, European and Asian differences are perhaps largely formed due to geographical differences. In his book On Liberty, John Stuart Mill (1806–1873) compares the fall of China and the rise of Europe as follows: "We have a warning example in China — a nation of much talent, and in some respects, even wisdom, owing to the rare good fortune of having been provided at an early period with a particularly good set of customs, the work, in some measure, of men to whom even the most enlightened European must accord, under certain limitations, the title of sages and philosophers.. .. On the contrary, they have become stationary. .. They have succeeded beyond all hope in what English philanthropists are so industriously working at — in making a people all alike, all governing their thoughts and conduct by the same maxims and rules; and these are the fruits.. .. What has made the European family of nations an improving, instead of a stationary portion of mankind? Not any superior excellence in them, which, when it exists, exists as the effect not as the cause; but their remarkable diversity of character and culture.... Europe is, in my judgment, wholly indebted to this plurality of paths for its progressive and many-sided development."

Marx argues: "The ideas of the ruling class are in every epoch the ruling ideas, i,e., the class which is the ruling material force of society, is at the same time its ruling intellectual force." China's tradition is to recruit people who pass national examinations to govern in different levels of government. Mao destroyed this tradition and Deng restored it. Except training effective labor forces for maintaining economic advancement, Deng wants to effectively control the entire country under a single party. In his study on the impact of natural, social, and economic conditions on human character formation, Montesquieu (1748: 25) concludes that the Chinese racial spirit was greedy, dishonest, industrious, and respectful of their elders. The quasi-nomad Manchus consoled the Han Chinese in a benevolent way by making Han Chinese "greedy, dishonest, industrious, and respectful of their elders". The harmonious co-existence of the two races could be maintained over 260 years as the racial characters are in equilibrium of the demand and supply. The society of brute nomadic man and rice-based farmer is different from the society of competitive pirates. Different societies evolved in different directions with miscellaneous combinations of basic characteristics. Montesquieu describes the typical farmer under the nomadic ruler.

In 1822, Hegel (1991: 138) concludes: "In China, however, the distinction between Slavery and freedom is necessarily, not great, since all are equal before the Emperor—that is, all are alike degraded. As no honor exits, and no one has an individual right in respect of others, the consciousness of debasement predominates, and this easily passes into that of utter abandonment. ...They are notorious for deceiving wherever they can. Friend deceives friend, and no one resents the attempt at deception...". Montesquieu (1689–1755) and Hegel (1770–1831) were living during the Qing dynasty (1644–1912) when (Han) Chinese were under the Manchus' ruling. The Han Chinese characteristics were servile. The Manchus could control vast China with its less 1% of the Qing dynasty's population by making the Han Chinese distrust to each other. In fact, as early as in 1697, Leibniz noted the Chinese character under Manchus: "The Chinese above all others have attained a higher standard. In a vast multitude of men they have virtually accomplished more than the founders of religious orders among us have achieved within their own narrow ranks. So great is obedience toward superiors and reverence toward elders, so religious, almost, is the relation of children toward parents, that for children to contrive anything violent against their parents, even by word, is almost unheard of, and the perpetrator seems to atone for his actions even as we make a parricide pay for his deed.. .. To us, not enough accustomed to act by reason and rule, these smack of servitude; yet among them, where these duties are made natural by use, they are observed gladly" (Cook and Rosemont 1994:47).

As far as politics and social sciences are concerned, the examinations which Chinese officials are taking are still made officials to be in conformity with whatever the party asks for. John Stuart Mill (1806–1873) points out: "A State which dwarfs its men in order that they may be more docile instruments in its hands even for beneficial purposes will find that with small men no great thing can really be accomplished." A modern human society flourishes individual characters. "It is a good thing", Lu Xun (1980, VI: 134) portrays, "that the Chinese want face; the pity is that this face is so flexible, so constantly changing, that it becomes confusing with not wanting face." Influential Chinese intellectuals of the May Fourth generation were capable of criticizing; but they failed to propose anything constructive for building a modern society. They advocated science and democracy; but did not support freedom and individualism. Writers, like Lu Xun and Bo Yang, succeeded in encouraging people to 'call names of political leaders' in streets. But they did not provide constructive ideas or thought systems for modernizing China. According to *The Great Learning*: "To see men of worth and not able to raise them to office; to raise them to office, but not so quickly - this is disrespect. To see bad men and not be able to remove them; to remove them, but not to do so to a distance: - this is weakness. To love those whom men hate, and to those who men love - this is to outrage the natural feeling of men. Calamities cannot fail to come down on him who does so."

China's economic achievement associated with spread market mechanism and encouraged capitalist spirit validates Adam Smith's thought on creation of national wealth. China has changed not only economically, but also bodily, personally, politically, institutionally, legally, socially, intellectually, technologically, academically, morally, ethically, ethnically, geographically, environmentally, culturally, sexually, inter-regionally, and internationally, in many areas in different speeds. These changes are closely interconnected to each other. China is confirming what Marx appreciates in capitalism for improving productivity and making technological progresses. China's 100 years history has proved what Marx says: "History repeats itself, first as tragedy, second as farce." The application of Marx's socialism by Mao produced a penurious socialist China with very low education (almost no higher education), while the application of Marx's progressive capitalism by Deng has resulted in the Chinese farce.

Theory works well if the basic assumptions upon which the theory is built corresponds to the reality. Marx's theory implies that if China aspires to be more effective, more rational, more innovative, and more progressive, China should move toward more capitalism in association with increasing social and economic evils as China is now still in stage of low capital per capita (or immature stage of capitalism).

In *The Problem of China* in 1921 Bertrand Russell predicts and suggests hundred years ago: "The change that has hitherto taken place is traceable ultimately to the military superiority of the West; but in future our economic superiority is likely to be quite as potent. I believe that, if the Chinese are left free to assimilate what they want of our civilization, and to reject what strikes them as bad, they will be able to achieve an organic growth from their own tradition, and to produce a very splendid result, combining our merits with theirs."

A Thucydides Trap Between America and China?

> A simple rule in dealing with those who are hard to get along with is to remember that this person is striving to assert his superiority; and you must deal with him from that point of view.
>
> Whitehead (1861–1947)

> The evil of men is that they like to be the teachers of others.
>
> Mencius (382–279 BC)

Society is organic. Its life expectancy can be long or short. So far, no society in human history lasts forever in terms of socioeconomic structure. Collective (national or racial) wisdom and stupidity oscillate if a large population survives long enough. National security, social order, and economic efficiency are interrelated, but each has its own principles and functions. Each generation of the society has its mindset which deviates from other generations even within the same culture. The history of construction, maintenance, and destruction of the Great Wall tells much about dynamics of Chinese mentality about international relations.

The USA, overseas Chinese communities, and some other contemporarily advanced regions in the world did not have long history of higher civilizations. These countries' relative high positions in global civilization are durable as they appear due to internal mechanisms of stagnation and collapse, not so much due to external competitive factors. Birth, youth, and aging are natural processes of national development. Collective stupidity or inefficiency tends to last long, and golden time is always transitory like an adult woman's natural beauty. Political economic theory (which is a collection of biased ideas while society is an organic whole) does not provide any solid theory to sustain national collective wisdom and efficiency. Man is sure about how to enter inefficient traps, but not sure about how to maintain a modern civilized (internationally fair) society. Self-destruction is an inevitable alternative for any society, at least so far, in the greatness.

With regards to modern civilization measured in terms of industrialization, modern politics (capitalism and socialism are modern concepts), knowledge, and information, China is far younger than America. Before the West came to influence China, over centuries China's international games were played between mobile nomadic societies (without any higher cultural components or sophisticated religions) and immobile rice-based societies. The equilibrium point is either to be invaded so that Han Chinese are ruled by nomadic peoples or to live essentially in isolation so that the emperor ruled the entire country, spending huge national budgets and human resources on the Great Wall. The West saved Han Chinese with its modern weapons and ships, in a historical perspective, from being ruled by nomadic peoples. Traditional skills of killing with swords and strategies of fighting mastered by nomads lost efficiencies in the front of modern guns. When the West was controlling the world, Bertrand Russell (1872–1970, 1922), who spent a long period in China, pointed out: "If intercourse between Western nations and China is to be fruitful, we must cease to regard ourselves as missionaries of a superior civilization, or worse still, as men who have a right to exploit, oppress, and swindle the Chinese because they are an "inferior" race." The American government still feels morally superior over the Chinese government as Fairbank (1986: 1) reveals: "Because the British did not open the India-China to us [the United States], we did less well in supplying opium to China; but that only enhanced our sense of moral superiority." As many Chinese people born in the New China have studied and lived in America over the last four decades, they do not feel any kind of moral superiority of America, even though they don't think of that for China either.

China has been changed under the influence of the West. No race is brave without its members strongly believing in something worthwhile to fight for. China's high IQ population and probably protectable national security implies that its people would be brave enough to fight against any invader. Bertrand Russell (1922) illustrates the history of interactions in the past: “I found one day in school, a boy of medium size ill-treating a smaller boy. I expostulated, but he replied: ‘The bigs hit me, so I hit the babies; that’s fair.’ In these words he epitomized the history of the human race.” Games might be repeated, but perhaps in different forms due to diffusion of nuclear powers, even if widely spread rational knowledge and accessible objective information cannot maintain the world in peace.

In many respects, China is Americanizing, the USA is trying to search ways to maintain its relatively declining superpower. Hermann Hesse (1877–1962) says: “If you hate a person, you hate something in him that is part of yourself. What isn’t part of ourselves doesn’t disturb us.” Both America and China are in their natural stage of social evolution as human race is convergingly, at least among rational cultures, becoming an organic whole. Civilization is the stock accumulated over its history. People born into one civilization might contribute nothing to high parts of that civilization but make many miserable memories of that civilization for its late generations to disguise. The opposite is also possible. The young generation of Americans, for instance, make not much interesting contribution to the progress of American civilization in comparison to, for instance, their grandparent and parent generations. But the young generation might perceive itself in a far higher position in the global stage than its spirit and capacity can hold. Between American civilization and Chinese civilization, the highest parts are not yet fully comparable, lowest parts are identical everywhere in the world, and middle parts are differentiated, useful, but mediocre. As Chinese and American students are educated almost with the same textbooks and playing similar social and economic games, their differences in interpreting reality and playing political games do not produce much differences in most basic aspects of social and economic life between the two peoples. Chinese farmers, different from quasi-nomadic Russians, would, perhaps, not be interested in something like the cold-war game. In high parts of Chinese culture, there is no such thing called cultural superiority by nature. Once if a nation stops learning, ancient Confucianism deems that it is not much from an animal society. One observes that if they are not politically “polluted” (brainwashed with shallow ideas), Chinese and American young people and IT workers can often communicate even more easily among their own countrymen. Young kids form the two cultures play games together for hours even without understanding each other's languages. In this digit-connected world, a large portion of the population in a modern rational society are no more "drug-addicted" to a single rationally unexamined belief or ideology. Before WWII, the share of the global population who received higher education was extremely low, which provided the conditions for simplified ideologies like socialism or capitalism to easily diffuse among the passionate and uneducated. The aged Trump generation is becoming quickly a history and future generations might not be blindly support some ideology which they have not proper understanding as a universal value system. The global last man is not yet born and man is still in a making process.

There are now trade wars between China and the USA. Trade theory predicts mutual harms due to trade wars if the two economies were market-based economies with full employment of input factors. Theoretical predictions can be meaningfully validified only when the assumptions have something to do with the reality. As China is not a market-dominated economy and the US is faced with problems of unemployment and trade deficits with the rest of the world, the net impact of trade wars on any side is difficult to evaluate. Contemporary economic theory cannot prove short-run and long-run consequences of trade wars between the two sides. American economists, who are mostly equipped with very narrow or partial economic theories, have only miscellaneous personal opinions, at best, on the net impact of trade wars. Trade wars between the two countries might be considered like quarrels between husband and wife—the results might theoretically benefit both, harm one and benefit another, or harm both. There are no certain consequences with trade wars, except that people of both sides learn much about each other.

In history Chinese did not fight for a religion or an ideology. To use a religion or an ideology to plunder is new for Chinese. The Chinese *yin-yang* theory does not justify any single man-made ideology or a universal religion with a single God. In Chinese mindset, any single-minded ideology is not sustainable in the long term. This does not imply that Han Chinese were kind and peaceful. Han Chinese were brute among themselves. Its history cycled the strengthening and falling of the Great Wall. The people within the Wall were obedient to the central power as farmers had an even worse alternative with nomadic invaders. Farmers emphasized social stability and would fight to death to protect their home when they were aware of some probability of a victory. As Bertrand Russell points out, "Neither a man nor a crowd nor a nation can be trusted to act humanely or to think sanely under the influence of a great fear." Long time ago, Deng Xiaoping told the Chinese government how to act: "Observe calmly; secure our position; cope with affairs calmly; hide our capacities and bide our time; be good at maintaining a low profile; and never claim leadership." But once equipped with modern military technologies and economic powers, Chinese government and Chinese people would behave differently in future, especially after having learned from the West over the last two centuries.

Bergsten (2018) analyzes whether there is a "Thucydides trap" in the world economy. He concludes a possibility of a "Thucydides trap" in the global economic order. The term implies that when a rising power rivals a ruling power, wars tend to occur between the powers. These kinds of conflicts happen everywhere between societies. Typical examples are Athens challenged Sparta, and Germany attacked Britain. Han Chinese within the Great Wall and neighboring nomads happened similarly over history. There are inherent dynamic forces for conflicts and wars between a declining prosperous and powerful nation and a rising and rude nation. There are such conflicts not only between nations, also between families in a village, gangsters in a city, firms in an industry, regions in a large area or so on. Since American-German Trump has become American president, conflicts between the US and China have increasingly become multi-dimensional and severe. So far conflicts are mainly limited to trading games. In the long term, there is nothing much for China to lose if conflicts are still limited to economic and political areas as China is still learning and modernizing. Chinese people have learned far more in the last few years about world and modern societies from the US under Trump's presidency. China has a greater confidence because Trump has valuated China so high. His "honest" lies about China as the top leader of the greatest power in human history has made Chinese people to have, for better or worse, more confidence in China as a nation. Napoleon Bonaparte, a great Western strategist, reveals: "You must not fight too often with one enemy, or you will teach him all your art of war." Trump's leadership has further separated American societies but has solidified the power of China's government in China.

Although history repeatedly confirms Thucydides traps, mankind enters a new stage of rational civilizations. The world is becoming a village in a way that has never occurred in mankind. In a traditional Chinese village, people living together over many generations do not quarrel about their beliefs or preferences. People from the same village tend to tolerate others' shortcomings as similar things might occur within one's own family. Lies and falsifying information cannot effectively cover hypocrisy of the faked gentleman. Sense of shame cannot be easily hidden or forgotten as neighbors will constantly warn you if you do not behave yourselves. In a village civilization, how to solve problems related to inherent conflicts between incumbents and challengers might be different from an open society because domestic lies are not so easy to hide as in the past in contemporary digital-connected world. For instance, the people in London got the news about the opium war in China in a few months after the international conflict took place. During these few months, British government and Chinese government had enough time and great capacities to make up the history to make their own citizens happy with their own governments. Nowadays people in the world know an airplane crash in seconds and can know more about the whole story, at least from varied perspectives, rather than a single-source fake news. In modern wars between two countries the one who has technical geniuses and nuclear powers has higher probability to vanish the other. The American nuclear bombs on Japan illustrate possible, but very light, consequences of nuclear wars. The destructive forces of early nuclear bombs are like those of toys in comparison with modern ones. Destructive powers of contemporary bombs in Russia or China, not to say in the USA, are far more powerful than the ones used by the US on Japan. The current pandemic, even if the virus is proved by scientists (if they can be trusted) not man-made, hints on potential risks of other types of international wars. Moreover, a few geniuses whose intellectual results are unpredictable can play a deterministic role in the final victory in nuclear wars. From now on there does not exist a higher probability for any country to gain from causing a world war. Even if China disappeared from the earth, America's relative position in the world would not be much changed in the long term as technologies and rational knowledge are diffused among the village.

Man does not easily give life to a claimed cause which he has neither trust, nor interest, nor understanding, nor benefit. Widely spread modern education and quickly diffused information enable men to doubt about meanings of wars. Bertrand Russell (1872–1970) says: "I would never die for my beliefs because I might be wrong." No ideology so far diffused among human societies has anything solidly related to universal truth. Man is far from understanding himself, not to say a symbol system to represent truth for all the people in a free (not a drug-addicted) society with large population. There is no need for ideology for a single man in isolated island. An ideology is a collectively accepted value system but built on sand. After all, it is only a rule in gaming dreamed of by some thinkers perhaps in isolation. In many modern societies, the law, ethic, and habit are developed on basis of the ideology the society accepts without deeply examining its root. Its role in society is like the rule in sport. The people self-train or are trained to play the life game, being framed by the ideology. The ideology is important for national building and functioning. In modern times, even national plundering is in the name of ideology. Since the ideology is meaningful within certain time in certain space, killing lives for economic benefits in the name of ideology tend to become increasingly ineffective in human evolution due to fast expanding technologies, rapidly growing knowledge, widely and quickly spread education based on science and rationality, and globalization.

Men, irrespective of their high education, might still be "brave" enough to die for causes they really understand nothing about. Man may give his life purely for the sake of love. Religion is purely performed for the sake of religion. But as far as collective behavior of nation is concerned, man has mostly behaved like a wolf irrespective of his appearance, religion, and education. There is no certainty about what man can do, especially against his own kind as Nietzsche observes: "In individual, insanity is rare, but in groups, parties, nations and epochs, it is the rule." Keynes (1883–1946) sees man's behavior as a consequence of anticipation: "Successful investing is anticipating the anticipation of others." Global peace in near future, if available, is perhaps due to spread nuclear powers. Man is just entering globally rationalized, information-digitalized, nuclear-covered, and virus-diffused epoch. No age in history is collectively faced with so many uncertainties like today. Once upon a long time, wars supported with religions, nationalism, or even justice were a profitable way for a society to enrich itself by killing and plundering. Nevertheless, due to destructive powers of modern weapons and widely and expeditiously travelled information, profitability tends to vanish. Even mutual neglection may be a better choice than mutual destruction, like modern marriage. Hemingway (1899–1961) reveals:

> They wrote in the old days that it is sweet and fitting to die for one's country. But in modern war, there is nothing sweet nor fitting in your dying. You will die like a dog for no good reason.

The Vietnam war might exemplify what he means. Global peace is never secured by peaceful talks among potential enemies but might be gained by constructing international institutions for maintaining global peace or through ubiquitous diffusion of destructive weapons among potential enemies as implied by Mozi's philosophy of universal love (Mozi 470–391 BC).

Can China Escape Middle-Income Trap with Its High IQ Population?

> There are cases in which the blade springs, but the plant does not go on to flower! There are cases where it flowers, but no fruit is subsequently produced.
>
> Confucius

China is a sizeable socialist market economy. Size matters in every aspect of individual life and social dynamics. In modern economies, large market sizes imply scale and scope economies. China and India are potentially important due to their potential market sizes. National population matters especially in this economically, politically, militarily, and emotionally well-connected organic world. The global village commonly connected with digitals and individually protected by nuclear powers implies that plundering and colonization could not be profitably conducted in large scales across countries. National large size implies dramatically increasing or catastrophically decreasing scale economy. Collective stupidity or wisdom is not proportionally linear in size. The application of a trivial idea in economics by Deng has caused the butterfly effect in China's modern development as well as global market structure due to China's population size.

China, like Japan and the four little tigers, has achieved rapid economic prosperity during the periods from poverty to per capita US$10,000. The common pattern of expansion is that foreign economies initially provide many ideas, technologies, and management methods for them to learn. This is not only true for Asian economies, but also for the greatest economy USA. The East Asian economies have grown with social and political stabilities with friendly relationships with the US or under the American surveillance (Japan has been under US control after WWII). After initial take-offs, for each economy, how to overcome the so-called middle-income trap is a challenging question. The concept refers to a phenomenon that most of the middle-income countries fail to become members of the high-income economies. They stop at further development and maintain long-term economic stagnation. They have comparative advantage in terms of labor costs to poor economies and have no capacities to compete with advanced economies, especially, in fields of high value-added industries and services. Confucianism-influenced cultural areas, Japan and the four little tigers, have succeeded in making the great escape and join the high-income group.

The successful East Asian economies are characterized by relatively low-income inequality. On the other hand, it is commonly argued that social inequality and the relative size of the middle-income group are key determinants of economic advancement. Li (2017) introduces a concept of double middle-income traps to describe China's situations. The concept refers to a situation that the per capita output stagnates, and the size of the middle-income group is unable to expand for an extended period. Applying China's data, Li concludes that the middle-income group is a key determinant in promoting mass communication and overcoming the double middle-income traps. In China, a family with the disposable household between RMB90,000 and RMB450,000 is defined as middle-income. The middle-income households shared about 24.3% of the national total in 2015, i.e., more than 300 million. Unlike its situations 40 years ago, China has accumulated huge amount of capital, built great infrastructures, and accumulated much knowledge and human capital. Opportunities and comparative advantages offered by poverty, low labor costs and a lowly educated population are disappearing in China. There seems one certain advantage left in China—potentials of high IQ population. If data of different estimations on the world's IQ distributions are reliable and IQ is an important determinant of productivity in future, China has great potentials for further development.

There are different studies in IQs among nations and regions. Ranking results are similar. China's IQ is in top and its economic performance in terms of GDP per capita is at low positions in the world as listed in Table 6.2. The table lists the average IQs for some selected countries. The data for 110 countries was made by a project called WorldData.info. The IQs in the table was averaged from the results of 9 international studies. IQ is a measurement of ability for combinations, comprehension, and learning. Average IQ of an economy seems increasingly important in an information-based and knowledge-based economy. If a society with a high

Table 6.2 Average IQs, GDP per capita, and happiness indexes

Country/Region	*IQ rank (IQ)*	*GDP per capita (US$) in 2017*	*Happiness rankings*
Singapore	1 (108)	57,713	34
Hong Kong	2 (108)	46,194	36
Taiwan	3 (106)	n.a.	26
South Korea	4 (106)	29,742	57
Japan	5 (105)	38,428	54
China	6 (104)	8,826	86
Switzerland	7 (102)	80,190	5
Germany	15 (100)	44,769	15
United Kingdom	16 (100)	59,720	19
France	26 (98)	38,477	23
United States	27 (98)	59,532	18

Notes The data on IQs are based on: https://www.worlddata.info/about.php; The Per capita nominal GDP in 2017 is from: https://data.worldbank.org/indicator/NY.GDP.PCAP.CD; The 2018 happiness index is from: https://en.wikipedia.org/wiki/World_Happiness_Report

average IQ and low deviations from the average, then it is expected that inequalities in income and wealth should be small, if the social environment is fair and work ethics is high, like Japan, Singapore, South Korea, and Taiwan.

The conclusions based on average IQs are controversial. Especially, the data do not reflect, for instance, whether the society has genius or not. A mediocre society may have very high average IQ. High IQ countries in East Asia are also well known for being lowly ranked in happiness. China's economic performance in GDP per capital are far below Singapore, Japan, Hong Kong, Taiwan, and Korea. USA's average IQ is much lower than China's and China's population is almost four times as the U.S. population. This implies that if China's population potential was properly cultivated and the national economy was not characterized by collective stupidity or inefficiency, China's GDP could easily be as twice, if not four times, as that of the USA's. Nevertheless, national development is a consequence of compounding legal systems, tradition, culture, education, politics, and military power under omnifarious possible fortunes. Today China is obviously far from being an effective society.

Irrespective of the largest population and low per capita income, China's population has average IQ within top 10 among all the national populations according to the research results conducted by different projects over years. Even during the Cultural Revolution, China's IQ was also high (similarly for poor North Korea). Cultural stocks might be important factors for this phenomenon. China's IQ is much higher than America's, and near to the Western European advanced countries', such as UK, Sweden, Germany, Italy, and France. In this millennium human capital is becoming increasingly more important for national development. In the light what has been achieved in Western economies and the four little tigers, China's economic reform has been a very small step towards cultivating and exploring Chinese human capital. China's astonishing expansion since 1978 is unprecedented in its scale, scope, and duration. No people could have dreamed of this. Now country's economy is relying on R&D to upgrade its economic structure. Chinese R&D is spending currently more than 15% of the world's total. If China succeeds in escaping the trap, implications for global environment, natural resources, poverty, and political and military stabilities are uncertain.

Since the West came to East Asia from the opium war to 1978, China collectively behaved in such a way that the low probability event became a historical factor. Since 1978–2018, China again collectively surprised the world, but in the opposite direction. The probability of straggling around middle-income for a modern economy with largest population whose average IQ is highest in the world should be very low. It would be a world wonder if China come back to the bottom of the world in per capita income.

China's Uncertain Future in Chaotic World

> It has yet to be proven that intelligence has any survival value.
>
> Socrates (470–399 BC)

Life is a learning process. China is still young as modern society. It chose the new path of modernization only from 1978 with poverty and low education as the starting point. Its conflicts with the superpower surfaced only a few years ago. The economic reform, irrespective of the butterfly effect, is short for a country's economic development, not to say a national development. China's political power is controlled by men born in the 1950s and the 1960s when the country did not even have sufficient food for survival. Soon after he became the General Secretary of the Central Committee of the CCP in November 2012, Xi Jinping stated the Chinese dream about being re-respected in the following way (Appelbaum et al. 2018: 1): "After the 170 or more years of constant struggle since the Opium Wars, the great revival of the Chinese nation enjoys glorious prospects ... Now everyone is discussing the Chinese dream, and I believe that realizing the great revival of the Chinese nation is the greatest dream of the Chinese nation in modern times." Even when a person succeeded in escaping from poverty and possibility of not-being directly humiliated, it will take a long way to earn and maintain cloudy respectability and worthiness in public. A basic condition for respectability and worthiness for a person is to constantly examine himself. A basic condition for national respectability is genuine freedom in speech and publishing. No nation is respectable if its citizens cannot even speak out obvious facts in society in modern times.

Man craves being respected and honored, but seldom self-examines respectability and worthiness. Nobility is earned. One society's social nobility is often laughingstock of other societies, especially in the contemporary digitally connected world. Aged—practically wise if not cunning—politicians of some countries with neither proper education nor proper manner provides no national hope for their young people. The past is made by the dead, the current is controlled by the aging, and the future is decided by the unborn. The history of Han Chinese was repeatedly a good servant and a no-effective master since the first emperor created a united country. The geography is perhaps the most important determinant of the Chinese cycles. Digital technologies and low transport costs make geography less effective in separating cultures. China is in its turning point into an unknown type of global civilizations.

China is somehow characterized by the early stage of capitalism. Karl Marx holds that capital-driven economy would produce massive and colossal productive forces. It enables the capitalist economy to have rapid advancement in technology due to profit-maximizing behavior of capitalists. The world market is expanded by increased capital. Capitalists enhance productivities to obtain profits, by exploiting the raw materials of the earth, perpetuating innovation, and pressing out of the workers as much as output as possible and using all inputs as rationally as possible. As China switches from socialism towards capitalism, it has some features of early capitalism as described by Charles Dickens in *A Tale of Two Cities* (Book the First, Chapter I): "It was the best of times, it was the worst of times, it was the age of wisdom, it was the age of foolishness, it was the epoch of belief, it was the epoch of incredulity, it was the season of Light, it was the season of Darkness, it was the spring of hope, it was the winter of despair, we had everything before us, we had nothing before us, we were all going direct to Heaven, we were all going the other way...".

Desires for wealth, power and sex are satisfied not only with virtue and diligence, but often in association with violence, criminals, and corruption. Chinese life is now an amalgam of hope and fear in depth, scale and scope that has never occurred in its recoded history. As Napoleon says, "Among those who dislike oppression are many who like to oppress." Han Chinese history has not yet experienced much sprit of individual freedom. Oppressing and being oppressed is the main character of Chinese history. "No period of history has ever been great or ever can be that does not act on some sort of high, idealistic motives.", Whitehead (1861–1947) points out. Sufficient food for the population, a stabilized society, and secured monopolistic power is the highest dream of the builder of each Chinese dynasty. Confucius (15: 33) points out: "When a man's knowledge is sufficient to attain and his virtue is not sufficient to enable him to hold, whatever he may have gained, he will lose again. When his knowledge is sufficient to attain, and he has virtue enough to hold fast, if he cannot govern with dignity, the people will not respect him. When his knowledge is sufficient to attain, and he has virtue enough to hold fast; when he governs also with dignity, yet if he try to move the people contrary to the rules of propriety—full excellence is not reached." This is the basic individual, racial, as well as national standard of sustainable development in Chinese culture.

National morality does not experience the butterfly effect as Confucius recognizes: "If a truly royal ruler were to arise, it would still require a generation, and then virtue would prevail." A man is decent because he decently treats himself internally as well as externally. A nation is civilized because it behaves decently towards its citizen and humanely to other members of global human societies. Among all the iffy ideologies, China still collectively chooses a non-effective one for its national decency and efficiency.

China was a great servant of global economies in the period 1978–2018. Napoleon warned the West not to open China for the sake of the West:

> China? There is a sleeping giant. Let him sleep. For when he wakes, he will move the world.

China had been, domestically and internationally, so ineffective, and servile during such a long time that when China was showing a sign of openness, no American leader would ever care about Napoleon's words. There was no sign for China to have a capacity to perturbate the developed world in 1976 when Mao was dying. America encouraged China to open door for its own military, political and economic purposes. The US now has an itch for China to remain in a low position in global division of labor and consumption, at least, in the level not exceeding the superpower.

This book reflects on why China's economy has not collapsed and is still becoming structurally stronger from the early 1980s. The period under consideration is a short, but an extremely interesting period, in China's history. It is the history of transformation in social, economic, political, cultural, and institutional interdependence between billion persons, millions of families, numerous firms, many industries, different levels of government, multiple cities and regions with the Chinese cultural stocks accumulated over many thousand years and towering global knowledge stock. China has been experiencing the bifurcation from the traditional social and economic structure into a modern one. China has been moving away from the bottom of the world in per capita income and per capita higher education. A nation often climbs half a way towards the highest potential point and stops there for a while before it moves backwards. China is still far away from a modernized status, irrespective of its recent achievements. It would be premature to predict how the wakened but not yet free China—with its highest average IQ and largest population in the world, very sophisticated cultural capital stocks in rational knowledge, very short history of modernization, and great scientific knowledge rapidly accumulated—evolves in this fast innovating, instantly informed, globally similarly educated, culturally communicative, ideologically ended and uncertain, militarily destructible, politically distrustful, and unequally enriching, rationalizing, and mediocre chaotic world.

References

Appelbaum, R. P., Cao, C., Han, X. Y., Parker, R., & Simon, D. (2018). *Innovation in China*. Medford: Polity.

Aristotle. (2009). *Nicomachean Ethics* (rev. ed.) (translated by W. D. Ross). Oxford: Oxford University Press.

Arnold, V. I. (1992). *Catastrophe Theory* (3rd rev ed.). Berlin: Springer-Verlag.

Bergsten, C. F. (2018). China and the United States: The Contest for Global Economic Leadership. *China and World Economy, 26*(5), 12–37.
Chan, F., & Sun, B. Y. (2018). The Centralisation of the Chinese Communist Party's Campaign against Corruption and Its Implications. *China Report, 54*(4), 403–420.
Chea, C. C. (2015). Empirical Studies: Corruption and Economic Growth. *American Journal of Economics, 5*(2), 183–188.
Chen, Y. J., Li, P., & Lu, Y. (2018, July). Career Concerns and Multitasking Local Bureaucrats; Evidence of a Target-Based Performance Evaluation System in China. *Journal of Development Economics, 133*, 84–101.
Cook, D. J., & Rosemont, H. (1994). *Introduction Writings on China*, see Leibniz (1994).
Fairbank, J. K. (1986). Introduction - Patterns and Problems. In E. R. May & J. K. Fairbank (Eds.), *America's China Trade in Historical Perspectives - The Chinese and American Performance*. Cambridge, MA: Harvard University Press.
Hegel, G. F. W. (1827/1975). *Lectures on the Philosophy of World History* (translated by D. Fordes). Cambridge: Cambridge University Press.
Hegel, G. W. F. (1991). *The Philosophy of History* (translated from the German origin by J. Sibree). New York: Prometheus Books.
Huntington, S. P. (1968). *Political Order in Changing Societies*. New Haven: Yale University Press.
Leff, N. H. (1964). Economic Development Through Bureaucratic Corruption. *The American Behavioral Scientist, 8*(3), 8–14.
Levy, R. (2002). Corruption in Popular China. In P. Link, R. P. Madsen, & P. G. Pickowicz (Eds.), *Popular China—Unofficial Culture in a Globalizing Society*. New York: Rowman & Littlefield Publishers.
Li, P. L. (2017). China's Path to Overcoming the Double Middle-Income Traps. *China & World Economy, 25*(6), 28–44.
Lu, X. (1980). *Selected Works* (in four volumes, translated from the Chinese origin by X. Y. Yang and G. Yang). Beijing: Foreign Languages Press.
Maslow, A. H. (1943). A Theory of Human Motivation. *Psychological Review, 50*(4), 370–396.
Maslow, A. H. (1987). *Motivation and Personality* (3rd ed.). Delhi: Pearson Education.
McLeod, S. A. (2018). *Maslow's Hierarchy of Needs*. Retrieved from https://www.simplypsycholy.org/maslow.html.
Montesquieu, C. (1748). *The Spirit of Laws* (edited with an introduction by D. W. Carrithers). Berkeley: University of California Press.
Myrdal, G. (1968). *Asian Drama*. New York: Random House.

Pan, Y., Fang, S., & Yang, Z. (2018, April). Living Arrangements of the Elderly: A New Perspective from Choice Constraints in China. *China Economic Review, 50*, 101–115.

Qin, A. (2017). *Fraud Scandals Sap China's Dream of Becoming a Science Superpower*. https://www.nytimes.com/2017/10/13/world/asia/china-science-fraud-scandals.html.

Qin, X. Z., Wang, S. Y., & Hsieh, C. R. (2018, October). The Prevalence of Depression and Depressive Symptoms among Adults in China: Estimation Based on a National Household Survey. *China Economic Review, 51*, 271–282.

Russell, B. (1922). *The Problem of China*. New York: Century.

Schwarcz, V. (1986). *The Chinese Enlightenment: Intellectuals and the Legacy of the May Fourth Movement of 1919*. Berkeley: University of California Press.

Singh, V. (2018). Ageing Society and Labor Policy in China: Analyzing Policy Challenges and Options. *Chinese Studies, 7*, 242–250.

World Bank. (2007). *Cost of Pollution in China Technical Report*. Washington, DC: World Bank, East Asia and Pacific Region.

Wright, T. (2018). *Popular Protest in China*. Medford: Polity.

Wu, G. L. (2018). Capital Misallocation in China: Financial Frictions or Policy Distortions? *Journal of Developmental Economics, 130*, 203–223.

Zhang, W. B. (1998). *Japan versus China in the Industrial Race*. London: Macmillan.

References

Andornino, G. B. (2017). The Belt and Road Initiative in China's Emerging Grand Strategy of Connective Leadership. *China & World Economy, 25*(5), 4–22.

Appelbaum, R. P., Cao, C., Han, X. Y., Parker, R., & Simon, D. (2018). *Innovation in China*. Medford: Polity.

Aristotle. (2009). *Nicomachean Ethics* (rev. ed.) (translated by W. D. Ross). Oxford: Oxford University Press.

Armes, R., & Hall, D. (1997). *Thinking Through Confucius*. New York: SUNY Press.

Arnold, V. I. (1992). *Catastrophe Theory* (3rd rev ed.). Berlin: Springer-Verlag.

Barmé, G., & Jaivin, L. (1992). *New Ghosts, Old Dreams*. New York: Times Books.

Bauer, J. R., & Bell, D. A. (1999, edited). *The East Asian Challenge for Human Rights*. Cambridge: Cambridge University Press.

Becker, J. (1996). *Hungry Ghosts: Mao's Secret Famine*. New York: Free Press.

Bell, D. A. (1978). *The Cultural Contradictions of Capitalism*. New York: Basic Books.

Bell, D. A. (1996). Afterword. In *The Cultural Contradictions of Capitalism*. New York: Basic Books.

Bergsten, C. F. (2018). China and the United States: The Contest for Global Economic Leadership. *China and World Economy, 26*(5), 12–37.

Berthrong, J. H. (1998). *Transformations of the Confucian Way*. Boulder: Westview Press.

Bhattachrya, P., Palacio-Torralba, J., & Li, X. (2018). On Income Inequality Within China's Provinces. *Chinese Studies, 7,* 174–182.

W.-B. Zhang, *The Butterfly Effect in China's Economic Growth*,
https://doi.org/10.1007/978-981-15-9889-0

Brodsgaard, K. J. (2018). China's Communist Party: From Mass to Elite Party. *China Report, 54*(4), 385–402.

Brook, T. (1998). *Quelling the People—The Military Suppression of the Beijing Democracy Movement*. Stanford: Stanford University Press.

Brook, T., & Blue, G. (1999, edited). *China and Historical Capitalism—Genealogies of Sinological Knowledge*. Cambridge: Cambridge University Press.

Burns, J. P. (1999). The People's Republic of China at 55: National Political Reform. In R. L. Edmonds (Ed.), *The People's Republic of China After 50 Years*. Oxford: Oxford University Press.

Chadde, D. D., & Qiu, F. (2003). Recent Trends and Emerging Patterns of Foreign Direct Investment in China. In I. Alon (Ed.), *Chinese Culture, Organizational Behavior, and International Business Management*. Westport: Praeger.

Chan, F., & Sun, B. Y. (2018). The Centralisation of the Chinese Communist Party's Campaign against Corruption and Its Implications. *China Report, 54*(4), 403–420.

Chan, K. W., & Zhang, L. (1999). The Hukou System and Rural-Urban Migration in China: Processes and Changes. *The China Quarterly, 160*, 818–855.

Chan, W. T. (1963). *The Way of Lao Tzu*. New York: The Bobbs-Merrill Company Inc.

Chan, W. T. (1973). *A Source Book in Chinese Philosophy* (translated and compiled). Princeton: Princeton University Press.

Chang, C. Y. (1975). *Tao: A New Way of Thinking*. New York: Harper & Row, Publishers.

Chea, C. C. (2015). Empirical Studies: Corruption and Economic Growth. *American Journal of Economics, 5*(2), 183–188.

Chen, A. H. Y. (2002). *An Introduction to the Legal System of the People's Republic of China*. Hong Kong: Butterworths.

Chen, C. L. (2019). *The Liberalisation of FDI Policies and the Impacts of FDI on China's Economic Development*. Retrieved from https://press-files.anu.edu.au/downloads/press/n4267/html/ch29.xhtml?referer=&page=41.

Chen, H. C. (1911). *The Economic Principles of Confucius and His School*. New York: The Faculty of Political Science of Columbia University.

Chen, J. P. (1990). *Confucius as a Teacher—Philosophy of Confucius with Special Reference to Its Educational Implications*. Beijing: Foreign Languages Press.

Chen, Y. J., Li, P., & Lu, Y. (2018, July). Career Concerns and Multitasking Local Bureaucrats; Evidence of a Target-Based Performance Evaluation System in China. *Journal of Development Economics, 133*, 84–101.

Cheng, H. S. (1993). Foreign Trade. In W. Galenson (Ed.), *China's Economic Reform*. San Francisco: The 1990 Institute.

Clarke, D. C. (2003). Puzzling Observations in Chinese Law—When Is a Riddle Just a Mistake? In C. S. Hsu (Ed.), *Understanding China's Legal System*. New York: New York University Press.

Coase, R., & Wang, N. (2012). *How China Became Capitalist*. Hampshire: Palgrave Macmillan.

Confucius. (1992). The Confucian Analects. In *The Four Book* (translated by J. Legge and revised and annotated by Z. Liu and Z. Luo). Hunan: Hunan Publishing House.

Constable, N. (1996). Introduction—What Does It Mean to Be Hakka? In N. Constable (Ed.), *Guest People—Hakka Identity in China and Abroad*. Seattle: University of Washington Press.

Cook, D. J., & Rosemont, H. (1994). *Introduction Writings on China*, see Leibniz (1994).

Dai, M., Maitra, M., & Yu, M. J. (2016, April). Unexceptional Exporter Performance in China? The Role of Processing Trade. *Journal of Development Economics, 121*, 177–189.

Deng, X. P. (1994). On Reform of the Political Structure. In *Selected Works of Deng Xiaoping*. Vol. III. Beijing: Foreign Language Press.

de Tocqueville, A. (1948) *Democracy in America*, vols. I and II. New York: Alfred A.Knopt.

Dickson, B. J. (1997). *Democratization in China and Taiwan—The Adaptability of Leninist Parties*. Oxford: Oxford University Press.

Doctrine of the Mean. (1992). In *The Four Book* (translated by J. Legge and revised and annotated by Z. Liu and Z. Luo). Hunan: Hunan Publishing House.

Du, J. L., & Zhang, Y. F. (2018, February). Does One Belt One Road Initiative Promote Overseas Direct Investments. *China Economic Review, 47*, 189–205.

Du, Y., & Lu, Y. (2018). The Great Opening Up and the Roadmap for the Future. *China and World Economy, 26*(2), 68–93.

Duncan, M. (2009, September 28). *Granddaughter Keeps Mao's Memory Alive in Bookshop*. Reuters.

Erbaugh, M. S. (1996). The Hakka Paradox in the People's Republic of China—Exile, Eminence, and Public Silence. In N. Constable (Ed.), *Guest People—Hakka Identity in China and Abroad*. Seattle: University of Washington Press.

Fairbank, J. K. (1986). Introduction - Patterns and Problems. In E. R. May & J. K. Fairbank (Eds.), *America's China Trade in Historical Perspectives - The Chinese and American Performance*. Cambridge, MA: Harvard University Press.

Fana, H. C., Lin, F. Q., & Tang, L. X. (2018, November). Minimum Wage and Outward FDI from China. *Journal of Development Economics, 135*, 1–19.

Fang, C., Garnaut, R., & Song, L. (2018). 40 Years of China's Reform and Development: How Reform Captured China's Demographic Dividend. In

R. Garnaut, L. Song, & C. Fang (Eds.), *China's 40 Years of Reform and Development 1978–2018*. Australia: ANU Press.

Fung, Y. L. (1952). *A History of Chinese Philosophy* (Vol. I, translated from the Chinese origin by D. Bodde). Princeton: Princeton University Press.

Fung, Y. L. (1953). *A History of Chinese Philosophy* (Vol. II, translated from the Chinese origin by D. Bodde). Princeton: Princeton University Press.

Gao, P. Y. (2018). China's 40 Years of Fiscal and Tax Reform: A Basic Trajectory. *China and World Economy, 26*(2), 94–106.

Garver, J. W. (1997). *The Sino-American Alliance - Nationalist China and American Cold War Strategy in Asia*. Armonk: M.E. Sharpe.

Golley, J., & Kong, S. T. (2018). Inequality of Opportunity in China's Educational Outcomes. *China Economic Review, 51*, 116–128.

Gong, B. L. (2018, May). Agricultural Reforms and Production in China: Changes in Provincial Production Function and Productivity in 1978–2015. *Journal of Development Economics, 132*, 18–31.

Gray, J. (1990). *Rebellions and Revolutions—China from the 1800s to the 1980s*. Oxford: Oxford University Press.

Great Learning. (1992). Translated by J. Legge and revised and annotated by Z. Liu and Z. Luo. Published in the Chinese English bilingual series of Chinese classics. Hunan: Hunan Publishing House.

Gu, M., Michael, R., Zheng, C., & Trines, S. (2019, December 17). *Education in China*. https://wenr.wes.org/2019/12/education-in-china-3.

Han, S. Y. (1965). *The Crippled Tree*. New York: G.P. Putnam's Sons.

He, B. G. (2001). *The Democratization of China*. London: Routledge.

Hegel, G. F. W. (1827/1975). *Lectures on the Philosophy of World History* (translated by D. Fordes). Cambridge: Cambridge University Press.

Hegel, G. W. F. (1991). *The Philosophy of History* (translated from the German origin by J. Sibree). New York: Prometheus Books.

Heidegger, M. (1971). *On the Way to Language* (translated by P. D. Hertz). New York: Harper & Row.

Hsieh, T. Y. (1929). Origins and Migrations of the Hakkas. *Chinese Social and Political Science Review, 13*, 208–228.

Hu, A. G. Z., Zhang, P., & Zhao, L. J. (2017, January). China as Number One? Evidence from China's Most Recent Patenting Surge. *Journal of Developmental Economics, 124*, 107–119.

Hume, D. (1994). *Political Essays* (edited by K. Haakonssen). Cambridge: Cambridge University Press.

Huntington, S. P. (1968). *Political Order in Changing Societies*. New Haven: Yale University Press.

Huntington, S. P. (1996). *The Clash of Civilizations and the Remaking of World Order*. New York: Touchstone.

I Ching (*Yi Jing*, Book of Changes) (1993). Translated by Legge, J. and revised and annotate edited by Y. Qin. Hunan: Hunan Publishing House.

Jones, D. M. (2001). *The Image of China in Western Social and Political Thought*. New York: Palgrave.

Jones, W. C. (2003). Trying to Understand the Current Chinese Legal System. In C. S. Hsu (Ed.), *Understanding China's Legal System*. New York: New York University Press.

Ju, J. D., & Yu, X. D. (2018). China's Opening up After 40 Years: Standing at a Historic Turning Point. *China & World Economy, 26*(2), 23–49.

Jung, C. G. (1965). *Introduction, Secret of the Golden Flower: A Chinese Book of Life* (translated by R. Wilhelm). New York: Harcourt Brace Jovanovich, Inc.

Jung, C.G. (1989). *Psychological Types* (a revision by R. F. Hull of the translation by H. G. Baynes). London: Routledge.

Ke, C. (1988). The Problem of the Floating Population in Large Cities and Countermeasures. *Cengxiang Jianshe* 5.

Keller, P. (2001, edited). *Chinese Law and Legal Theory*. Dartmouth: Ashgate.

Khrushchev, N. (1974). *Khrushchev Remembers—The Last Testament* (translated and edited by S. Talbott). Boston: Little, Brown.

Landes, D. S. (1998). *The Wealth and Poverty of Nations: Why Some Are So Rich and Some So Poor*. New York: North & Company.

Lao, T. (1963). *Tao Te Ching* (translated with an introduction by D. C. Lau). London: Penguin Books.

Lau, L. J. (2008). Thirty Years of Chinese Economic Reform: Reasons for Its Success and Future Directions. In C. Papadimitriou & S. Zhang (Eds.), *Internet and Network Economics*. Lecture Notes in Computer Science, vol. 5385. Berlin: Springer.

Leff, N. H. (1964). Economic Development Through Bureaucratic Corruption. *The American Behavioral Scientist, 8*(3), 8–14.

Leibniz, G. W. (1994). *Writings on China* (translated by D. J. Cook and H. Rosemont). Chicago: Open Court.

Levy, R. (2002). Corruption in Popular China. In P. Link, R. P. Madsen, & P. G. Pickowicz (Eds.), *Popular China—Unofficial Culture in a Globalizing Society*. New York: Rowman & Littlefield Publishers.

Li, H. B., Liu, P. W., & Zhang, J. S. (2012, May). Estimating Returns to Education Using Twins in Urban China. *Journal of Developmental Economics, 97*, 494–504.

Li, K. W., & Jiang, W. (2019). *China's Foreign Trade: Reform, Performance and Contribution to Economic Growth*. Retrieved from https://press-files.anu.edu.au/downloads/press/n4267/html/ch28.xhtml?referer=&page=40.

Li, P. L. (2017). China's Path to Overcoming the Double Middle-Income Traps. *China & World Economy, 25*(6), 28–44.

Li, T. T., & Wang, Y. (2018, October). Growth Channels of Human Capital: A Chinese Data Study. *China Economic Review, 51*, 309–322.

Li, Z. S. (1996). *The Private Life of Chairman Mao—The Memoirs of Mao's Personal Physician* (translated from the Chinese origin by H. C. Tai). New York: Random House.

List of Jewish Nobel Laureates. (2018). Retrieved from https://en.wikipedia.org/wiki/List_of_Jewish_Nobel_laureates.

Liu, Y. L., Lu, M., & Xiang, K. H. (2018). Balance Through Agglomeration: A Race Between Geography and Policy in China's Regional Development. *China & World Economy, 26*(6), 72–96.

Lu, X. (1980). *Selected Works* (in four volumes, translated from the Chinese origin by X. Y. Yang and G. Yang). Beijing: Foreign Languages Press.

Mah, J. S., & Yeo, M. (2014). The Role of the Government in R&D Promotion and the Development of Technology—Intensive Industries in China. *China Report, 50*(2), 91–107.

Mao, Z. D. (1977). *Selected Works of Mao Tse-Tung* (in five volumes, published in varied years). Beijing: Foreign Language Press.

Maslow, A. H. (1943). A Theory of Human Motivation. *Psychological Review, 50*(4), 370–396.

Maslow, A. H. (1987). *Motivation and Personality* (3rd ed.). Delhi: Pearson Education.

McLeod, S. A. (2018). *Maslow's Hierarchy of Needs*. Retrieved from https://www.simplypsycholy.org/maslow.html.

Mencius. (1992). The Works of Mencius. In *The Four Book* (translated by James Legge and revised and annotate edited by Liu and Z. Luo). Hunan: Hunan Publishing House.

Mendoza, O. M. V. (2018, October). Heterogeneous Determinants of Educational Achievement and Inequality Across Urban China. *China Economic Review, 51*, 129–148.

Montesquieu, C. (1748). *The Spirit of Laws* (edited with an introduction by D. W. Carrithers). Berkeley: University of California Press.

Mungello, D. E. (1977). *Leibniz and Confucianism—The Search for Accord*. Honolulu: The University Press of Hawaii.

Myrdal, G. (1968). *Asian Drama*. New York: Random House.

Pan, Y., Fang, S., & Yang, Z. (2018, April). Living Arrangements of the Elderly: A New Perspective from Choice Constraints in China. *China Economic Review, 50*, 101–115.

Qin, A. (2017). *Fraud Scandals Sap China's Dream of Becoming a Science Superpower*. https://www.nytimes.com/2017/10/13/world/asia/china-science-fraud-scandals.html.

Qin, X. Z., Wang, S. Y., & Hsieh, C. R. (2018, October). The Prevalence of Depression and Depressive Symptoms among Adults in China: Estimation Based on a National Household Survey. *China Economic Review, 51*, 271–282.

Rummel, R. J. (1991). *China's Bloody Century - Genocide and Mass Murder since 1900*. London: Transaction Publishers.

Russell, B. (1922). *The Problem of China*. New York: Century.

Schurmann, F. (1968). *Ideology and Organization in Communist China*. Berkeley: University of California Press.

Schwarcz, V. (1986). *The Chinese Enlightenment: Intellectuals and the Legacy of the May Fourth Movement of 1919*. Berkeley: University of California Press.

Schwartz, B.I (1972, edited). *Reflections on the May Fourth Movement*. Cambridge, MA: Harvard University Press.

Seldes, G. (1985). *The Great Thoughts*. New York: Ballantine Books.

Shapiro, J. (2001). *Mao's War Against Nature—Politics and the Environment in Revolutionary China*. Cambridge: Cambridge University Press.

Shi, X., & Wu, Y. R. (2017, December). The Effect of Internal and External Factors on Innovative Behaviour of Chinese Manufacturing Firms. *China Economic Review, 46*, S50–S64.

Singh, V. (2018). Ageing Society and Labor Policy in China: Analyzing Policy Challenges and Options. *Chinese Studies, 7*, 242–250.

Smith, A. (1759/1982). *The Theory of Moral Sentiments* (edited by D. D. Raphael and A. L. Macfie). Indianapolis: Liberty Press.

Smith, A. (1776/1976) *An Inquiry into the Nature and Causes of the Wealth of Nations* (edited by E. Cannan). Chicago: The University of Chicago Press.

So, A. Y., & Chu, Y. W. (2016). *The Global Rise of China*. Cambridge: Polity Press.

Spence, J. D. (1992). *Emperor of China—Self-Portrait of K'ang-his*. London: Pimlico.

Stromberg, R. N. (1996). *Democracy—A Short, Analytical History*. New York: M.E. Sharpe.

The Economist. (2020). Retrieved from https://www.google.com/search?rlz=1C1OKWM_jaJP857JP857&source=univ&tbm=isch&q=number+of+students+in+China&sa=X&ved=2ahUKEwik5q_95s7qAhXFzIsBHRIeBBMQsAR6BAgJEAE&biw=878&bih=380imgrc=gWbyGekODkaVNM.

Toffefson, J. (2018). China Declared World's Largest Producer of Scientific Articles. *Nature, 553*, 390.

Vogel, E.F. (2011) *Deng Xiaoping and the Transformation of China*. Cambridge, MA: Harvard University Press.

Xiong, A. L., Li, H. Y., Westlund, H., & Pu, Y. J. (2017, April). Social Networks, Job Satisfaction and Job Searching Behavior in the Chinese Labor Market. *China Economic Review, 43*, 1–15.

Wan, G. H., Wang, C., Yin, H., & Zhang, Y. (2018). From Equality of Deprivation to Disparity of Prosperity: The Poverty-Growth-Inequality Triangle in Post-reform China. *China & World Economy, 26*(2), 50–67.

Wan, G. H., & Zhang, Y. (2018, June). The Direct and Indirect Effects of Infrastructure on Firm Productivity: Evidence from Chinese Manufacturing. *China Economic Review, 48*, 143–153.

Wang, C. (2020, March 4). *The Evolution of China's Consumer Market in the Past Decade*. Retrieved from https://food.chemlinked.com/news/food-news/the-evolution-of-chinas-consumer-market-in-the-past-decade.

Wang, X., Xie, Z., Zhang, X. B., & Huang, Y. P. (2018, June). Roads to Innovation: Firm-Level Evidence from People's Republic of China (PRC). *China Economic Review, 49*, 154–170.

Weber, M. (1951). *The Religion of China—Confucianism and Taoism* (translated from the German original by H. H. Gerth with an introduction by C. K. Yang). New York: The Free Press.

Weng, Y. L., & Xu, H. (2018, October). How Guanxi Affects Job Search Outcomes in China? Job March and Job Turnover. *China Economic Review, 51*, 70–82.

Woo, W. T. (2019). *A US Perspective on China's External Economic Disputes in the Past 40 Years and in the Coming 40 Years*. Retrieved from https://press-files.anu.edu.au/downloads/press/n4267/html/ch31.xhtml?referer=&page=43.

World Bank. (2007). *Cost of Pollution in China Technical Report*. Washington, DC: World Bank, East Asia and Pacific Region.

Wright, T. (2018). *Popular Protest in China*. Medford: Polity.

Wu, G. L. (2018). Capital Misallocation in China: Financial Frictions or Policy Distortions? *Journal of Developmental Economics, 130*, 203–223.

Wu, N., & Wang, Q. Y. (2018, August). Wage Penalty of Overeducation: New Micro-Evidence from China. *China Economic Review, 50*, 206–217.

Xun, Z. (1963). *Basic Writings* (translated from the Chinese origin by B. Watson). New York: Columbia University Press.

Yu, X. Z. (1989). Legal Pragmatism in the People's Republic of China. *Journal of Chinese Law, 3*, 29–51.

Yuan, G., & Zhang, L. (2015). Public Education Spending and Private Substitution in Urban China. *Journal of Developmental Economics, 115*, 124–139.

Zhang, W. B. (1991). *Synergetic Economics*. Heidelberg: Springer-Verlag.

Zhang, W. B. (1998). *Japan versus China in the Industrial Race*. London: Macmillan.

Zhang, W. B. (1999). *Confucianism and Modernization*. London: Macmillan.

Zhang, W. B. (2000). *Adam Smith and Confucius—The Theory of Moral Sentiments and The Analects*. New York: Nova Science.

Zhang, W. B. (2001). On Lao Tzu—His Impact on Chinese Thinking. In D. E. Andersson & J. P. H. Poon (Eds.), *Asia-Pacific Transition*. New York: Palgrave.
Zhang, W. B. (2003). *The American Civilization Portrayed in Ancient Confucianism*. New York: Algora.
Zhang, W. B. (2007). *New China's Long March from Servility to Freedom*. New York: Nova Science.
Zhang, W. B. (2010). *Fukuzawa Yukichi: The Pioneer of East Asia's Westernization with Ancient Confucianism*. Frederick, MD.: PublishAmerica.
Zhang, W. B. (2011). *The Rise and Fall of China's Last Dynasty: The Deepening of the Chinese Servility*. New York: Nova Science.
Zhang, W. B. (2020). *The General Economic Theory: An Integrative Approach*. Switzerland: Springer International Publishing.
Zhou, T. C. (2018). Capitalization of Public School Quality into Housing Prices: An Empirical Analysis Based on School District Housing for Public Primary Schools in Shanghai. *Chinese Studies, 7*(4), 287–327.

Name Index

W.-B. Zhang, *The Butterfly Effect in China's Economic Growth*,
https://doi.org/10.1007/978-981-15-9889-0

Subject Index

W.-B. Zhang, *The Butterfly Effect in China's Economic Growth*, https://doi.org/10.1007/978-981-15-9889-0

The manufacturer's authorised representative in the EU is Springer Nature Customer Service Centre GmbH, Europaplatz 3, 69115 Heidelberg, Germany. If you have any concerns regarding our products, please contact ProductSafety@springernature.com

Printed and bound by CPI Group (UK) Ltd, Croydon, CR0 4YY
30/09/2026
02225286-0007